Teaching Economics Online

ELGAR GUIDES TO TEACHING

The Elgar Guides to Teaching series provides a variety of resources for instructors looking for new ways to engage students. Each volume provides a unique set of materials and insights that will help both new and seasoned teachers expand their toolbox in order to teach more effectively. Titles include selections of methods, exercises, games and teaching philosophies suitable for the particular subject featured. Each volume is authored or edited by a seasoned professor. Edited volumes comprise contributions from both established instructors and newer faculty who offer fresh takes on their fields of study.

For a full list of Edward Elgar published titles, including the titles in this series, visit our website at www.e-elgar.com.

Teaching Economics Online

Edited by

Abdullah Al-Bahrani

Professor of Economics, Haile College of Business, Northern Kentucky University, USA

Parama Chaudhury

Professor, Department of Economics, University College London, UK

Brandon J. Sheridan

Associate Professor of Economics, Economics Department, Elon University, USA

ELGAR GUIDES TO TEACHING

 Edward Elgar
PUBLISHING

Cheltenham, UK • Northampton, MA, USA

Published by
Edward Elgar Publishing Limited
The Lypiatts
15 Lansdown Road
Cheltenham
Glos GL50 2JA
UK

Edward Elgar Publishing, Inc.
William Pratt House
9 Dewey Court
Northampton
Massachusetts 01060
USA

A catalogue record for this book
is available from the British Library

Library of Congress Control Number: 2024939177

This book is available electronically in the **Elgar**online
Economics subject collection
http://dx.doi.org/10.4337/9781803921983

MIX
Paper | Supporting
responsible forestry
FSC
www.fsc.org   FSC® C013056

ISBN 978 1 80392 197 6 (cased)
ISBN 978 1 80392 198 3 (eBook)

Printed and bound in Great Britain by
TJ Books Limited, Padstow, Cornwall

Contents

Figures

Tables

Contributors

Abdullah Al-Bahrani is Professor of Economics and Associate Dean for Graduate Studies and Research at Northern Kentucky University's Haile College of Business, USA. He is the recipient of the Kenneth G. Elzinga Distinguished Teaching Award from the Southern Economic Association (SEA). He is an advocate for making economic education accessible and engaging. Abdullah produces a weekly YouTube, podcast, and newsletter series devoted to increasing awareness of economics and its influence on our decisions. He is also a co-founder of The Econ Games.

Fabio R. Aricò is Professor of Higher Education and Economics in the School of Economics and Director of the Centre for Higher Education Research Practice Policy and Scholarship, University of East Anglia, UK. He is a member of the Executive Group of the Economics Network, the Editorial Board of the International Review of Economic Education, and the Assessment in Higher Education Conference Executive Committee. He has also recently served as member of the QAA Advisory Group for the review for the Subject Benchmark Statement for Economics. Fabio was awarded a National Teaching Fellowship in 2017 for his work on Student Self-Efficacy and Learning Gain.

Parama Chaudhury is Professor in the Department of Economics and Pro-Vice Provost (Education) at University College London, UK. She is also Founding Director of the Centre for Teaching and Learning Economics (CTaLE), a member of the Royal Economic Society's Council and the Education and Training Committee, and recently chaired the QAA's 2023 Economics Subject Benchmark Statement.

Paul D. Cowell is Head of Economics at Forward College, France, a contributor to CORE Econ and an Associate of the Economics Network. Prior to arriving at Forward, he has held leadership roles as an elected member of the University Court, the Deputy Associate Dean for Learning and Teaching, and chair of the institutional pedagogy group.

Flower Darby is an Associate Director of the Teaching for Learning Center at the University of Missouri, USA and the co-author of several books including *The Norton Guide to Equity-Minded Teaching* (2023) and *Small Teaching*

Online: Applying Learning Science in Online Classes (2019). She has taught in multiple disciplines and modalities in higher education for over 28 years.

Michael Enz is the Director of Professional Development for the Center for Excellence in Teaching and Learning at Virginia Polytechnic Institute and State University, USA. Prior to this appointment he taught economics for 25 years at 6 different higher education institutions.

Simon D. Halliday is Associate Professor of Economics Education in the School of Economics at the University of Bristol, UK, and co-author (with Sam Bowles) of an intermediate microeconomics textbook *Microeconomics: Competition, Conflict and Coordination* published with Oxford University Press (2022).

Cloda Jenkins is Associate Dean, Education Quality and a Professorial Teaching Fellow in the Department of Economics and Public Policy in the Imperial College Business School, UK, where she is also Head of Year for BSc Economics, Finance and Data Science. Cloda also serves as Associate Director of the Centre for Teaching and Learning Economics (CTaLE), member of the RES Education and Training Committee and member of the EEA Education Committee.

Alice Louise Kassens is the John S. Shannon Professor of Economics at Roanoke College, USA, Founding Director of the Centre for Economic Freedom, Research Fellow with the Institute for Economic Equity at the Federal Reserve Bank of St. Louis, and Associate Editor of the *Journal of Economics Teaching*. Her publications include the book *Intemperate Spirits: Economic Adaptation during Prohibition* (2019).

Humberto Llavador is an Associate Professor of Economics at Universitat Pompeu Fabra (UPF), an affiliate professor at the Barcelona School of Economics, and a researcher at the Institute of Political Economy and Governance, Spain. He has held visiting positions at Yale University and the Grantham Research Institute on Climate Change and the Environment at LSE, and he is a past scholar of the School of Social Science at the Institute for Advanced Studies in Princeton, USA. In addition to his teaching at UPF and BSE, he has offered courses at Yale, INSEAD-Singapore, Korea University, and the University of California. He has given talks on teaching innovation at the meetings of the European Economic Association and at the Symposium of the Spanish Economic Association. Currently, he is the Delegate of the Dean for Teaching Innovation at UPF, a member of Committee on Education in Economics of the Spanish Economic Association, a contributor to the CORE-econ project, and an editor of *Experiencing Economics*. In 2012 he received the *Recognition Jaume Vicens-Vives* for teaching quality and innovation from the Catalan Government.

Rebecca L. Moryl is a passionate economics educator with 20 years' classroom experience. In addition to serving as Associate Professor and Department Chair of Economics at Emmanuel College, her work on innovative and effective economics pedagogy has won awards and been featured in several publications. She is the creator of audioecon.com, a resource library of podcasts and instructional materials used by thousands of economics instructors across the globe since 2013. An avid traveller, she has conducted research, taught students, trained faculty, and developed curricula around the world, including as Fulbright Scholar at the University of Kigali, Rwanda. Currently living in Ireland, she provides professional workshops and guest lectures in economics, effective pedagogy, curriculum development, assessment, online instruction, and learning.

Ramin Nassehi is an Associate Professor (Teaching) at the Department of Economics at University College London, UK. He is a longstanding member of the Centre for Teaching and Learning Economics (CTaLE), leading their work in connecting students with research through organising the annual undergraduate conference, Explore Econ, and designing innovative ways for communicating economics to the public, notably the London Economics Walk.

Stefania Paredes Fuentes is a Principal Teaching Fellow at the University of Southampton, UK, Senior Fellow of the Higher Education Academy and Diversity Champion for the Royal Economic Society. As a member of the Executive Board of the Economics Network, and Associate of the Centre for Teaching and Learning Economics (CTaLE) she actively promotes pedagogical excellence in economics education. Her pedagogical research focuses on addressing inequalities in higher education and advancing diversity within economics. Stefania has contributed to the development of innovative teaching and assessments methods for Macroeconomics, aiming to narrow awarding gaps across diverse student demographics. Her other research interest extends into the fields of institutional economics, inequality, and Latin American development.

Darshak Patel is a Senior Lecturer of Economics and the Director of Undergraduate Studies at The University of Kentucky Gatton College of Business and Economics, USA. His goal as an educator is to increase the level of engagement among students by developing lectures and assignments that focus on generating a high level of energy, interest, and motivation towards the subject of economics. He is also a co-founder of The Econ Games.

Phil Ruder is a Distinguished Professor of Economics at Pacific University in Forest Grove, Oregon, USA. Phil teaches all his classes with team-based learning (TBL) student-centred pedagogy. Since 2015, Phil has taught numerous online and hybrid TBL economics courses to undergraduate and MBA students. With Scott Simkins and Mark Maier, Phil has led an effort to make it easier for economic teachers to include student group work in economics classes, conducting workshops, developing materials, and constructing the TBL module and activity library at the Starting Point: Teaching and Learning Economics website. With Mark Maier, Phil coedited *Teaching Principles of Microeconomics* (Elgar 2023) which offers a wide range of strategies to improve the traditional introductory course.

Daria Sevastianova is an Associate Professor of Economics at the University of Southern Indiana in Evansville, Indiana, USA. She also serves as the Center for Economic Education Director, helping to promote financial literacy in the region by developing and presenting materials for high school teachers. In addition, she developed her university's most successful and longest standing international exchange with a sister city in Germany.

Brandon J. Sheridan is an Associate Professor in the Department of Economics at Elon University, located in Elon, North Carolina, USA. He is also a founding member of the Economic Education Network for Experiments, which is a worldwide collaboration of instructors working together on synchronized studies in their classrooms.

James E. Tierney is an educator, entrepreneur, and improv artist. James combines his diverse skills to bring innovative approaches to teaching economics. He holds a master's degree in economics from UC-Irvine and has extensive experience in academia, including a significant tenure teaching economics at Penn State University, USA. Co-owner of Happy Valley Improv and the Blue Brick Theatre in State College, PA, James integrates his passion for the performing arts into his educational methods. He is also the founder of Tierney Education, where he specializes in tutoring and academic coaching, further demonstrating his commitment to fostering educational excellence and student success.

Acknowledgments

Abdullah, Parama, and Brandon would like to thank the dedicated educators committed to enhancing teaching methods and creating learning environments that empower student growth. Parama Chaudhury would also like to thank the UCL Laidlaw Research and Leadership Programme for financial support for research assistance during the initial stages of planning and developing this book idea.

Introduction to *Teaching Economics Online*

Teaching online or in a blended format, and how to do it well, has become an area of much discussion in recent years. Interest in effective online instruction was increasing even before the Covid-19 pandemic of 2020 moved most universities at least partly online. Within Economics, this topic has resonance as Economics programmes tend to be large so there are clear benefits of online provision to address the challenges related to physical teaching and learning space, while at the same time, much of the fundamentals of Economics involve technical and relatively abstract material which can make the online environment even trickier as students may be less likely to engage with such material.

In this book, we bring together a collection of experts from across the UK, Europe, and the US on both technical and design elements of teaching Economics online and in a blended format, as well as the pedagogical benefits that can be derived from this setup and how to mitigate the complications presented by being online. We start with some of the common (and big) challenges of the online setup, work our way through the more traditional ways of teaching Economics and how best to move these online, to more innovative formats, and end with a look at extra- and co-curricular teaching online. This provides a relatively complete picture of how to take the full student experience to a format which could potentially be more inclusive and accessible than the traditional setup. The goal of this book is to serve as a foundation for instructors considering online education and ways to improve student engagement in online or hybrid instruction.

Given the experience of the Covid-19 pandemic, university instructors have a chance to use the lessons learned over the last few years during the emergency move online to fashion a new way to teach and learn Economics. It is our view that, when done well, online education can make the higher education model more resilient to shocks such as the pandemic or geopolitical disturbances which make it harder to provide education in a traditional in-person setting. Compared with the traditional classroom, online education can also provide students with deep learning opportunities in an environment more like their future workplaces. Finally, online education can potentially make Economics education more accessible and inclusive. This book aims to use the collective wisdom of some of the leading innovators in the field to help Economics instructors bring about this transformation.

One of the key issues related to any education setting is how to create an environment conducive to learning. Part 1 of this book explores how to make learning online more effective and inclusive. We start with a chapter by Flower Darby that looks at what the research on learning science can tell us about how people learn in an online setting and how to use this knowledge to design an appropriate online classroom. Michael Enz's chapter continues with this theme by looking at how to apply the science of learning effectively in the context of online Economics education. Next, Simon Halliday and James Tierney address the rise of artificial intelligence (AI), perhaps one of the most consequential developments in the education sector. They consider the opportunities and challenges provided by AI to enable instructors to become more effective and students to learn more efficiently. Finally, Fabio Aricò and Paul Cowell address various challenges of making the online classroom inclusive. In addition to considering demographic elements of inclusivity and provision for students with legally protected characteristics, this chapter takes a deep dive into ways to make the online environment as inclusive and accessible as possible, from suggestions about the best type of graphic and audio formats to activities that may enhance inclusion in the online format.

Part 2 presents ways instructors can adapt their traditional approach for the online context. Many instructors were forced to adapt quickly during the pandemic and this section provides multiple examples and best practices for a range of different learning environments. We start with Parama Chaudhury and Cloda Jenkins discussing a co-curricular community building programme for first-year students. They show how to prepare students who are new to the university environment for success, and how this can be run partly online, in a programme which is mostly in-person. Next follow two chapters on different contexts for online teaching and learning of Economics. Alice Louise Kassens discusses how to design effective synchronous teaching and learning in an econometrics course, one of the most technical and potentially less-engaging parts of an Economics programme. Rebecca Moryl discusses online learning in a liberal arts context, where student engagement, quality instruction, and institution mission are paramount concerns. She discusses the research on how using best practices in online education can address issues arising from blended instructional formats when they are at odds with some of the fundamentals of the institution's liberal arts education model. In the final chapter in this section, Stefania Paredes Fuentes grapples with assessment, a source of much concern and consternation in Economics across all modalities. She considers how careful design can both build the skills we expect of our students and alleviate some of the worries about academic integrity in an online setting.

Part 3 focuses on innovative and interactive modes of teaching Economics, with chapters on teaching with games and experiments (Humberto Llavador), case studies and project-based learning (Cloda Jenkins), and team-based learning (Phil Ruder). These are all methods that have been used within Economics for some time, but the online format presents obstacles where the design calls for physical activities or interactions. At the same time, the default passivity in an online setting necessitates more built-in interactivity in such a teaching and learning format. As many discovered during the pandemic years, careful redesign using technological tools that many universities subscribe to already can adequately substitute for the in-person setup and provide an additional dimension to the pedagogical approach.

Part 4 considers how extra- and co-curricular learning in Economics can be implemented in an online environment. We start with Ramin Nassehi's chapter on how to take a blended approach to a student research conference, a culminating experience in an education model focused on developing students' research skills broadly defined. Ramin discusses how taking such an offering online provides an opportunity to broaden its impact and addresses the challenge of providing requisite support to a large cohort. Next, Abdullah Al-Bahrani, Darshak Patel, Daria Sevastianova, and Brandon Sheridan discuss how they took The Econ Games, an international data skill "internship for a day" competition, online and reflect on the benefits and challenges compared to the in-person version. Finally, Parama Chaudhury and Cloda Jenkins discuss their blended approach to continuous professional development in the form of Economics training for government employees. They argue that this is an effective way to roll out training to employees posted in different locations around the country and the world, and discuss how it has influenced their approach to online learning for university students.

We aim for this book to serve as a resource available to instructors when thinking about how to re-optimise their teaching and learning design to make it appropriate for a blended or online modality. Higher education institutions are settling into a new normal after the Covid-19 pandemic, with students expecting multiple educational modalities to be available. The future of education will likely leverage a portfolio of engagement options from which students may choose. We hope this book provides those involved in education provision with a toolbox to address the opportunities and challenges of this exciting new world.

Abdullah Al-Bahrani, Parama Chaudhury and Brandon J. Sheridan

PART I

EFFECTIVE LEARNING IN AN ONLINE
CLASSROOM

1. What does the literature say about learning online?

Flower Darby

Online education is poised to continue a decade-long growth trend, even as in-person enrollments decline (Seaman et al., 2018). While this form of education is the way of the future, and while it offers increased access and strategic equity-focused affordances, it is not without its challenges. Attrition rates are higher in asynchronous online classes than in person (Shaikh & Asif, 2022). Students require more autonomy and self-regulation skills to be successful online (UDL on Campus, n.d.). Blended and hybrid courses, in which some class time takes place in-person and some takes place online (live or asynchronous), are increasingly available as colleges and universities seek to enact the affordances of technology and accommodate students' complex lives. And many instructors struggle to interact with the people in their online environments to facilitate learning.

These challenges can exacerbate issues related to teaching Economics. Students may come to this discipline with little prior knowledge of or experience with the subject matter (P. Chaudhury, personal communication, July 10, 2022). Material can be technical and class sizes may be large. All of these factors combine to create conditions that may not foster teaching and learning, which can be enhanced by a relationship-focused approach that facilitates effective communication (Felten & Lambert, 2020). Additionally, post-pandemic, as postsecondary institutions move toward blended models, significant components of class take place in online environments. Such virtual spaces create distance between educators and students, and may feel inhospitable and isolating, further limiting meaningful communication that facilitates robust learning (Darby & Lang, 2019).

Yet it doesn't have to be this way. Based on the body of literature on teaching and learning online, there is much we can do to foster equitable outcomes in online classes and to enhance teaching and learning in online environments. When we implement evidence-based strategies for effective online course design and teaching, we'll create lively, invigorating settings where both we and our students can thrive. Whether our courses are fully online (asynchronous or synchronous), blended, or in-person with some online elements, such as publisher materials or online activities and assessments, the evidence-based principles and strategies that follow can improve our collective experience in virtual spaces.

First, a word about what I mean by "online teaching and learning." The definition of online education has expanded since the Covid-19 pandemic, with universities and colleges increasing offerings beyond what used to be the primary online education offering, asynchronous classes. Now when we talk about teaching and learning online, we refer to a range of modalities and variations. We can think of this as a continuum, with fully asynchronous online classes at one end and fully in-person classes at the other end. Indeed, we might even consider that *all* classes are online classes (Cohn, 2021). Given the fact that students can (and want to be able to) attend classrooms via live synchronous video if needed, and given the fact that Learning Management Systems (LMSs) such as Canvas, D2L, Moodle, and Blackboard Learn are almost universally available for every class, we would do well to hone our ability to engage students in online spaces to facilitate both ease of access and productive learning behaviors.

The good news is that these environments offer advantages and strengths that we lack in physical classrooms. We can apply learning science, emotion science (the neuroscience of how emotion and cognition interrelate), and online teaching and learning theory to facilitate meaningful time on task that enables today's students to engage, persist, and learn, no matter the mode of our classes. Most importantly, we can advance equity when we do.

WHAT THE LITERATURE TELLS US ABOUT EFFECTIVE ONLINE LEARNING

Many instructors who are new to online teaching haven't had an opportunity to become familiar with the rich body of knowledge about what works (and what doesn't) in online education. In this section, I'll alternate brief summaries of key theoretical frameworks as well as principles drawn from learning science and emotion science. This approach enables us to explore practical course design and teaching strategies based on a solid, scholarly foundation.

The Community of Inquiry Framework

In the late 1990s a team of researchers wanted to understand what goes into a good online class. Historically, and regrettably still today, online classes can feel like electronic correspondence courses, impersonal, transactional, and not like "real" (in-person) classes. To enrich this learning environment, and to highlight the importance of interactions online, Garrison et al. (2000) devised the now well-established Community of Inquiry (CoI) framework which includes three presences. Cognitive presence represents the thought work involved in online teaching and learning, both the instructor's and the students'. That is, cognitive presence represents your decision-making process about the textbook or other materials, learning activities you provide to help students interact with and practice new concepts, and the assessments you design to check for understanding and attainment of course learning outcomes. For students, cognitive presence refers to their cognitive processes involved in learning new information: understanding it, remembering it, and applying it to solve problems or analyze case studies, for example. Teaching presence speaks to the necessity of guiding and facilitating learning. When we teach in person, we respond in the moment to verbal and non-verbal cues. We observe confused expressions on students' faces, so we stop and ask for questions. Or we respond to students' answers to our questions, providing additional information or asking guiding questions to draw out important concepts. Online, it's important to figure out how to be responsive without the explicit cues we detect in person. This guidance comes from fellow students, too, as they share their experiences with each other as well as from the instructor. Social presence reminds us that we are all people in the online class, a fact which is all too easy to forget when all we see of each other may be names and gray silhouette avatars in an impersonal learning environment or names in black Zoom boxes. This model has been widely studied, tested, and is well regarded as authoritative in the way we facilitate effective learning online.

In 2012, Cleveland-Innes and Campbell proposed the addition of emotional presence. Originally represented within social presence, these researchers found that emotions play a significant part in the way we teach and learn online, such that this should be a separate, fourth, presence. Think about how you feel about teaching online. Are you excited about the opportunity? Do you feel isolated from your students? Frustrated? Energized? Thankful to be able to help students make meaningful progress while enjoying a remote work schedule?

Chances are you've felt all these things, or you will, if you haven't already started teaching in online spaces. Emotional presence recognizes that we bring our emotions into online environments with us—we don't check them at the door. And neither do our students. Today's new majority students lead complex lives (Artze-Vega & Taylor, 2020). Frequently, they're juggling schoolwork, family caregiving responsibilities, and a job—if not more than one job. Offering robust online components for in-person or hybrid classes helps students learn and succeed, given this complexity. But they still bring their emotions into online learning spaces. If it's been a stressful day, or they're worried about paying for groceries, or they doubt they'll be successful in this class—these emotions impact their experiences in online (and in-person) learning environments. Further, people who choose online classes frequently do so because of the flexibility it affords them. Of course, this isn't the only reason. Some people prefer this modality because as introverts or neurodivergent students they feel more comfortable in an online environment than they do in person. But broadly speaking, for most distance learners, flexibility is a primary factor.

However, many online students still feel uncertain in online classes. They may experience anxiety related to a perceived lack of instructor availability or support. Virtual learning spaces can feel confusing, overwhelming, or not intuitive, if we're most familiar with physical classrooms and behavioral norms. Students bring these emotions into online spaces, as well as any positive emotions that promote learning, such as hope, optimism, or joy. Essentially, emotions impact everything that happens in online classes and thereby impact learning online.

As we'll see later in this chapter, emotions powerfully affect cognition, for better or for worse. We'll consider how we can maximize positive, productive experiences and minimize negative experiences to promote effective learning online.

Learning Science: An Overview of How We Learn

In addition to theoretical frameworks, neuroscience can help inform our teaching practice to maximize student learning and engagement. Recent research has revealed much about how people learn and how we can therefore teach most effectively. What follows is a brief exploration of some of the salient evidence-based principles that help students learn and retain new information.

First, it is important to recognize that you, as an economist, possess rich expertise that your students do not. You are an expert in this field. As such, you have a dense neural network of information that is easily accessible when you need to recall various facts or concepts (Miller, 2014). You understand how ideas and theories relate, and this provides you with an overall understanding of how things work in Economics.

By contrast, the neural network of novice learners—that is, your students—is sparse. People who are new to a field of study lack context; they possess limited information about the discipline. Consequently, there are few connections between the few concepts they know. The result is a lack of overall comprehension which can make it difficult to understand individual concepts and ideas. Without context, it's harder to make sense of new information (Lang, 2016). Thus, explicitly introducing new topics, that is, an overview or background information, can help students process and understand new ideas more easily.

It's not only about telling students things, however. Educational philosophers have argued that we can't simply transmit knowledge into the minds of our students like pouring into an empty vessel. Neuroscience has shown that people learn by relating new information to what they already know (Ambrose et al., 2010). Students have to construct their own understanding by situating new information within their existing knowledge of a topic. By doing so, they begin to densify their own neural network, which leads to better comprehension overall. You can facilitate this process by asking students to identify connections between new concepts and existing knowledge and experiences. This can take many forms; one simple approach is to ask students to write or record a short reflection or create an electronic or paper-and-pen concept map, early in a module, to show how new topics relate to former topics in the class.

We also know that foundational information is necessary for higher-order cognition (Miller, 2014). Think about the difficulty of solving a quadratic equation without having your multiplication table memorized. To engage in more complicated mental tasks such as analysis, argumentation, and synthesis, as well as critical thinking and creative problem-solving, students must develop automaticity with basic concepts: that is, they don't have to stop to think about every little step in the process. We can understand automaticity when we think about driving a car, for example, or riding a bicycle. We undertake these everyday activities without needing to consciously process every decision or action involved. To help our students master complicated skills and tasks, we should design learning activities which promote automaticity with basic information. This can be achieved through skill drill kinds of exercises and homework sets.

Another key consideration is the importance of retrieval practice. We can take advantage of the so-called "testing effect," which refers to our ability to remember information better when asked to recall or retrieve it (think self-quizzing using paper or app-based flash cards). Auto-graded quizzes in the LMS make it easy to structure retrieval practice for our students, since we know that many students are unlikely to quiz themselves (Miller, 2014). These quizzes also promote the development of automaticity, and you can get creative with how you structure these assessments. If, for example, you think of module quizzes as opportunities for assessment *as* learning in addition to assessment *of* learning, you might offer multiple attempts so that students have an opportunity to immerse themselves in material they missed on their first try, thereby exploring new concepts and cementing new learning in long-term memory.

These auto-graded quizzes serve many purposes. They also provide important feedback for both you as the instructor and the students themselves. Based on quiz scores and item analysis, you can see where students are still struggling. This perspective may prompt you to record a quick, casual, explanation video in which you provide a clarifying example or illustration. Or you may choose to share helpful external resources such as YouTube explainer videos provided by other Economics educators.

And when students score more poorly than they expected to (false confidence is common in higher education assessments), this feedback can nudge them to seek additional assistance such as tutoring or to develop better study habits. Indeed, we do our students a disservice when the only assessments in our courses are high-stakes exams. Giving students feedback that is early and often—through, for example, weekly module quizzes—helps them accurately assess their own readiness for tests and exams (Miller, 2014).

We also know from the literature that spaced practice (studying in short sessions over multiple days) is more effective than massed practice (cramming for a test). In the short term, cramming works. Students can perform better on the next day's test than if they hadn't studied for hours and hours the day before. But that learning is shallow. It doesn't stick. When asked to recall the same information on the final exam or in subsequent classes, students will struggle.

An effective way to apply this principle is to space out assignment, discussion, and quiz due dates throughout each week. Online learners are busy and may underestimate the amount of time needed to succeed. They may expect to be able to do the entire week's work in one day. Spacing out due dates throughout each week holds students accountable to engage regularly with course concepts. Be sure to develop a consistent routine though: our brains crave structure (Mays Imad, personal communication, April 18, 2022). Following the same weekly schedule will help students know what to expect and plan accordingly.

An additional consideration is that, as social beings, we understand new information better when we talk about it with other people. This point is especially true in some collectivistic or interdependent cultures, and is why I advocate for the effective use of discussion forums. "Talking" about course concepts, even in asynchronous, written posts, helps students learn from other students and thereby attain a deeper understanding overall. Some LMSs such as Canvas make it easy to record discussion posts, enabling students to literally talk about ideas they're learning about. This activity can support students from oral cultures as well as verbal processors. Consider offering students the choice of whether to write or record discussion submissions, an easy way to begin applying Universal Design for Learning.

One final principle to consider here: we have limited attentional resources at any given time (Cavanagh, 2016). Contrary to popular belief, we can only focus on one narrowly defined thing at a time. That's why texting and driving is so dangerous. We fool ourselves into thinking we can attend to road and traffic conditions while also reading, thinking about, and replying to text messages. It's simply not possible. Given this reality, we should reduce distractions and tasks that are unrelated to course concepts yet require cognitive processing. A common pitfall in asynchronous online classes is confusing organization and navigation. If students have to search to find where to upload an assignment or send you a message, their attentional resources are depleted. Creating clear and intuitive navigation frees up capacity for the learning task at hand. Consider asking students or colleagues for feedback on the "usability" of your class. Is it confusing and hard to find things? That makes it hard to use and therefore hinders focus and learning.

This overview has been a very cursory introduction to learning science. There's more, much more, to know about how we learn, but this chapter provides a few ideas about how to structure online class interactions to apply learning science.

Universal Design for Learning

Another important theoretical framework that guides our approach is Universal Design for Learning, or UDL (CAST, n.d.). Originally developed by neuroscientists in the 1980s, UDL is based on Universal Design in the built, physical world. Universal Design emerged in the 1960s with a goal of reducing the need for accommodations or special assistance for anyone with varying needs and abilities. For example, a door with a doorknob assumes that individuals who need to enter the area can easily turn the doorknob. An automatic sliding door, by contrast, increases access for everyone (Hedtke, 2022). UDL represents the same idea. This framework helps us work toward the goal of lowering barriers to learning for everyone.

Research has shown that the way we learn is unique (CAST, n.d.). No two people learn in the same way, and certainly we all have differing preferences, needs, and circumstances. UDL accounts for individual learner variability through three guiding principles based on the neuroscience of how we learn. Briefly, this approach is about offering options and supports that are part of the very design of the class. Applying UDL makes it less likely that students will have to request accommodations to successfully access and navigate our online spaces, both of which are necessary to learn. Further, restricting access, even inadvertently, fosters inequity. UDL principles guide our ability to create and teach engaging and inclusive classes in all modalities.

First, we offer multiple means of engagement. Put simply, we offer choices. Students can choose topics or formats that they find most relevant or interesting for their particular goals, strengths, and abilities, activities in which they can best demonstrate mastery of class concepts. The second principle is to offer multiple means of representation. How can students get to the information they need? Are all class materials in written form? If so, we present a barrier to those who prefer media-based learning experiences. If we add audio recordings or mini-video lectures, we offer alternative pathways for these learners as well as for students who want to learn while commuting to work, for example, (Tobin

& Behling, 2018). Third, we offer multiple means of action and expression. Providing options for how students interact with, explore, and practice new concepts and skills empowers them to develop and demonstrate their learning in ways that support their individual success (Novak & Van Rees, 2019).

Offering all these options can seem overwhelming, so we would do well to take Tobin and Behling's (2018) advice to start small and to be strategic. They propose a "+1" approach. Identify a pinch point in a class you've taught a few (or several) times. Is there an assignment that students consistently struggle with? A concept that stumps many? You'll end up reducing your workload when you add alternatives for that topic or activity. Here's what I mean: if students comprehend a concept more fully because you added, say, a mini-video explanation or analogy to the assigned reading, it's likely they'll ask fewer questions by email or during your office (or student) hours. Likewise, investing time in devising options for an artifact students create to show their knowledge (e.g., a paper or a video presentation) may, in the long run, both reduce grading time and increase your grading enjoyment as you assess a variety of well-developed submissions instead of marking the same paper assignment over and over again.

In short, applying UDL is not likely to be a task we'll ever be done with, but beginning to think about baking alternatives and choices into the design of our classes helps us advance equity and support our well-being and success, too. For example, in a large enrollment, technical class, it could benefit students to provide a Guided Notes document or partial PowerPoint slides as an option for students who benefit from structured note-taking exercises. Or you could provide a transcript or bulleted outline (with timestamps) for video-recorded lectures, to help students grasp the overall organization of a recorded lecture and skip to a section for review if needed. Both of these approaches facilitate learning for students with differing needs and preferences, and the better learning that is likely to result can help reduce emailed questions or those posed in office hours.

Emotion Science: The Power Tool of Engaging and Effective Teaching

To supplement our understanding of how people learn we can turn to emotion science. This field of study tells us that emotions and cognition are inextricably linked; that is, we can't think without involving our emotions, contrary to popular belief (Immordino-Yang & Damasio, 2007). Indeed, emotions impact everything that happens in online classes, for better or for worse. Our task is to apply emotion science in our online spaces to motivate students, capture and keep their attention, and help them persist, learn, and remember what they've learned long-term. Doing so will likely also result in our increased enjoyment of and improved efficacy in online teaching.

Researchers have studied the effect of positive academic emotions such as hope and joy on academic achievement (Pekrun et al., 2007). In multiple studies across varying contexts, findings suggest that cultivating positive experiences through creating psychologically safe learning environments and through building students' self-efficacy, as examples, predicts student engagement, motivation, and persistence, all of which boost learning.

It may not be surprising to know that the opposite is true, too. Negative experiences shut down cognition. Students who experience mistrust, fear, and anxiety (perhaps because of an innocuous reason such as a well-intentioned but still confusing online class layout) have fewer available cognitive resources to focus, attend, and process. Test anxiety is a well-known manifestation of this phenomenon. Think about it as bandwidth. Our capacity for cognitive engagement is reduced when there are negative drains on our mental capacity (Verschelden, 2017).

The overarching principle here is, as noted above, to minimize negative and maximize positive experiences in our classes. Following are some affective-science-based principles and applications to promote engaged learning.

To begin, let's consider a key finding from the work of leading affective researcher Mary Helen Immordino-Yang: we can only think deeply about what we care about (2016). Earlier we considered the automaticity of activities like driving a car or riding a bike. When you aren't wholly focused on the task underway, your mind drifts to topics that you care about: perhaps the potential for conflict in today's departmental meeting with a contentious colleague, or what's for dinner, or maybe where you plan to take your next vacation. When we care about something, we are more deeply invested in that topic or task.

We can apply this finding to great effect simply by asking ourselves, "Why will my students care about what they're learning or doing in this lesson or activity?" This question also taps into UDL principles of providing multiple means of engagement (Novak & Van Rees, 2019). One practical way of helping students care about the task at hand is to highlight, or better yet, invite students to identify for themselves, how what they're doing is relevant or useful for them (Yeager et al., 2014). Point out to students how they'll apply this week's learning in an upcoming project, or on the final exam, or in the subsequent class, or on the job. Ask students to reflect, in a short written or recorded response, on how this week's concepts relate to their daily lives. Or assign forward-looking assessments that invite them to use new skills to solve problems or answer questions they'll likely encounter in the future in a professional or home or community setting (Artze-Vega et al., 2023). When students see the utility value of even tedious tasks like homework sets or practice exercises, they are more likely to willingly set aside distractions such as social media or online videos and focus on the task at hand (Yeagar et al., 2014).

In addition to helping students care about, and therefore engage more deeply with, course concepts, emotion science suggests further principles for application. In the words of Sarah Rose Cavanagh, author of *The Spark of Learning: Energizing the College Classroom with the Science of Emotion* (2016), "Cognitive resources are limited. Emotion trumps" (2019). Emotions grab our attention, help us focus, motivate productive learning behaviors (or not), and consolidate information and experiences into long-term memory. Creating class experiences that evoke an emotional response is a primary way to attract and hold students' limited attention. If you're worried about what your students are doing on the other side of their screen, with their camera off in Zoom, for example, design emotionally arousing activities.

How to do this? Take a cue from advertisers and the media, who use images, videos, and audio to appeal to our emotions. In your slides, include a poignant photo of people impacted by a policy or principle you're discussing. Share TED Talk videos with compelling speakers, or news items that show how class concepts are important in real life.

Tell stories from your own experience to demonstrate principles in action and ask students to tell their stories or share their experiences in discussion posts or individual reflections. Create assignments which offer a narrative option: write a story (or create a graphic novel or record a video) that shows how a character could navigate a disciplinary problem in the workplace, for example. Offering options such as these taps into UDL principles, too, as learners can choose how best to show what they've learned.

Further, assign activities that are fun or inherently interesting. A biology professor I know asks his students to collect a sample from the shopping cart handle at the local supermarket, then analyze it for the microbes it contains. Gross! But also, fascinating! Offer quiz games as an engaging way to structure retrieval practice. Or ask students to engage in a more sobering exercise to explore the gravity of course concepts. Such activities hook students' emotions, prompt deeper engagement, and facilitate better learning in turn.

The above principles and suggestions have to do with harnessing the power of emotions in positive ways (Darby, 2018). We would do well to briefly consider how online classes might inadvertently foster negative experiences, as those are highly demotivating (for us as well as for our students).

First, for many people, online classes are isolating, creating a sense of loneliness and a lack of connections with others in the class. Whether asynchronous or synchronous, online classes typically operate at a distance. Because we are such social beings, this isolation can hinder engagement and learning. Many online students struggle to feel part of a group, which in turn decreases their sense of belonging. Multiple studies show that belongingness predicts academic achievement; for one example, see Pedler et al. (2020). We can foster online students' sense of belonging by designing classes which include social and emotional presences from the CoI framework. Further chapters in this volume explore how to do so in more depth.

We can also work to anticipate and prevent confusion, since that leads to frustration and disengagement. In an asynchronous class, students can't raise their hand in real time to ask for clarification of a concept or task. Even in online live lessons, the distance created by the screens hinders students' connection with you and may therefore limit their willingness to ask a question during class. Knowing this, make an effort to provide explicitly clear guidance for class organization and topic and task instructions. A short screen capture video tour of your online class space (not more than three minutes, if possible) helps alleviate fears and anxiety about how the class is set up, what to do first, etc. A slide or document with clear breakout group directions, including time expectations for tasks, structures the time and reduces nerves or reluctance to engage ("Take ten minutes to discuss these three questions on the chapter. Then take another five minutes to create a bullet-point summary of main ideas from your discussion."). And clear instructions for any task, such as discussion forums, tests, papers or projects, and group work, likewise helps to reduce anxiety and free up cognitive resources for learning. Consider using rubrics, checklists, and examples of good work to provide even more direction.

Emotions are powerful. Like any power tool, we must wield them carefully. Attending to both emotional presence and emotion science, in informed and thoughtful ways, can result in increased student engagement, motivation, focus, and memory, all of which are necessary for learning.

PRACTICAL RAMIFICATIONS: DESIGNING AND TEACHING EFFECTIVE, EQUITY-FOCUSED ONLINE CLASSES

In addition to the suggestions woven throughout the above sections, here are six key takeaways, based on what we've explored in the literature, to facilitate effective learning online.

1.   Forefront Interactions with Other People in the Class

To prevent online classes from feeling like electronic correspondence courses, regularly interact with your students, and structure purposeful interactions among students (Darby, 2019). It's possible, and important, to prioritize "presence" such that your online students know you're there, and that you're a real person. This need for social interaction can also be met by other students, as we'll see next. Regarding yourself, help your students see and get to know you a bit. Make frequent appearances in asynchronous online classes through strategic one-to-many communications such as announcements, reminders, and discussion posts. Share one or more photos of yourself, not only in professional settings, but also in real life, perhaps sharing pictures of pets or favorite hobbies or travel destinations. If you're an emoji person, include these in text-based communications such as assignment comments or announcements. Return student work in a timely fashion. Take advantage of functions within your LMS (such as the "Message students who…" tool in the Canvas gradebook, which allows targeted communications based on student performance on assessments and activities). Respond quickly to student emails. No, you are not an online chatbot, but the most frequent student complaint in online classes is the lack of an actively participating instructor (Glazier & Harris, 2020). Communicate and honor your availability policy, when students can expect an email reply, etc.

Intentionally foster connections among students, too. Introduction discussion forums, icebreaker and community-building activities, and well designed and facilitated module discussions and breakout groups all help students feel like they're not alone, while also promoting peer-to-peer learning. A helpful source for building community online is the Equity Unbound website (OneHE, 2024), filled with a variety of culturally relevant and inclusive activities and ideas to build all-important connections and relationships in online spaces.

2.   Protect Your Time and Energy to Be Your Best Online Teaching Self

Although instructor presence is highly important, it's easy to overdo this component, leading you to spend hours and hours grading, answering emails, and more. When you are depleted, it's impossible to teach effectively. It's essential to protect downtime for yourself, which can be challenging if you're new to online.

In your syllabus and via announcements, inform students of your general availability as well as unexpected absences. For example, tell your students that you're offline after 6:00pm, and that if they email you after that time, they can expect a response prior to 6:00pm on the following weekday. Are you online on weekends? Explain when you're available, and when you're not. Share what your typical turnaround time is when grading assignments. These approaches give you and your students peace of mind by helping everyone know what to expect. Similarly, if you have a planned or unplanned absence, send a quick announcement to let students know when you'll be back. Online students just want to know that you're there and engaged. Communicating about brief absences not only helps students know what to expect, which reduces anxiety, it also helps them see you as a real person, which fosters engagement and motivation to learn.

3. To Save Time in the Long Run, Provide Explicit Guidance

You'll likely reduce the number of email and office-hour questions you receive when students clearly know what you're asking them to do. Creating detailed instructions, rubrics, checklists, and mini-explainer videos are well worth the time involved, as these can promote student confidence and self-efficacy. You'll likely find that students submit higher quality work, requiring less time for individual grading and feedback.

4. Offer Options Where Possible

In line with UDL, add options for engaging with class materials, exploring and practicing concepts and skills, and demonstrating knowledge. Can students watch a mini-lecture video or print and take notes on a text transcript (or both at the same time)? Can they write a discussion post or record a video? Can they engage in a breakout group or complete and submit an in-class exercise on their own? Can they choose a topic of interest and relevance to them and their local community for a major assessment? Can they present their work in a format of their choosing? When we build options and alternatives into the very design of our online classes, we lower barriers to learning and facilitate achievement and success.

5. Structure Intentionally Sequenced Modules and Activities Based on Learning Science

Many asynchronous classes follow a predictable, yet ineffective pattern: each week or module contains readings (and sometimes videos), static slide decks, quizzes, stilted discussion forums, and paper or project assignments. Very often, all activities are due at the end of the module week, which fosters procrastination and works against the spaced practice principle.

Instead, include deliberately paced active learning exercises that work well in virtual environments. Publisher materials may provide options for practice or homework sets and quizzes or checks for understanding built into course readings or videos. If so, take advantage of these opportunities to get students doing something rather than passively reading or watching materials. Create additional interactive tasks in online modules or Zoom sessions: prior knowledge surveys, concept maps or other advanced organizers, connection activities, and retrieval practice and reflection activities such as writing or recording three key takeaways from a module or discussion forum. If synchronous class meetings are an option for you, consider how best to use the valuable time you have together. For example, ask students to submit questions about what's still confusing on a discussion board or anonymous survey (Artze-Vega et al.,

2023). Then use synchronous time to address the confusing concepts, since students can ask additional questions of you, the expert, in real time. These and other ideas are worth considering as you begin to build interactive tasks into your online classes.

6.   Design for Emotion

One of the most effective ways to keep students engaged is to get them emotionally invested in their learning (Cavanagh, 2016). Even (or especially) in STEM fields where the content seems neutral or objective, we can attract and keep students' attention, focus, and time on task by creating emotionally evocative lessons, materials, and activities. Tell stories. Highlight relevance. Ask why your students will care about what they're learning. Create emotional appeals through media and prompts. Offer tasks that are fun, or poignant, or funny (such as Bungee-Jumping Barbie, a well-known exercise in statistics classes, where students calculate linear regressions to determine the ideal length of cord before the Barbie doll goes splat on the rocks). In careful and well-structured ways, invite emotional connections with course concepts, and you'll likely see better learning as a result.

CONCLUSION

Teaching online requires different approaches than teaching in person. It also offers creative opportunities to engage students in their learning. To become adept at facilitating effective learning in virtual environments, we can look to principles and practices drawn from the literature. Additionally, the chapters in this book provide evidence and strategies to equip instructors for teaching online Economics classes. Since online offerings are on the rise, investing time and effort in developing as online educators is worth doing for the well-being of yourself as well as for the well-being and equitable success of your students.

REFERENCES

Ambrose, S. A., Bridges, M. W., DiPietro, M., Lovett, M. C., & Norman, M. K. (2010). *How learning works*. Jossey-Bass.

Artze-Vega, I., Darby, F., Dewsbury, B., & Imad, M. (2023). *The Norton guide to equity-minded teaching*. W. W. Norton & Company.

Artze-Vega, I., & Taylor, E. (2020). Foreword. In P. Felten & L. M. Lambert, *Relationship-rich education: How human connections drive success in college*. Johns Hopkins University Press.

CAST. (n.d.). The UDL Guidelines. https://udlguidelines.cast.org/

Cavanagh, S. R. (2016). *The spark of learning: Energizing the college classroom with the science of emotion*. West Virginia University Press.

Cavanagh, S. R. (2019, March 11). How to make your teaching more engaging. *The Chronicle of Higher Education*. https://www.chronicle.com/article/how-to-make-your-teaching-more-engaging/

Cleveland-Innes, M., & Campbell, P. (2012). Emotional presence, learning, and the online learning environment. *The International Review of Research in Open and Distributed Learning, 13*(4), 269–292. https://doi.org/10.19173/irrodl.v13i4.1234

Cohn, J. (2021, September 21). *Enhancing the student experience.* [Virtual Forum]. The Chronicle of Higher Education.

Darby, F. (2018, January 3). Harness the power of emotions to help your students learn. *Faculty Focus*. https://www.facultyfocus.com/articles/teaching-and-learning/harness-power-emotions-help-students-learn/

Darby, F. (2019, April 17). How to be a better online teacher. *The Chronicle of Higher Education*. https://www.chronicle.com/article/how-to-be-a-better-online-teacher/

Darby, F., & Lang, J. M. (2019). *Small teaching online: Applying learning science in online classes*. Jossey-Bass.

Felten, P., & Lambert, L. M. (2020). *Relationship-rich education: How human connections drive success in college*. Johns Hopkins University Press.

Garrison, D. R., Anderson, T., & Archer, W. (2000). Critical inquiry in a text-based environment: Computer conferencing in higher education. *The Internet and Higher Education, 2*(2–3), 87–105. https://doi.org/10.1016/S1096-7516(00)00016-6

Glazier, R. & Harris, H. S. (2020). How teaching with rapport can improve online student success and retention: Data from two empirical studies. *The Quarterly Review of Distance Education, 21*(4), 1-17.

Hedtke, A. (2022, April 12). *Network.* [Discussion board post]. EDUCAUSE Learning Lab. https://academy.educause.edu.

Immordino-Yang, M. H. (2016). *Emotions, learning, and the brain*. W. W. Norton & Company, Inc.

Immordino-Yang, M. H., and Damasio, A. (2007). We feel, therefore we learn: The relevance of affective and social neuroscience to education. *Mind, Brain, and Education, 1*(1), 3–10. https://doi.org/10.1111/j.1751-228X.2007.00004.x

Lang, J. M. (2016). *Small teaching: Everyday lessons from the science of learning*. Jossey-Bass.

Miller, M. D. (2014). *Minds online: Teaching effectively with technology*. Harvard University Press.

Novak, K. and Van Rees, S. (2019). 3 questions to kickstart Universal Design for Learning in your classroom. *Think Inclusive*. https://www.thinkinclusive.us/post/3-questions-to-kickstart-universal-design-for-learning-in-your-classroom

OneHE. (2024). *Equity Unbound*. https://onehe.org/equity-unbound/

Pedler, M. L., Willis, R., & Nieuwoudt, J. E. (2020). A sense of belonging at university: student retention, motivation, and enjoyment. *Journal of Further and Higher Education, 46*(3), 397–408. https://doi.org/10.1080/0309877X.2021.1955844

Pekrun, R., Frenzel, A. C., Perry, R. P., & Goetz, T. (2007). The control-value theory of achievement emotions: An integrative approach to emotions in education. In P. A. Schutz & R. P. Perry (Eds.), *Emotion and education* (pp. 13–36). Academic Press.

Seaman, J. E., Allen, I. E., & Seaman, J. (2018). *Grade increase: Tracking distance education in the United States*. Babson Survey Research Group. https://www.bayviewanalytics.com/reports/gradeincrease.pdf

Shaikh, U. U., & Asif, Z. (2022). Persistence and dropout in higher online education: Review and categorization of factors. *Frontiers in Psychology*, 13, 1–14. https://doi.org/10.3389/fpsyg.2022.902070

Tobin, T. J., & Behling, K. T. (2018). *Reach everyone, teach everyone: Universal Design for Learning in higher education.* West Virginia University Press.

UDL on Campus (n.d.). *Executive functioning in online environments.* http://udloncampus.cast.org/page/teach_executive

Verschelden, C. (2017). *Bandwidth recovery: Helping students reclaim cognitive resources lost to poverty, racism, and social marginalization.* Stylus Publishing.

Yeager, D. S., Henderson, M. D., Paunesku, D., Walton, G. M., D'Mello, S., Spitzer, B. J., & Duckworth, A. L. (2014). Boring but important: A self-transcendent purpose for learning fosters academic self-regulation. *Journal of Personality and Social Psychology, 107*(4), 559–580. https://doi.org/10.1037/a0037637

2. Making learning stick in online education

Michael Enz

INTRODUCTION

During your academic career, you might have heard someone say either "that person is a natural teacher" or "I am good at mathematics, but not so good at writing." Becoming a good teacher, a good writer, and gaining mathematical skills all require one basic concept: learning. Unfortunately, learning is hard. However, every one of us is capable of learning and the science of learning literature can help each instructor understand how to place our students in the best position to learn. The following chapter provides six concepts from the science of learning literature and how to implement these concepts in an online course.

GET STUDENTS INVOLVED

Before presenting each of the six key concepts, it is crucial to create student buy-in for what you are asking them to do. Learning is hard and you are going to ask them to depart from what many of them see as a "normal" classroom. Gary Smith (2008) provides great insights on getting students to buy in on a learning-centered classroom. On the first day of class, he asks them the following question: "Thinking of what you want to get out of your college education and this course, which of the following is most important to you? 1. Acquiring information (facts, principles, concepts) 2. Learning how to use information and knowledge in new situations 3. Developing lifelong learning skills." I ask this same question to my students and find similar results to Smith: most of the students choose the second and third tasks. Then the instructor can follow up with "Of these three goals, which do you think you can make headway outside of the class by your own reading and studying, and which do you think would be best achieved in class working with your classmates and me?" I also ask my students this and find similar results to Smith, that almost all students select the second and third options. This process allows the instructor to make sure that students understand the course design and the importance of working during class on different activities. It also stresses the importance of working outside of class to be prepared and to get the most out of each class.

Concept 1: Practice

Many of the examples of implementing the science of learning in an online classroom that this chapter covers are from Enz (2021). At one point in their lives, many of our students have participated in a sport or played a musical instrument and know the importance of practice when it comes to improving that activity. However, few of our students make the same connection between practice and learning in their classes. A story that I often tell in my classes is my first attempt at running a marathon at the age of 28 and finishing in four and a half hours. At the age of 40, I ran a marathon in two hours and fifty-five minutes. The primary explanation for the improvement in time is the amount and type of practice in preparing for a race and what I learned about running a marathon over those years. In *Make it Stick: The Science of Successful Learning* (Brown et al., 2014), the authors describe their study of the retrieval practice of testing. They approach a middle school principal and eventually team with Patrice Bain (a social studies teacher) and Pooja Agarwal (a research assistant) to develop test questions. Students who were quizzed on material scored a full grade better than the students who were not quizzed. The effect of higher scores is found in additional studies of different grade levels, different subjects, and in longer-term testing (McDermott et al., 2014). Using quizzes is one form of practice that can assist in the learning process.

Another form of practice is using class time to work through problems. Willingham (2009) notes that students can improve their performance on a cognitive task through classwork. A common strategy in face-to-face classes is to give students a problem to work on in small groups and have the instructor walk around the classroom providing the appropriate scaffolding as students tackle the problems. Then, you can bring everyone back together as a class and discuss the solutions that the groups created.

This process of assigning a problem in small groups is relatively easy to transfer to a synchronous online course. Using most video communications platforms, you can assign students to breakout rooms to work on the problems. These breakout rooms can be created with pre-planned groups that you have chosen, or Zoom (for example) allows for a random assignment of groups. As Dan Levy (2020) notes, the breakout rooms tool can replace the think/ pair/share activities that many educators use in a face-to-face classroom. The ability of an instructor to join a group (whether requested by the group or initiated by the instructor) simulates the process of walking around the classroom and providing the appropriate scaffolding. After groups have been given a chance to prepare a solution to a problem, you can call them all back into the main group and call on members of each group to discuss the different answers. In a face-to-face classroom, it is easy to check with students to find out how far each group has been able to progress on a given problem. In Zoom, you can use broadcast messages that are sent to each group letting them know how much time they have left to work on a problem and encouraging them to invite you to their group if they are struggling to progress.

It is important to note that not all practice is the same. As Bjork and Bjork (2020) note, some conditions can rapidly improve short-term performance, but fail to enhance long-term retention. Learning in conditions where students are challenged, and the rate of apparent learning is slowed, can optimize long-term retention. The authors reference a previous work titled "Making things hard on yourself, but in a good way: Creating desirable difficulties to enhance learning" to reiterate the importance of desirable difficulties (Bjork and Bjork, 2011). In a study by McDaniel, et al. (1986), the authors find that strategies that slow readers down like leaving out letters in words result in readers remembering more. A key challenge for instructors is to create problems that have a level of difficulty that is appropriate for the students' previous knowledge. One way of assessing the students' current knowledge is to have them complete problems before class using software provided by publishers such as Achieve, Mindtap, MyEconLab, Inquizitive, etc. Each software provides the instructor with a breakdown of how students performed on each topic.

It is important to decide what you want your students to practice. For example, at the start of each face-to-face class, I want my students to practice retrieving concepts from the assigned reading. When students first encounter new material, they encode and store the new information. As instructors, we can have students practice retrieving that information from storage and preparing to use it. Roediger and Karpicke (2006) conducted a study to examine the impact of simply rereading a passage versus being asked to write down everything that one can remember. Students who were asked to reread were able to score better when quizzed only five minutes later. However, when quizzed a week later, the students who wrote down everything they could recall outperformed the group that reread the passage. This result is consistent with the previous section regarding desirable difficulties. The task that is easier results in more short-term memory but less long-term memory. As Butler and Roediger (2007) find, the design of the recall activity can impact the ability of the student to recall information over time. In my face-to-face classes, I focus on asking questions that require students to generate their answers rather than choosing from a list of multiple-choice answers. In an online class, this initial retrieval practice becomes slightly more challenging. However, you can pose a question and ask all students to create their answers in the Chat tool in Zoom.

Be careful to note that all students should immediately record their answers, but not submit them in the Chat until you ask them to do so, so that all students are submitting their answers at the same time and not simply copying what someone else has written. Derek Bruff (2019) and Dan Levy (2020) provide many excellent tips on using the polling feature in Zoom as a quick way to gauge whether students can recall information.

Concept 2: Motivation

Many instructors had no problem being motivated as undergraduate or graduate students. Early on in my teaching career, I attempted to motivate my students to learn the material by making the material more entertaining or connecting it to pop culture examples that were fun. As the previous section notes, learning is hard, and making concepts fun or easy may not encourage long-term memory. In *How Learning* Works (Ambrose, et al., 2010), the authors argue that one approach to motivation breaks it down into two separate parts: subjective value and expectancies. The subjective value is the extent to which the topic is important to the learner while the expectancies represent how much the learner believes that practice will lead to a positive outcome. One way to increase motivation is to make sure that students have some voice or agency in their learning. Mitra and Gross (2009) describe student voice as an opportunity for individuals to influence decisions that will shape their lives. This is a good description of the general sense of voice or agency. I am particularly fond of the description from Toshalis and Nakkula (2012) where they state, "student voice is the antithesis of depersonalized, standardized, and homogenized educational experiences because it begins and ends with the thoughts, feelings, visions, and actions of the students themselves." From the start of the class, make sure that the expectations are clear for each assessment and stress the opportunities for students to make decisions regarding their assessment. Instead of assigning a task that can be completed by writing a paper, creating a podcast, or recording a presentation, make sure that the students know what a successful form of each will involve. Providing choice for students allows them the opportunity to own their work because it came from their choice.

Joshua Eyler (2018) tells a wonderful story about Donald Saari in the book *How Humans Learn*. Saari attempts to motivate his students by joining them in an exploration of a topic and collectively building connections to the material. In a face-to-face classroom, I often use storytelling as a method of creating motivation. To motivate the impacts of increasing and decreasing marginal products of labor I use an example of fast-food production (Enz, 2016). This example is familiar to many students who have either worked in the fast-food industry, have seen a fast-food kitchen, or would desperately like to avoid fast-food employment. The example usually provides the students with some humor as the instructor acts out the production process in a fast-food restaurant. As Cavanaugh (2016) notes, activating emotions in students begins a process through the body and brain which makes the memory stronger. The student experience of listening to a story over a video communications platform is quite different than being in a room during an impassioned tale that is collectively experienced with your classmates. However, you can still create emotional responses in your students that can enhance learning. For example, in a face-to-face class I might tell a story that elicits an emotional response because of the way I move around the classroom. This type of story would not translate well unless my camera were able to track my physical movement. Instructors need to consider why a particular teaching method is effective and whether that translates from face-to-face to the online environment.

Another way to increase motivation is by building better relationships with your students. This allows you to relate to them personally as you discuss how to experience success in the class. In a face-to-face class, many instructors might show up to class 10 minutes early to have casual conversations with their students to learn more about them and their general interests. This can be repeated in Zoom class by opening the class early and allowing students to enter early. Even in an 8:30 am class, I show up to a Zoom class at least 10 minutes ahead of time to chat with anyone as they enter the class.

It is important to stress different connections: both between instructor and student and between student and student. In a face-to-face classroom, there are many opportunities for students to interact with one another and the instructor. On the first day of online class, I make sure the students can interact with a few different groups of students and encourage them to create online study groups. I attempt to use personal examples to connect with my students so that they can view me as a human and not as a screen. I offer a video presentation of our syllabus where I add my views on the importance of policies or why I have designed this class in a certain manner. Finally, I provide a video introducing myself to the class where I present pictures of me from my childhood forward so they can see me as a person. To increase the connections between students, Darby and Lang (2019) recommend requiring peer-to-peer interactions in the class. This can be done through some of the breakout rooms group activities that I described or by having students create an introduction video of themselves and having students respond to one another. One word of caution is for you to select a genuine activity. Students have been in enough classes now where they are asked to post something on a discussion board and provide "x" number of comments on other student's posts. If students view the task as simply checking boxes, then they will not experience the motivation as a genuine interaction.

Concept 3: Connections

As a student moves from novice to expert in a discipline, they develop the ability to make connections between different concepts within and outside of the discipline. Ambrose and Lovett (2014) note that the knowledge students bring with them to a class plays a crucial role in the learning of new material. When you start a face-to-face class, you might have a no-stakes quiz or activity generated to learn what type of knowledge students are bringing with them to the class. In an online course, this might be even easier to implement because you can create the assessment through your Learning Management System and students will already be accustomed to accessing materials online. Do not assume that your students have the knowledge or skills from a prerequisite course. Instead, perform an initial assessment to determine their previous knowledge. This step allows you to determine how much time you will have to spend reviewing concepts as you progress. If you do not want to prepare a specific assessment to learn what your students already know from prerequisite courses, you can pose specific questions and ask your students to formulate their answers in the Chat. Once again, remind them to write their answers, but wait until instructed to send to the Chat. After class, you can check the Chat Transcript to review answers given by students.

In addition to connecting new material to previous knowledge, students can also connect the material to their daily lives. Darby and Lang (2019) note that students who connect course material to their daily experiences can achieve deeper processing and a richer understanding of the material. In reference to the previous section, this is an excellent opportunity for students to gain some voice or agency in their responses. Instead of preparing an activity where you ask students to explain what type of price discrimination is occurring at a movie theater, you can simply ask students to provide an example of and explain the type of price discrimination from their daily lives. This forces the student to make the connection between the concept and their personal experience. It is also a great opportunity to have students create examples that might cover several different types of price discrimination. If you have them create their answers in the Chat and have them wait until everyone submits at once, you can find different examples of third-degree and second-degree price discrimination and probably some that come close to first-degree price discrimination. You could also look at all the examples that are given and issue a few polls where you ask the students to answer a multiple-choice question: "What type of price discrimination is taking place in the following example?"

The study of economics has an opportunity to make important human connections with our students, something that unfortunately is often overlooked. Students learn more when they think that the subject matter can be used to increase the well-being of other human beings (Yeager, Henderson et al.,

2014). Showing students how using economics can improve the well-being of a society is something we can easily do in a face-to-face class and online. While conducting an online course, it is crucial to have your students see you as a human being instead of a box on a screen. Covering examples of how economics can improve the well-being of people's lives allows students to think of you as more than a screen. For example, when covering positive externalities, you can use an example of flu shots to understand that the market outcome fails to maximize the well-being of society. However, through different forms of intervention, society can increase its net benefit with greater production and consumption of flu shots.

Finally, bring enthusiasm to your teaching. In *Uncommon Sense Teaching* (Oakley et al., 2021), the authors summarize work by educational psychologist Richard Mayer (Mayer, 2014; Mayer et al., 2020) by emphasizing that "when you are in front of a camera, you need to be bold and bigger than life." As we have learned during the COVID-19 pandemic, sitting in front of a computer screen for hours each day can be physically and emotionally draining. If students can engage in a class where the instructor is enthusiastic, it takes less energy for the student to be engaged.

Concept 4: Mindset

In Carol Dweck's seminal work on mindset (Dweck, 2006), a fixed mindset is one where abilities are believed to be fixed while a growth mindset is one where abilities can be developed. Dweck shows how success in a broad variety of areas, including school, is dependent on a growth mindset. Mueller and Dweck (1998) find that when children are praised for their natural abilities they perform worse than children who are praised for effort. Focusing on ability can lead an individual to think they will always perform well and therefore practice and work on something less. However, when praised for effort, an individual will be more motivated to work harder or practice more. Kray and Haselhuhn (2007) perform a study with their MBA students and find that students who have a growth mindset perform better in their negotiation activity than those who have a fixed mindset. One activity that I have implemented is presenting a copy of a transcript that has varying degrees of success as defined by most of the students. I eliminated the personal information so the students do not know the person behind the transcript. After asking the students to view the transcript, I ask the students what their opinions are of the students on the transcript. Many of the students comment on how "average" the student looks and wonders how the student could get a "C" in a Survey of Music Literature course and an "A" in a Senior Economics Seminar. Finally, I ask the students to identify in which class this student states they learned the most. The most common responses are classes where the student earned an "A."

I love using this example because the student on the transcript is me and the class that I learned the most in was an English Literature course my first year in college. During the discussion, students learn that I entered college with a below-average Verbal SAT score for my class. If I had adopted the mindset that "I am just not good at writing" then I would have never improved my writing. Instead, I knew I could improve my writing and worked very hard throughout the semester. Even though the course grade was a "B" the amount of learning was tremendous.

Our shift to online education in Spring 2020 provided another excellent example of a growth mindset. In February 2020, I knew nothing about Zoom. In March 2020, I was holding all my classes via Zoom. When I would try something new in class and it worked, I would usually comment that I had never tried that before and was hoping it would work. If I tried something new and it did not work, I explained what I had attempted, what I learned from my failure, and that I would work on it in the future. As Joshua Eyler (2018) suggests, students' fear of failure jeopardizes learning. As instructors, we need to create opportunities where students can fail and learn from that process. Unfortunately, many courses are designed where a single failure on an assessment can greatly damage the student's grade. In my principle online courses, I use the Learning Curve Assignments in Achieve where my students are graded by completion or incompletion. Their task is to reach a level of points for completion. The "penalty" for an incorrect response is that it takes longer to reach completion. This allows a student the opportunity to fail without encountering a large grade penalty.

How can you tell if your students have a fixed or growth mindset and are there steps you can take to change that mindset? For the first question, there is a short quiz developed by Dweck (2006) that you can issue to your students online. For the second, a group of researchers (Yeager, Johnson et al., 2014) created a short (under an hour), online growth mindset intervention that improved student performance. In addition to a one-time intervention, I would suggest reminding students throughout the semester about the ability to grow and to learn more. One point at which this reminder can be particularly important is when it comes to providing feedback.

Concept 5: Feedback

In *Powerful Teaching: Unleash the Science of Learning* (Agarwal & Bain, 2019), readers are given four powerful teaching tools to increase student learning. One of the tools, feedback-driven metacognition, focuses on how we can deliver feedback to our students in a way that will maximize learning for all students. The authors provide two illusions common among our students. The first illusion is that when students think they got something correct, they probably did. Agarwal et al. (2008) ask their college students to predict how well they will do in remembering a passage on a given topic. On average, the students estimated they would recall 64% of the reading passages, however when quizzed, they only remembered 49%. The second illusion from Agarwal and Bain (2019) is that students' confidence is always in sync with their learning. Students often claim that they felt like they knew the material until they took the test, or even after the test, they were confident that they did well.

To address these two illusions, instructors need to focus on the type of feedback they are giving their students. Brown, et al. (2014) reference Mike Ebersold's quote describing the peer review process, "if there are other neurosurgeons around you, it's a safeguard. If you are doing something that's not acceptable, they'll call you to task for it." This is not to encourage a hostile environment with your students, but they need feedback to understand what they know and what they do not know. Agarwal and Bain (2019) advise giving feedback for both correct and incorrect answers, prioritizing elaborative feedback, and encouraging students to make mistakes. For example, if a student provides a response of "supply goes up and the price increases and quantity increases," you can provide the following feedback: "You are correct that supply has increased because of the decrease in the price of an input. However, this shifts the supply curve to the right which means that price will decrease, and quantity will increase." This type of feedback allows the student to see all of the elements of their work that were correct and incorrect.

For most face-to-face classes, instructors have students turn in an assignment or test, and then the instructor provides written feedback after the assessment is marked. In an online class, you can provide this same type of feedback assuming the assessment is turned in online. Assuming the class size is manageable (a term that is up to you to define), you can create a video using Zoom and the student's work and record yourself going through the test with oral, rather than written feedback. In economics classes where there might be a lot of graphs that are provided in the answers, the instructor can draw the correct version of the graph while recording the video, so the student can receive feedback on exactly where the mistakes were made. If you worry about students being less inclined to read the feedback that you have provided if they earn a low score on an assessment, you can return the assessment with feedback only and ask students to provide the grade they thought they earned given their responses and your feedback. This also provides some of the voice or agency that was discussed earlier. Finally, you can record your classes online so students can access the feedback that you are giving on problems that you have worked on during a class or feedback that you are providing to an answer that was given by a student during class.

Concept 6: Interleaving

In *How We Learn*, Benedict Carey (2014) describes an experiment run by two researchers, Robert Kerr and Bernard Booth (1978). They recruited thirty-six eight-year-olds to toss a bean bag to a target. They separated them into two groups for practice sessions: one group threw at a target that was three feet away and another group alternated between a target two feet away and a target that was four feet away. Each person would throw a bag while their vision was obstructed, then their performance would be revealed before throwing again with vision obstructed. After twelve weeks of practice, they tested the performance of these two groups on a target that was three feet away. The group with the varied practice outperformed the group that practiced from three feet away. The researchers conducted the same experiment on an older group of twelve-year-olds and the varied practice group performed better than the fixed distance practice group by an even wider margin. This example of varied practice or interleaving applies to academic as well as physical pursuits.

Rohrer and Taylor (2006) had one group of students study math using blocked practice and another group use interleaving. They quizzed the groups right after the practice was complete and the blocked practice group outperformed the interleaving group with an average of 100% compared to 81%. However, when the same students were quizzed a day later, the scores of the blocking group dropped to 38% while the interleaving group only fell to 77%. Thus, the interleaving group essentially doubled the performance of the blocking group after twenty-four hours.

Interleaving does not improve learning in all cases. Agarwal and Bain (2019) provide a few cautionary notes when considering the adoption of interleaving. First, mixing everything up doesn't mean it's always beneficial for learning. A study examining different subjects finds that using interleaving in chemistry and history does not increase learning (Hausman & Kornell, 2014). A possible explanation is that the topics being interleaved are too different from one another. The benefits of interleaving are found in concepts that are similar rather than different so that students can begin to recognize the subtle differences in the similar concepts. The second note of caution is that taking one concept and presenting it in different ways is not interleaving. If a problem is presented in different ways, students might be able to apply the same solution strategy to each, rather than being forced to choose a different strategy that assists in the learning process. The final note of caution is that some students need scaffolding when encountering interleaving. Some students may not be able to access an interleaved approach directly and could benefit greatly from a mixed approach where the student encounters some blocking before the interleaving. As noted by Benedict Carey in *How We Learn* (2014), climbers and hikers have a saying: it's not an adventure until something goes wrong.

Each day in life we deal with situations that arise when something has gone wrong. If we only prepare for life by approaching a problem-solving process that involves blocking, then we will not be prepared for when something goes wrong.

When considering implementing interleaving in an online class, you can apply it to many of the teaching approaches that have been discussed throughout this chapter. A recall question at the start of class can apply to the assigned reading for that day or could cover a concept that was discussed the class period before or even a week before. When creating group problems in class, you can include a problem from the previous week or ask students to compare the problem they just solved to a problem on a similar concept that was covered the previous week. In *Small Teaching* (Lang, 2016), James Lang recommends setting aside a reasonable amount of quiz questions on previous material, for those who use quizzing. For example, if you use a weekly quiz of ten questions, he recommends you set aside two of those questions to address previous material. He also suggests that you can open a class session by posting a test question from a previous test or a question that applies to previous material that could be on the next test or cumulative final exam. If you choose to use interleaving, remember that the benefits from interleaving arise from covering related, yet distinct material.

CONCLUSION

Learning is hard, yet instructors can implement teaching techniques and develop courses that implement the science of learning to put their students in the best possible position to maximize learning. The implementation of the science of learning is possible in both face-to-face and online course formats. In each class modality, the instructor can improve the learning environment by becoming familiar with the science of learning literature. This chapter covers six concepts from the science of learning and how an instructor can implement them in an online modality. However, the use of the science of learning literature should not end with these six. If you are interested in the concepts covered in this chapter or simply want to know more about the science of learning, I recommend reading the following books (listed in alphabetic order): *How Humans Learn* by Joshua Eyler (2018); *How We Learn* by Benedict Carey (2014); *Make It Stick* by Peter Brown, Henry Roediger, and Mark McDaniel (2014); *Powerful Teaching: Unleash the Science of Learning* by Pooja Agarwal and Patrice Bain (2019); *Small Teaching: Everyday Lessons from the Science of Learning* by James Lang (2016); *Small Teaching Online* by Flower Darby and James Lang (2019); *Uncommon Sense: Practical Insights in Brain Science to Help Students Learn* by Barbara Oakley, Beth Rogowsky, and

Terrence Sejnowski (2021); and *Why Don't Students Like School?* by Daniel Willingham (2021).

REFERENCES

Agarwal, P. K. & Bain, P. M. (2019). *Powerful teaching: Unleash the science of learning.* Jossey Bass Inc.

Agarwal, P. K., Karpicke, J. D., Kang, S. H., Roediger, H. L., & McDermott, K. B. (2008). Examining the testing effect with open- and closed-book tests. *Applied Cognitive Psychology, 22*(7), 861–876. https://doi.org/10.1002/acp.1391

Ambrose, S. A., Bridges, M. W., DiPietro, M., Lovett, M. C., & Norman, M. K. (2010). *How learning works: Seven research-based principles for smart teaching.* John Wiley & Sons.

Ambrose, S. A., & Lovett, M. C. (2014). Prior knowledge is more than content: Skills and beliefs also impact learning. In V. A. Benassi, C. E. Overson, & C. M. Hakala (Eds.), *Applying science of learning in education: Infusing psychological science into the curriculum* (pp. 7–19). Society for the Teaching of Psychology.

Bjork, E. L., & Bjork, R. A. (2011). Making things hard on yourself, but in a good way: Creating desirable difficulties to enhance learning. In M.A. Gernsbacher, R. W. Pew, L. M. Hough, & J. R. Pomerantz (Eds.), *Psychology and the real world: Essays illustrating fundamental contributions to society* (pp. 56–64). Worth Publishers.

Bjork, R. A., & Bjork, E. L. (2020). Desirable difficulties in theory and practice. *Journal of Applied Research in Memory and Cognition, 9*(4), 475–479. https://doi.org/10.1016/j.jarmac.2020.09.003

Brown, P. C., Roediger, H. L., & McDaniel, M. A. (2014). *Make it stick: The science of successful learning.* Belknap Harvard.

Bruff, D. (2019). Intentional tech: Principles to guide the use of Educational Technology in college teaching. West Virginia University Press.

Butler, A. C., & Roediger, H. L. (2007). Testing improves long-term retention in a simulated classroom setting. *European Journal of Cognitive Psychology, 19*(4–5), 514–527. https://doi.org/10.1080/09541440701326097

Carey, B. (2014). *How we learn: The surprising truth about when, where, and why it happens.* Random House.

Cavanaugh, S. R. (2016). *The spark of learning: Energizing the college classroom with the science of emotion.* West Virginia University Press.

Darby, F., & Lang, J. M. (2019). Small teaching online: Applying learning science in online classes. Jossey-Bass, a Wiley Brand.

Dweck, C. S. (2006). *Mindset: The new psychology of success.* Random House.

Dweck, C. S. (2008). *Mindset: The New Psychology of Success: How We Can Learn to Fulfill Our Potential.* Ballantine Books.

Enz, M. J. (2016). Teaching the production function using fast food royalty. *Journal of Economics and Finance Education, 15*(3), 12–14.

Enz, M. (2021). Moving the Science of Learning From Face-to-Face to Online. *Journal of Economics Teaching, 5*(4), 171–177.

Eyler, J. (2018). How humans learn: The science and stories behind effective college teaching. West Virginia University Press.

Hausman, H., & Kornell, N. (2014). Mixing topics while studying does not enhance learning. *Journal of Applied Research in Memory and Cognition, 3*(3), 153–160. https://doi.org/10.1016/j.jarmac.2014.03.003

Kerr, R., & Booth, B. (1978). Specific and varied practice of motor skill. *Perceptual and Motor Skills*, *46*(2), 395–401. https://doi.org/10.1177/003151257804600201

Kray, L. J., & Haselhuhn, M. P. (2007). Implicit negotiation beliefs and performance: Experimental and longitudinal evidence. *Journal of Personality and Social Psychology*, *93*(1), 49–64. https://doi.org/10.1037/0022–3514.93.1.49

Lang, J. M. (2016). Small teaching: Everyday lessons from the science of learning. Jossey-Bass.

Levy, D. (2020). Teaching effectively with zoom: A practical guide to engage your students and help them learn. Dan Levy.

Mayer, R. E. (2014). Introduction to multimedia learning. *The Cambridge Handbook of Multimedia Learning*, 1–24. https://doi.org/10.1017/cbo9781139547369.002

Mayer, R. E., Fiorella, L., & Stull, A. (2020). Five ways to increase the effectiveness of instructional video. *Educational Technology Research and Development*, *68*(3), 837–852. https://doi.org/10.1007/s11423–020–09749–6

McDaniel, M. A., Einstein, G. O., Dunay, P. K., & Cobb, R. E. (1986). Encoding difficulty and memory: Toward a unifying theory. *Journal of Memory and Language*, *25*(6), 645–656. https://doi.org/10.1016/0749–596x(86)90041–0

McDermott, K. B., Agarwal, P. K., D'Antonio, L., Roediger, H. L., & McDaniel, M. A. (2014). Both multiple-choice and short-answer quizzes enhance later exam performance in middle and high school classes. *Journal of Experimental Psychology: Applied*, *20*(1), 3–21. https://doi.org/10.1037/xap0000004

Mitra, D. L., & Gross, S. J. (2009). Increasing student voice in high school reform. *Educational Management Administration & Leadership*, *37*(4), 522–543. https://doi.org/10.1177/1741143209334577

Mueller, C. M., & Dweck, C. S. (1998). Praise for intelligence can undermine children's motivation and performance. *Journal of Personality and Social Psychology*, *75*(1), 33–52. https://doi.org/10.1037/0022–3514.75.1.33

Oakley, B. A., Rogowsky, B., & Sejnowski, T. J. (2021). *Uncommon sense teaching: Practical insights in brain science to help students learn*. TarcherPerigee, an imprint of Penguin Random House LLC.

Roediger, H. L., & Karpicke, J. D. (2006). Test-enhanced learning. *Psychological Science*, *17*(3), 249–255. https://doi.org/10.1111/j.1467–9280.2006.01693.x

Rohrer, D., & Taylor, K. (2006). The effects of overlearning and distributed practise on the retention of mathematics knowledge. *Applied Cognitive Psychology*, *20*(9), 1209–1224. https://doi.org/10.1002/acp.1266

Smith, G. A. (2008). First-day questions for the learner-centered classroom. *The National Teaching & Learning Forum*, *17*(5), 1–4. https:// doi .org/ 10 .1002/ ntlf .10101

Toshalis, E., & Nakkula, M. (2012). *Motivation, engagement, and Student Voice*. Jobs for the Future.

Willingham, D. T. (2009). Is it true that some people just can't do math. *American Educator*, *33*(4), 14–19.

Willingham, D. T. (2021*). Why don't students like school?: A cognitive scientist answers questions about how the mind... works and what it means for the classroom*. Jossey-Bass.

Yeager, D. S., Henderson, M. D., Paunesku, D., Walton, G. M., D'Mello, S., Spitzer, B. J., & Duckworth, A. L. (2014). Boring but important: A self-transcendent purpose for learning fosters academic self-regulation. *Journal of Personality and Social Psychology*, *107*(4), 559–580. https://doi.org/10.1037/a0037637

Yeager, D. S., Johnson, R., Spitzer, B. J., Trzesniewski, K. H., Powers, J., & Dweck, C. S. (2014). The far-reaching effects of believing people can change: Implicit theories of personality shape stress, health, and achievement during adolescence. *Journal of Personality and Social Psychology, 106*(6), 867–884. https:// doi .org/ 10 .1037/ a0036335

3. Revolutionizing teaching economics online with AI: leveraging LLMs for enhanced communication, creativity, and efficiency in education[1]

Simon D. Halliday and James E. Tierney

INTRODUCTION

In the ever-evolving landscape of technology, Artificial Intelligence (AI) has emerged as a force for increasing firm productivity (Czarnitzki et al. 2023), exposing jobs to automation (Acemoglu et al. 2022), and transforming numerous sectors, including education. The growth of AI in educational settings has been remarkable, with applications ranging from grading to scheduling (Moore et al. 2022, Bernius et al. 2022). With the advent of generative AI—artificial intelligence software that can generate human-like outputs such as text, images, or videos—much of the early debate on its use in education has centered on its ability to enable student cheating and to undermine the ability for instructors to assess student learning (Geerling et al. 2023, Kornbluh 2023). These tools nonetheless enable instructors and students to be more productive and to improve learning in new and surprising ways.

Instructors may be overwhelmed by email, may struggle to provide individual contact with and tutoring for their students, may be challenged by a lack of new assessments, and may struggle with employing lessons from the learning sciences to implement what Darby and Lang (2019) call "small teaching online" or to incorporate more clearly the learning strategies proposed by Weinstein et al. (2018).[2] Large Language Models (LLMs) offer a way to alleviate administrative burdens, provide opportunities for tailored tutoring, enable quick creation of new assessments (quizzes, discussion questions, exam questions), and help the instructor to cultivate opportunities for teaching informed by the learning sciences.[3] We thus focus on using LLMs to alleviate administrative and teaching burdens for faculty and to enable improved student learning through collaboration with AI tools.

In what ways is AI in the economics classroom—online, hybrid, or in-person—important? First, the advent of AI heralds economic problems that fascinate our students, from the importance of AI and its relationship to automation with many jobs being shown to be vulnerable to AI (Acemoglu et al. 2022, Acemoglu and Restrepo 2020) to the great promise that AI offers for economic growth and for human flourishing if we create the incentives—the institutions—to use it to promote social good (Athey 2021) while recognizing that poorly designed incentives between humans and AIs may create bias (Athey et al. 2020). Panels of economists have been asked about their attitudes towards AI: whether it will help to create growth in the twenty-first century and whether it will alleviate or exacerbate contemporary economic inequalities (Clark Center Economic Experts Panel 2017, 2023). These questions make excellent hooks for teaching. Second, people can achieve significant productivity gains through the judicious use of AI. For example, Dell'Acqua et al. (2023) show that productivity improves by 40% with access to LLMs and Noy and Zhang (2023) show improvements in coding when using ChatGPT.

Given such relevance, we highlight several benefits of AI in teaching. First, using LLMs can lower an instructor's administrative burden. Second, LLMs allow an instructor to improve assessment and lower the costs of student-tailored teaching (Chen et al. 2023, Eicher et al. 2018, Goel and Joyner 2017). Third, LLMs permit instructors to engage in new ways of teaching that can enable improved metacognition, to facilitate "small teaching online" (Darby and Lang 2019), and to help students overcome the cognitive challenges of learning (Chew and Cerbin 2021, Goffe 2021). Fourth, students can use LLMs to improve their learning, clarify their thinking and metacognition, and unveil aspects of the hidden curriculum, which first-generation students, English-language learner students, and under-represented and minority students may not be as privy to. AI can thus help instructors with the imperative of improving the inclusivity of our classrooms (Bayer, Hoover et al. 2020, Bayer, Bhanot et al. 2020). Lastly, along with the competencies we currently understand our students require for completing an economics major or degree (Allgood and Bayer 2016, Quality Assurance Agency for Higher Education 2023), a new kind of literacy—AI Literacy—will likely become part of the portfolio of literacies and competencies we expect our students to have by the time they graduate and will likely be an employability skill. Evidence on employability skills suggests that employers will soon demand AI literacy, alongside expectations for clear written and verbal communication, disciplinary writing, critical thinking, data literacy, and quantitative literacy (Allgood and Bayer 2016, Jenkins and Lane 2019, Marshall and Underwood 2019, Halliday 2019, Dvorak et al. 2019, Batt et al. 2020, Department for Education 2023).

The literature about using LLMs in teaching is new. A variety of working papers discuss how to use LLMs and prompting in teaching (Mollick and Mollick 2022, 2023a) and in teaching economics specifically (Cowen and Tabarrok 2023). Cowen and Tabarrok (2023) show how to use LLMs to solve specific models, answer economic questions, and address other needs in economics teaching. We do our best to cover needs they do not address. Mollick and Mollick (2023b) provide an excellent video introduction to the tools and how to implement them in one's teaching. Kasneci et al. (2023) provide a broad range of ways for thinking about including LLMs in teaching and learning. Kaplan-Rokowksi et al. (2023) emphasize the conversational way students can learn with LLMs, consistent with existing literature on good learning practices with AI (Chen et al. 2023, Eicher et al. 2018, Goel and Joyner 2017). Sharples and Pérez y Pérez (2022) and Sharples (2022) explain how to think about AI with student writing. Sharples (2023) provides a framework for thinking about how to situate such practices in the humanities and social sciences. Cheating is not the literature's emphasis.

Although a variety of papers propose ways to integrate LLMs into teaching, we contribute to the literature by emphasizing modes in which LLMs lower administrative burdens (teaching and service-wise) for already taxed instructors, and we explicitly tie our recommended practices to evidence in the learning sciences. Because the technology remains in its infancy, we do not yet have experimental evidence for the effectiveness of some of our proposals, but because they connect to existing, well-evidenced practices, we expect that adopting similar practices in our teaching and learning will be beneficial.

We start by providing a brief introduction to AI and LLMs. We then show examples of LLMs applied to support instructors, first, to alleviate the administrative burden, and second, to improve and add to online or hybrid economics instruction. We proceed to show how students can use LLMs for their learning, based on insights from the learning sciences and recent research. We conclude by asking about the future directions for adoption and growth of AI in economics education.

OVERVIEW OF AI AND LLMS

AI encompasses a range of technologies that emulate human intelligence, with Large Language Models (LLMs) as our focus here: Open AI's GPT, Google's BERT and Bard, Anthropic's Claude, Microsoft's Bing, among others. LLMs are powerful tools designed to interpret and generate human-like text. LLMs are neural networks trained on datasets encompassing large portions of the publicly available text online. LLMs use mathematical functions called transformers to analyze words and recognize patterns and relationships within the text. By using context, LLMs can predict what comes next in a sentence or provide relevant responses to inquiries. This contextual "understanding" allows LLMs to offer responses to complex prompts and perform tasks that traditionally require significant human effort, such as content creation, data analysis, and coding. Crucially, LLMs do not *know* anything, they *predict* what should "come next" based on the contextual cues provided by the prompt as governed by the training documents.[4]

Thinking about Prompts

We assume the instructor and student will interact with an LLM through the chat interface, using prompts to get the output they wish to achieve.[5] We can recommend many introductions to writing prompts, such as Mollick and Mollick (2022, 2023a, 2023b) and Su (2023). Mollick and Mollick (2023a) highlight the importance of what they call "Explanation, Examples, and Analogies"; that is, giving some foundational explanation, providing examples for the LLM to work with, and drawing analogies that the LLM can use to produce better output.

One of the most important ways to improve a prompt is to ask the LLM to "act as [insert role]." Asking the LLM to take a specific role provides context for the LLM to provide output. Evidence suggests that asking the LLM to "reason step-by-step," or similar, will also improve the output that it produces, based on "chain of thought" (Kojima et al. 2022). LLMs do not have emotions, but treating them as if they do and appealing to those emotions can improve output (Li, Tamkin et al. 2023).

We encourage you to show students poor or vague prompts compared to well-crafted prompts. Whereas with economics knowledge, the instructor is a master of their knowledge who may thus suffer under the curse of knowledge, with respect to using AI, you can demonstrate to your students how you are a novice building towards mastery (Goffe 2021, Wieman 2007). Your mastery of economic knowledge will enable you to differentiate good output from bad, which, as we show later, proves crucial in how best to use LLMs. You and your students will learn how to better predict when the output produced by given prompts will be better quality, exercising judgment, and honing expertise.

Instructors, using this expertise, can craft prompts that target learning outcomes and better serve student needs. The difference between a poorly constructed prompt and an effective one can be significant. A vague prompt like "Tell me about economics" may result in a broad and generic response, whereas a better prompt should yield a more targeted and valuable response, for example, "Act like an economics professor teaching an introductory-level college class. Explain the concept of supply and demand in economics. Use an example that will be popular with students, such as the supply and demand for popular candy in the lead-up to Halloween."

New work suggests that prompting may not be as important as the LLM technology develops and they start to ask the prompter what they want, eliciting from us the optimal output through a chain of questions (Li, Tamkin et al. 2023). Acar (2023) argues we should not care so much about prompt engineering per se, but rather that users need to be clear about how best to formulate the problem we wish to solve. At this stage, though, good prompt writing informed by critical thinking dramatically alters the usefulness of the output one obtains.

EMPOWERING TEACHING AND LEARNING WITH LLMS

We separate our discussion of the use of LLMs into two sides: the instructor side and the student side. For the instructor side, we discuss the ways in which using LLMs can alleviate the administrative and teaching burden of the instructor. For the student side, we highlight how students can use LLMs to improve their learning and tailor their learning to personal needs.

The Instructor Side: Alleviating Administration and Supplementing Learning Materials

Alleviating communication burdens

Much of our time as instructors is taken up with responding to emails, producing documents like class syllabi or handbooks, drafting announcements, etc. LLMs can alleviate the burden of writing these communications or responding to students who ask questions that an LLM can respond to (and which we could therefore use to produce a template response). Please refer to Communication Prompts in the Appendix[6] for examples of vague and well-crafted prompts that can assist you as the instructor with alleviating your communication burden and crafting emails in response to students, writing announcements, and producing documents for your students.

Creating engaging assignments

Assignments are opportunities to spark curiosity, foster critical thinking, and build creativity. LLMs can assist faculty in crafting exercises that go beyond rote learning. Consider the corresponding prompts in the Appendix. We show how we have used ChatGPT to create discussion questions for an elective course, and we showed students the prompt used (which was not well-crafted). The intention was two-fold: both to use an LLM to produce work and to show students (in a scaffolded way across the semester) how to improve their own prompting. It remains important for the instructor to assess the questions produced and we show one potential use of a "bad" question, when the LLM hallucinates (makes up responses).

Drafting exam questions

Crafting multifaceted exam questions requires precision and time. LLMs offer a sophisticated solution, enabling educators to create diverse questions aligned with specific learning objectives. The power lies in the partnership between instructors and AI, transforming a tedious process into an efficient and creative endeavor. We offer examples in the Appendix of problem-set, discussion, and debate-sparking questions crafted with assistance from AI on specific papers and their authors.

Drafting quiz questions

Many instructors are concerned with the ways in which LLMs can now "ace" multiple-choice tests in economics (Geerling et al. 2023). Students still benefit from the deliberate practice, testing, spaced repetition, and interleaving that regular testing and contact with questions can provide (Weinstein et al. 2018). Devising new questions based on content that students may have not seen before costs instructors' time. LLMs can create many new questions at low cost and a variety of prompts work. We provide suggestions for the kinds of prompts that work to produce multiple-choice questions in the Appendix. Other suggestions can be found in Cowen and Tabarrok (2023).

Teaching examples with tailored figures and tables

In the Appendix we provide an example where we asked ChatGPT to explain comparative advantage. The example demonstrates ChatGPT's strengths and weaknesses: it devises an excellent example of two countries where one has absolute advantage in producing both goods and comparative advantage in producing one. But when asking ChatGPT to draw the corresponding production possibilities frontiers (PPFs) it makes mistakes. But, if you take what ChatGPT gives you, acknowledge its weaknesses, and ask it for code to produce the PPFs (in the programming language you prefer), it outputs correct figures and can produce a figure like Figure 3.1. It is hard to overstate how quick this process is and how much time an instructor can save in devising examples, creating new figures, and creating solutions for homework.

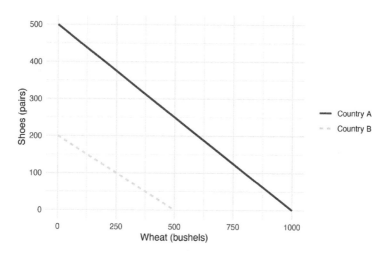

Figure 3.1   *Two production possibilities frontier from R code provided by ChatGPT*

Coaching students about plagiarism and using citations

Students often do not understand how to use citations and what to do with them. ChatGPT and Bing can help students to understand how to use citations by providing the correctly formatted citation for the reference list and on when to use citations. To do these exercises you need to have an LLM that connects to the internet, like Bing, but ChatGPT 4 with internet access works too. We will assume that you have shown students how to use Google Scholar and how Google Scholar citations can be copied and pasted into the relevant projects or citation software. If a student isn't sure how to produce the correct citation, they can ask Bing to produce a "Harvard style formatted citation for an economics class" (or similar as we show in the prompts). The LLM provides output that can coach the student on what plagiarism is, show them the correct way to cite the article, and provide the reference in a correctly formatted way. Moreover, you can show the students how the LLM itself will cite the relevant sources, ask it for academic-specific resources, ask it to play the role of one of the authors of a specific citation and explain the arguments, and so on. These are all incredibly helpful aspects of LLMs that a static "Guide to references" cannot achieve.

Diagnosing texts and output: Honing an expert intuition

Earlier, we discussed researchers testing AIs for grading: Moore et al. (2022) show how GPT-3 can be used for grading chemistry assignments and Bernius et al. (2022) demonstrate how it can alleviate text grading by about 85%. But grading is not the only way we can use AI for thinking about diagnosing and understanding the output of assessments. Sailer et al. (2023) show how AI can be used to improve pre-service teachers' diagnostic reasoning. The results suggest we can use LLMs to produce output to train teaching assistants and to show students what makes a good- or poor-quality answer. As with earlier tasks, this process would help both students and teaching assistants to improve their metacognition and their ability to diagnose good output from bad, especially in dialog with experts like the instructor. An example helps here: when using TAs, Simon has had the experience of those TAs referring to indifference curves as utility curves (a common error). An instructor could get AI output, seed it with the error they expect, show it to TAs and to students as an answer to a question they might have been asked, and then ask them to correct the error.

Furthermore, instructors can show students live responses by LLMs in class in response to a class discussion and demonstrate how to improve on the prompts a student might give and how to analyze the output given by the LLM as if it were a student doing an assessment. Students become better at understanding what an assessment prompt and a corresponding rubric mean when they later construct their own answers. They can consequently use AI to improve their own answers and to improve how they think about the answers they and AI give to similar questions.

Cheating and AI detection
It cannot be stated strongly enough that no technology can currently detect the use of AI. Trying to use technologies that claim to detect AI will harm students, as discussed in Salem et al. (2023). The technologies that claim to detect AI instead produce many false positives and regularly penalize students who are English language learners or otherwise not as comfortable with academic language with high misclassification rates (Liang et al. 2023). Watermark-based schemes can be spoofed and should not be relied on (Jiang et al. 2023). Because AI detection tools do not work reliably, we should adapt our teaching to how best to use AI in our assessments and how to coach our students to use AI to improve the work they do.

The Student Side: Tailored Learning and Overcoming Barriers

Improving student communication
Among the many skills that workplaces are asking of students graduating with an economics degree, effective spoken and written communication are among the most important (Allgood and Bayer 2016, Jenkins and Lane 2019). Moreover, clear communication is often a part of the so-called "hidden cur-

riculum" which first-generation students, under-represented and minority students, or international students from certain backgrounds may not be exposed to (Chatelain 2018). Correcting these inequalities remains a challenging task for an instructor who may not have the time to coach each student in large in-person or online classes. We suggest that students learn to use LLMs to improve their academic writing, email communication, resume/CV, and other professional documents. Students can learn to use LLMs iteratively, with prompts suggested in the Appendix, including coaching students on the most appropriate ways to pitch professional communication.

Personalized tutoring

LLMs can be used for coaching students especially when LLMs are asked (as suggested earlier) to think "step-by-step." Doing so could highlight reasoning steps that a student may have missed. Experimental evidence from Handa et al. (2023) suggests that LLMs tuned with growth-mindset supportive language (GMSL) can improve student outcomes better than LLMs that are not so equipped. Furthermore, companies like Kahn Academy (Kahnmigo) and Quizlet (Q-chat) have invested in their own LLMs that are geared more towards educational coaching and step-by-step reasoning.

Jia et al. (2021) show how BERT can be used to improve peer assessments to help students learn how to improve peer feedback. Tack and Piech (2022) show how GPT-3 and Blender can be used for personalized tutoring, suggesting that these models are not quite up to the level of human teachers, and suggesting we need to advance our evaluation tools better to understand the appropriate use of chatbots as tutors. Moreover, as Bryan (2023) shows, an instructor could train an LLM on their own class's documents to create a class-specific chat bot. The results suggest that for students who do not have access to a human instructor or when the human instructor has limited time a chatbot is a reasonable, though not perfect, substitute.

The online economics instructor who has many students may feel even greater urgency to leverage these tools as their opportunities for one-on-one interaction may be inhibited by missing the more casual moments of passing interaction at the end or start of class, in in-person office hours where students also interact with and coach each other, etc. To be sure, the instructor may facilitate similar interactions and moments of serendipity in their online class through careful architecture, but the personal coaching offered by LLMs may offer a reasonable, if inferior, substitute.

Detecting errors and metacognition

In asking ChatGPT to create discussion questions, ChatGPT hallucinated and said a paper contained a discussion of "the holdout problem," when the paper does not mention the holdout problem. Instead of deleting the question, though, Simon added another question about ChatGPT having made up content. Students had to work out, first, that a previous discussion question was hallucinated output from the AI (they were told previously that AI had helped Simon devise questions). They were "primed" to reflect on the quality of the output ChatGPT provided. Second, many were curious as to why ChatGPT had hallucinated and about the holdout problem itself. Sparking a student's curiosity engages them in learning! Students can act like detectives discovering when and to what extent an LLM hallucinates. Consequently, they learn and improve their metacognition, their ability to reflect on what they do and don't know in a course or about a subject (Chew and Cerbin 2021).

Elaboration
Having seen the discussion questions above, students were later asked to use AI to come up with questions, to reflect on the quality of the questions, and to help them make connections across different materials. This task provides students the opportunity to engage in reflection on the quality of questions that ChatGPT asks and to see how prompts change. It helps students to engage in elaboration (defined as in Weinstein et al. [2018] as "asking one's self about connections between ideas and how things work deepens understanding"). It asks students to reflect on and improve the questions by iterating and engaging in deliberate practice. These are all tasks a student can do by herself online and report on through the class's LMS.

Dual coding
The learning sciences suggest that dual coding improves learning. Dual coding is when a student engages in different representations of a concept (mathematical, text, tabular, graphical, etc.) to enhance their understanding (Weinstein et al. 2018). Users can request that an LLM create a certain type of output, and they can ask LLMs to give prompts for other AIs. For example, ChatGPT can be asked to give output that will prompt AI image generators like DallE or MidJourney. If they use LLMs to produce images, tables, or output that can create images like Figure 3.1, then they are engaging in dual coding—they are practicing thinking through what different depictions of similar ideas mean with different outputs. AI tools allow students to lower the costs of engaging in dual-coding activities they might be less skilled at or which they find effortful. It thus becomes ever more important for students to pay attention to what they do, what the output means, and why encoding ideas differently improves learning.

CONCLUSION

We showed a variety of ways in which instructors and students can employ LLMs to improve teaching and learning informed by the learning sciences and to alleviate administrative burdens. We have not explored many of the capabilities of LLMs, some of which are in preliminary stages and others which appear on the horizon. There are tasks that the authors have not yet tested, but which should be technologically feasible with LLMs like ChatGPT. For example, having ChatGPT use plug-ins to "listen" to a lecture, transcribe it, and provide summaries to students; later, ChatGPT could be used at the end of the semester to provide a summary of a class. Similarly, ChatGPT could listen to a technical lecture (e.g. in statistics) and provide simulations of the tasks done by the instructor. With respect to tools on the horizon, Open AI has recently released the capability for people to create their own tailored GPTs more easily (along the lines of what Bryan (2023) highlighted, before that release). Creating class-specific GPTs that students and instructors can use to improve teaching and learning, and attempting to get the GPT to improve the class content with learning science methods, would make for better classes.

Existing evidence and the likely future potential of LLMs reinforces the idea that instructors and administrators will not be able to detect the use of AI. If, in response to the existence of AI, instructors return to assessment methods based purely on in-person exams we will fail to exploit the benefits of spaced repetition and the testing effect to improve students' learning with regular quizzes and other forms of continuous assessment, while undermining students' futures by failing to coach them on the use of a transformative technology. Employers, on the other hand, will want AI-literate graduates who know how to use LLMs to improve their productivity and augment their creativity (Department for Education 2023). We thus need substantial research to assess how best to deploy LLMs in teaching and how to coach students and instructors alike on the most effective and appropriate uses of LLMs to improve teaching, learning, and even research. Leveraging these technologies will offer the chance to transform the online classroom through personalized coaching, improved and authentic assessments, and enhanced student learning and metacognition.

NOTES

1. With ChatGPT and Grammarly.
2. See also Chapter 1 by Darby and Chapter 2 by Enz in this volume.
3. In crafting the chapter, we have occasionally combined human insight with technological assistance from ChatGPT and Grammarly, much like a statistician uses statistical software.

4. Visual Storytelling Team and Murgia (2023) provide an excellent introduction to what LLMs do and how important transformers are. Wolfram (2023) explains how and why ChatGPT works.
5. The authors have also used the GPT API for more tailored engagement with GPT-4. But doing so is beyond what most students and instructors need to take advantage of the capabilities of GPT.
6. Appendix content is hosted at http://simondhalliday.com/teachingecononline _ai/.

REFERENCES

Abramoff, M. D., Whitestone, N., Patnaik, J. L., Rich, E., Ahmed, M., Husain, L., ... and Wagner, B. D. 2023. Autonomous artificial intelligence increases real-world specialist clinic productivity in a cluster-randomized trial. *NPJ Digital Medicine*, *6*(1), p. 184.

Acar, O. 2023. AI Prompt Engineering Isn't the Future. (6 June). *Harvard Business Review*. Retrieved from https:// hbr .org/ 2023/ 06/ ai -prompt -engineering -isnt -the -future. Accessed on 16 October 2023.

Acemoglu, D., Autor, D., Hazell, J. and Restrepo, P. 2022. Artificial intelligence and jobs: evidence from online vacancies. *Journal of Labor Economics*, *40*(S1), pp. S293–S340.

Acemoglu, D. and Restrepo, P. 2020. The wrong kind of AI? Artificial intelligence and the future of labour demand. *Cambridge Journal of Regions, Economy and Society*, *13*(1), pp. 25–35.

Allgood, S. and Bayer, A. 2016. Measuring college learning in economics. In R. Arum, J. Roksa and A. Cook (eds.), *Improving quality in American higher education: Learning outcomes and assessments for the 21st century*. Jossey-Bass, pp. 87–134.

Athey, S. 2021. Artificial Intelligence for Social Good. Stanford GSB Virtual Alumni Week 2021. (28 September). Retrieved from https:// youtu.be/ CcQAj5spD1A ?si= FfTpW7eYNai9YbBm

Athey, S. C., Bryan, K. A. and Gans. J. S. 2020. The Allocation of Decision Authority to Human and Artificial Intelligence. *AEA Papers and Proceedings*, *110*, pp. 80–84.

Batt, S., Grealis, T., Harmon, O., and Tomolonis, P. 2020. Learning Tableau: A data visualization tool. *The Journal of Economic Education*, *51*, pp. 3–4, 317–328, DOI: 10.1080/00220485.2020.1804503

Bayer, A., Hoover, G. A. and Washington, E. 2020. How You Can Work to Increase the Presence and Improve the Experience of Black, Latinx, and Native American People in the Economics Profession. *Journal of Economic Perspectives*, *34*(3), pp. 193–219.

Bayer, A., Bhanot, S. P., Bronchetti, E. T. and O'Connell, S. A. 2020. Diagnosing the Learning Environment for Diverse Students in Introductory Economics: An Analysis of Relevance, Belonging, and Growth Mindsets. *AEA Papers and Proceedings*, *110*, pp. 294–98.

Bernius, J. P., Krusche, S. and Bruegge, B. 2022. Machine learning based feedback on textual student answers in large courses. *Computers and Education: Artificial Intelligence*, *3*, p. 100081.

Brown, P. C., Roediger III, H.L. and McDaniel, M. A. 2014. *Make it stick: The science of successful learning*. Harvard University Press.

Bryan, K. 2023. A User's Guide to GPT and LLMs for Economics Research. (11 May). Talk at Princeton Bendheim Center for Finance. Retrieved from https://youtu.be/ LJGQjozWr0E?si=JUjDczGwzJielA_5. Accessed on 26 October 2023.

Chatelain, M. 2018. We must help first-generation students master academe's hidden curriculum. *The Chronicle of Higher Education, 21.*

Chen, Y., Jensen, S., Albert, L. J., Gupta, S. and Lee, T. 2023. Artificial intelligence (AI) student assistants in the classroom: Designing chatbots to support student success. *Information Systems Frontiers, 25*(1), pp. 161–182. https:// doi .org/ 10 .1007/s10796-022-10291-4

Chew, S. L. and Cerbin, W. J. 2021. The cognitive challenges of effective teaching. *The Journal of Economic Education, 52*(1), pp. 17–40.

Clark Center Economic Experts Panel. 2017. Robots and Artificial Intelligence. (30 June). Kent A. Clark Center for Global Markets, Chicago Booth, University of Chicago. Retrieved from https:// www .kentclarkcenter .org/ surveys/ robots -and -artificial-intelligence/. Accessed on 6 November 2023

Clark Center Economic Experts Panel. 2023. AI and Productivity Growth (27 April). Kent A. Clark Center for Global Markets, Chicago Booth, University of Chicago. Retrieved from https:// www .kentclarkcenter .org/ surveys/ ai -and -productivity -growth-2/. Accessed on 6 November 2023.

Cowen, T. and Tabarrok, A. T. 2023. How to Learn and Teach Economics with Large Language Models, Including GPT. (17 March). GMU Working Paper in Economics No. 23–18. Retrieved from https://ssrn.com/abstract=4391863 or http://dx.doi.org/ 10.2139/ssrn.4391863

Czarnitzki, D., Fernández, G. P. and Rammer, R. 2023. Artificial intelligence and firm-level productivity. *Journal of Economic Behavior & Organization, 211,* pp. 188–205.

Darby, F. and Lang, J. M. 2019. *Small teaching online: Applying learning science in online classes.* John Wiley & Sons.

Devlin, J., Chang, M. W., Lee, K., and Toutanova, K. 2018. BERT: Pre-training of deep bidirectional transformers for language understanding. *arXiv preprint.* Retrieved from https://arxiv.org/abs/1810.04805

Dell'Acqua, F., McFowland, E., Mollick, E. R., Lifshitz-Assaf, H., Kellogg, K., Rajendran, S., ... and Lakhani, K. R. 2023. Navigating the Jagged Technological Frontier: Field Experimental Evidence of the Effects of AI on Knowledge Worker Productivity and Quality. (15 September). Harvard Business School Technology & Operations Mgt. Unit Working Paper No. 24–013. Retrieved from https://ssrn.com/ abstract=4573321 or http://dx.doi.org/10.2139/ssrn.4573321

Department for Education. 2023. Generative Artificial Intelligence (AI) in Education. 26 October. Retrieved from https:// www .gov .uk/ government/ publications/ generative-artificial-intelligence-in-education/generative-artificial-intelligence-ai-in -education. Accessed on 3 November 2023.

Dvorak, T., Halliday, S. D., O'Hara, M. and Swoboda, A. 2019. Efficient empiricism: Streamlining teaching, research, and learning in empirical courses. *The Journal of Economic Education, 50*(3), pp. 242–257.

Eicher, B., Polepeddi, L. and Goel, A. 2018. Jill Watson doesn't care if you're pregnant: Grounding AI ethics in empirical studies. *Proceedings of the 2018 AAAI/ACM Conference on AI, Ethics, and Society, 7.*

Geerling, W., Mateer, G. D., Wooten, J. and Damodaran, N. 2023. ChatGPT has aced the test of understanding in college economics: Now what? *The American Economist,* p. 05694345231169654.

Goel, A. K. and Joyner, D. A. 2017. Using AI to teach AI: Lessons from an online AI class. *AI Magazine, 38*(2), pp. 48–58.

Goffe, W. L. 2021. Online implementation of portions of "the cognitive challenges of effective teaching." *The Journal of Economic Education, 52*(1), pp. 82–88.

Grammarly. 2023. *Grammarly.* https://www.grammarly.com/

Handa, K., Clapper, M., Boyle, J., Wang, R. E., Yang, D., Yeager, D. S., and Demszky, D. 2023. "Mistakes Help Us Grow": Facilitating and Evaluating Growth Mindset Supportive Language in Classrooms. In: *Proceedings of the 2023 Conference on Empirical Methods in Natural Language Processing.*

Halliday, S. D. 2019. Data literacy in economic development. *The Journal of Economic Education, 50*(3), pp. 284–298. DOI: 10.1080/00220485.2019.1618762

Jenkins, C. and Lane, S. 2019. Employability Skills in UK Economics Degrees. Report for the Economics Network. Retrieved from https://www.economicsnetwork.ac.uk/research/employability/executivesummary or https://doi.org/10.53593/n3245a

Jia, Q., Cui, J., Xiao, Y., Liu, C., Rashid, P. and Gehringer, E. F. 2021. All-in-one: Multi-task learning BERT models for evaluating peer assessments. *arXiv preprint arXiv:2110.03895.*

Jiang, Z., Zhang, J. and Gong, N. Z., 2023. Evading Watermark based Detection of AI-Generated Content. *arXiv preprint arXiv:2305.03807.*

Kaplan-Rakowski, R., Grotewold, K., Hartwick, P. and Papin, K. 2023. Generative AI and Teachers' Perspectives on Its Implementation in Education. Journal of Interactive Learning Research, 34(2), pp. 313–338. Association for the Advancement of Computing in Education (AACE). Retrieved from https://www.learntechlib.org/primary/p/222363/. Accessed on 14 October 2023.

Kasneci, E., Sessler, K., Küchemann, S., Bannert, M., Dementieva, D., Fischer, F., … and Kasneci, G. 2023. ChatGPT for good? On opportunities and challenges of large language models for education. *Learning and Individual Differences, 103*, pp. 102274.

Kojima, T., Gu, S. S., Reid, M., Matsuo, Y. and Iwasawa, Y. 2022. Large language models are zero-shot reasoners. *Advances in neural information processing systems, 35*, pp. 22199–22213.

Kornbluh, K. 2023, The chatbot that's cheating college campuses. *The Atlantic.* (5 May). Retrieved from https://www.theatlantic.com/technology/archive/2023/05/chatbot-cheating-college-campuses/674073/. Accessed on 18 October 2023.

Li, B. Z., Tamkin, A., Goodman, N. and Andreas, J. 2023. Eliciting Human Preferences with Language Models. *arXiv preprint arXiv:2310.11589.*

Li, C., Wang, J., Zhu, K., Zhang, Y., Hou, W., Lian, J. and Xie, X. 2023. Emotionprompt: Leveraging psychology for large language models enhancement via emotional stimulus. *arXiv preprint arXiv:2307.11760.*

Liang, W., Yuksekgonul, M., Mao, Y., Wu, E. and Zou, J. 2023. GPT detectors are biased against non-native English writers. *Patterns, 4*(7).

Liu, Y., Ott, M., Goyal, N., Du, J., Joshi, M., Chen, D., … and Stoyanov, V. 2019. RoBERTa: A robustly optimized BERT pretraining approach. *arXiv preprint.* Retrieved from https://arxiv.org/abs/1907.11692

Marshall, E. C. and Underwood, A. 2019. Writing in the discipline and reproducible methods: A process-oriented approach to teaching empirical undergraduate economics research. *The Journal of Economic Education, 50*(1), pp. 17–32.

Mollick, E. R. and Mollick, L. 2022. New Modes of Learning Enabled by AI Chatbots: Three Methods and Assignments. (13 December). Retrieved from https://ssrn.com/abstract=4300783 or http://dx.doi.org/10.2139/ssrn.4300783

Mollick, E. R. and Mollick, L. 2023a. Using AI to Implement Effective Teaching Strategies in Classrooms: Five Strategies, Including Prompts. (17 March). The Wharton School Research Paper. Retrieved from https://ssrn.com/abstract=4391243 or http://dx.doi.org/10.2139/ssrn.4391243

Mollick, E. and Mollick, L. 2023b. Practical AI for instructors and students. Wharton School YouTube Channel. Retrieved from https:// youtu .be/ t9gmyvf7JYo ?si = HmAicwEamUC-cpYs Accessed on 3 November 2023.

Moore, S., Nguyen, H. A., Bier, N., Domadia, T. and Stamper, J. 2022. Assessing the quality of student-generated short answer questions using GPT-3. In: *Educating for a new future: making sense of technology-enhanced learning adoption: 17th European Conference on Technology Enhanced Learning*, EC-TEL 2022, Toulouse, France, 12–16 September, Proceedings. Springer-Verlag, pp. 243–257.

OpenAI. 2023. ChatGPT. https://www.openai.com/

Noy, S. and Zhang, W. 2023. Experimental evidence on the productivity effects of generative artificial intelligence. *Science 381*, pp. 187–192. DOI: 10.1126/science.adh2586

Quality Assurance Agency for Higher Education (QAA). 2023. Subject Benchmark Statement: Economics. Retrieved from https:// www .qaa .ac .uk/ the -quality -code/ subject-benchmark-statements/ subject-benchmark-statement-economics. Accessed on 16 October 2023.

Sailer, M., Bauer, E., Hofmann, R., Kiesewetter, J., Glas, J., Gurevych, I. and Fischer, F. 2023. Adaptive feedback from artificial neural networks facilitates pre-service teachers' diagnostic reasoning in simulation-based learning. *Learning and Instruction, 83*, pp. 101620.

Salem, L., Fiore, S., Kelly, S. and Brock, B. 2023. Evaluating the Effectiveness of Turnitin's AI Writing Indicator Model. Center for the Advancement of Teaching, Temple University.

Sharples, M., 2022. Automated essay writing: An AIED opinion. *International journal of artificial intelligence in education, 32*(4), pp. 1119–1126.

Sharples, M. 2023. Towards social generative AI for education: theory, practices and ethics, *Learning: Research and Practice, 9*:2, pp. 159–67. DOI: 10.1080/23735082.2023.2261131

Sharples, M. and Pérez y Pérez, R. 2022. *Story machines: How computers have become creative writers*. Routledge.

Su, J. 2023. Master the Perfect ChatGPT Prompt Formula (in just 8 minutes)! Retrieved from https:// youtu .be/jC4v5AS4RIM ?si = YoSyO1X3UFLrzZHZ. Accessed on 16 October 2023.

Sun, Y., Wang, S., Li, Y., Feng, S., Tian, H., Wu, H., … and Liu, Z. 2019. ERNIE: Enhanced representation through knowledge integration. *arXiv preprint*. Retrieved from https://arxiv.org/abs/1904.09223.

Tack, A. and Piech, C. 2022. The AI teacher test: Measuring the pedagogical ability of blender and GPT-3 in educational dialogues. *arXiv preprint arXiv:2205.07540*.

Trust, T., Whalen, J. and Mouza, C. 2023. Editorial: ChatGPT: Challenges, Opportunities, and Implications for Teacher Education. Contemporary Issues in Technology and Teacher Education, 23(1), pp. 1–23. Society for Information Technology & Teacher Education. Retrieved from https:// www .learntechlib .org/ primary/p/222408/. Accessed 14 October 2023.

Visual Storytelling Team and Murgia, M. 2023. Generative AI exists because of the transformer: This is how it works. *The Financial Times*. 12 September. Retrieved from https://ig.ft.com/generative-ai/. Accessed on 26 October 2023.

Weinstein, Y., Madan, C. R. and Sumeracki, M. A. 2018. Teaching the science of learning. *Cognitive research: principles and implications*, *3*(1), pp. 1–17.

Wieman, C. E. 2007. The "curse of knowledge" or why intuition about teaching often fails. APS News–The back page. *American Physical Society News, 16*(10), pp. 8. https://www.aps.org/publications/apsnews/200711/backpage.cfm.

Wolfram, S. 2023. What Is ChatGPT Doing... and Why Does It Work? *Stephen Wolfram Blog*. 14 February. Retrieved from https://writings.stephenwolfram.com/2023/02/what-is-chatgpt-doing-and-why-does-it-work/ Accessed on 26 October 2023.

Wu, J., Yang, S., Zhan, R., Yuan, Y., Wong, D. F. and Chao, L. S., 2023. A Survey on LLM-generated Text Detection: Necessity, Methods, and Future Directions. *arXiv preprint arXiv:2310.14724*.

Yang, Z., Dai, Z., Yang, Y., Carbonell, J., Salakhutdinov, R. and Le, Q. V. 2019. XLNet: Generalized autoregressive pretraining for language understanding. arXiv preprint. Retrieved from https://arxiv.org/abs/1906.08237

4. Accessibility, inclusivity, and diversity in teaching economics online

Fabio R. Aricò and Paul D. Cowell

INTRODUCTION

You do not need to be an expert in accessibility, inclusivity, or diversity to ensure that your teaching is accessible and inclusive to all. Similarly, being an experienced economics instructor does not automatically beget these qualities in the student learning experience. Instead, the most important factors are a sincere approach to the value of equality of learning opportunity and a commitment to using student diversity as a source of richness in the learning activities.

Nevertheless, economics as a discipline presents some unique challenges to accessibility, particularly in its graphical and mathematical content, and teaching economics in an online setting can additionally create important considerations. However, the online learning environment also presents significant opportunities to address student learning barriers in a more powerful manner than in-person instruction. Moreover, the discipline's emphasis on evidence-based theory, empirical application, and individual and collective behaviours (American Economic Association, 2023; Quality Assurance Agency for Higher Education, 2023) can be leveraged to create a learning experience that empowers student agency for change in tackling societal issues.

This chapter explores the three major themes of accessibility, inclusivity, and diversity in the context of teaching economics online. These themes can be thought of as sequential: first, students should be able to access the learning opportunities without disadvantage or barrier (accessibility); second, students should be equally included in the learning activities and experience irrespective of any characteristic (inclusivity); and third, the learning experience should both promote and celebrate student diversity and ensure that economics is not singularly seen through any one lens or voice (diversity). Each theme is explored with reference to the particular considerations in teaching economics in the virtual learning space, or combining virtual spaces and in-person experiences, with all ideas and approaches given clear rationale.

ACCESSIBILITY

Why Accessibility Is Important

The most immediate and crucial aspect of teaching is that of accessibility. If students face barriers in accessing their learning, then all other considerations – the learning activities, assessments, and syllabi – are rendered completely moot. Simply, accessibility is the foundation upon which *all* learning takes place. Therefore, it should be the instructor's first consideration when preparing to design or deliver any learning activity, since it is much harder to reverse engineer accessibility after the fact, not unlike addressing the deficient foundations of a pre-existing physical structure.

In teaching economics online, this consideration necessitates an important emphasis from the instructor on digital accessibility, however it is additionally important to consider accessibility in the context of how students are physically engaging with the virtual learning environment. Barriers may exist for students using computer equipment in the form of physical disabilities, so it is important that clear signposting is made to institutional support. Students may be interacting with the online learning activities from a wide range of physical and social situations (including students with caring responsibilities), so it may be significantly beneficial to offer asynchronous avenues of engagement with instructors, the activities, and their peers in the online space. Additionally, financial and/or geographical barriers may result in digital poverty,[1] hence the need for clear setting of expectations for synchronous activity engagement, the required/recommended specification of hardware and software (including whether students need access to a webcam, microphone, or touch-screen device, and how students with physical disabilities will be supported if these are not appropriate). Notwithstanding the design of the learning activities, assessments, and the digital learning environment, the instructor will not normally be responsible for providing solutions to physical support needs, but setting expectations and signposting is both helpful and importantly explicitly promotes equality of learning opportunity (Iosad, 2020).

Digital Accessibility

For an instructor teaching economics online, digital accessibility is of paramount importance. In essence, it involves preventing unnecessary barriers to access by providing materials and experiences in a manner that benefits all, regardless of disability or circumstance (Russ & Hamidi, 2021; Kulkarni,

2019). For instance, by using headings correctly in documents and online content to allow any students (or indeed instructors) with visual impairments to be able to use screen reading software to listen to and navigate around the content. This measure not only gives clarity in presentation, but also ensures that all students and colleagues have equal access to the learning environment and its content, irrespective of how they wish or how they require to do so. The principles of digital accessibility are also an important component of Universal Design for Learning (UDL), which calls for accessibility, inclusivity, and flexibility in the design stage of every learning activity (Burgstahler & Cory, 2008).

An economics instructor in the online space is creator and facilitator, both of activities and of content. Careful consideration needs to be paid to accessibility in the design of both. If the institution is accepted to be responsible for ensuring the physical accessibility of its physical learning spaces and buildings, the instructor is equally responsible for ensuring all their learners find the virtual learning space free of barriers and easy to navigate. As a content creator, it is important for instructors to regularly use in-built accessibility checking software, available in most Learning Management Systems (LMSs) and in document editors, to ensure accessibility. It is also good practice to provide editable formats of documents (e.g. a Word document rather than a pdf; a raw table rather than a picture of a table) so that students who have a visual impairment or who have Specific Learning Difficulties (SpLDs) such as dyslexia, can readily use screen readers or change font styles and sizes (Coxon et al., 2020). Images used in learning materials should have alternative (or ALT) text descriptions, which also applies to graphs (Naples, 2017). Given the regular importance of the latter in economics, it may be helpful to provide an audio description of the diagram to aid visualisation, which could take the form of a live narration in a synchronous activity or a downloadable audio file in an asynchronous resource. Graphs should also be saved and used as a Scalable Vector Graphic (SVG) format, since this format is more accessible than a simple image as it allows greater magnification, axis reading, and editing; the latter of which can be important for different types of colour blindness. Furthermore, when referring to graphs and identifying data series or curves, it is best practice to identify the different elements in a variety of ways to help support students who have visual impairments or lower vision, especially as this is not typically considered an official disability in most countries, yet graphical modelling is ubiquitous in economics. This step can be done relatively concisely, such as: 'the new indifference curve, which is blue and steeper'. Accurate labelling of elements on a diagram can provide a further source of support for visually impaired students, and ease understanding and clarity for all students at the same time; i.e., referring to shifts in curves and changes in equilibrium can be done visually, identifying colours, but also symbolically: 'the demand shifts from AD_1 to AD_2 and the equilibrium moves from E_1 to E_2'. The general principle is simple: use different means to convey the same concepts, so that students can identify which ones work best for them. Economics also requires at times a proficiency in algebraic and quantitative problem solving, so any such materials pertaining to this content should be digital and able to be read by a screen reader.

If producing asynchronous video content – which in itself is a more accessible and inclusive format for content delivery than a live lecture (MacCullagh et al., 2017) – then it is important to ensure that captions are provided accurately. Though educational video streaming services may provide auto-captions, these may be rendered widely ineffective if they contain inaccuracies, which can often be the case when discussing specific economics or algebraic terms. Hence, care should be taken to ensure accuracy, particularly around threshold concepts.[2] However, this is another example of accessibility that benefits all, since accurate video captions are helpful not only for audibly impaired students, but also for learners whose first language is not the medium of instruction, as can be the case with economics owing to its popularity amongst international students.

In synchronous activities, such as live workshops, lectures, or small-group teaching, the principles of UDL are important in ensuring accessibility. When asking students to participate, some students may not be able to use a microphone or webcam due to a disability or because of caring responsibilities, and it is critical to fostering a sense of belonging and learning community that such barriers are not highlighted amongst peers to prevent marginalisation and 'othering'. Instead, instructors should both be proactive in checking for any disclosures of situations or disabilities before asking students to engage with learning activities, particularly those that are synchronous. Additionally, and independent of disclosure, instructors should consider allowing – and equally valuing – a variety of avenues for live participation. Whilst not all learners who are reluctant to engage with audio/visual participation may be genuinely experiencing a barrier to engaging, it is important not to force participation from everyone due to the potential for unintentional marginalisation. If using live collaborative activities such as class digital whiteboard activities for graph work, consider that some students may not have access, or be able to use, a graphics tablet, touch-screen device, or in the case of some physical disabilities, a mouse. Instead, allow for text and/or audio contributions and act as a scribe by adding those contributions as the instructor. Issues connected to digital poverty can be addressed by signposting to the institution's available resources or using alternative options (such as OpenOffice or Google Suite in lieu of paid document editors). Learning and teaching design can also foster accessibility; by reflecting on the balance between synchronous and asynchronous events the instructor makes choices about the endowments and resources students will need to access. Pedagogical effectiveness includes considerations on accessibility that cannot be neglected.

Digital Skills

Even if all materials and activities are accessibly designed and produced, and curated in an accessible virtual learning environment, this may still not guarantee that students do not encounter barriers in engaging with their learning, if they do not possess the requisite digital skills to do so. Unlike the physical classroom, the online learning environment may present challenges for students who are not used to using particular forms of software, engaging in particular online activities (such as breakout rooms), or even just projecting their presence and their engagement into a digital environment. Clear expectations should be set at the beginning of any course or set of activities regarding what students will be asked to do in the online learning activities (ideally in conjunction with learning outcomes so that students can see both the what and the how) and references should be made to institutional policies or open-source instructional guides. Instructors should also consider designing opportunities for no-stakes practice, such as providing practice runs of creating and submitting digital assignments or engaging with discussion boards as a social icebreaker, to allow digital proficiency and confidence to build.

Online vs In-Person Accessibility

Accessibility is the foundation of all learning, and teaching economics online requires instructors to be aware of not only the materials and virtual learning environment they create, but also of the discipline's challenges on accessibility, particularly around graphical exposition and algebraic modelling. Yet teaching in an online context offers some unique opportunities to overcome these challenges. Writing on a whiteboard (or chalkboard) in a physical classroom was never an accessible practice, nor was delivering content in the form of a live lecture to students with an audio or visual impairment. Irrespective of how much an instructor is engaging with their students in the physical classroom in addition to online learning, the virtual learning space can be a powerful tool for good in economics. In creating the digital content and environment with accessibility at the very start, instructors can ensure no barriers exist to students' learning in a far more powerful way than could be achieved in a physical space alone.

INCLUSIVITY

Ensuring that we facilitate the creation of an inclusive environment in economics classrooms is an important step. But what can we do to ensure that all students feel valued, empowered to work collaboratively to meet their learning outcomes, and exploit the countless opportunities offered by university education? In other words, how can we build on accessibility to establish inclusivity in the context of economics education?

Inclusive Induction Sessions: Challenging Stereotypes

The process starts with induction. At the beginning of their journey, when students meet in a large venue for the first time (whether in-person, virtual or blended), the visual impact of diversity in the classroom can already represent a strong enabler to the development of a sense of belonging. Many induction sessions are often dense and packed with information that schools and departments are eager to share with the students to help them navigate the university environment. Nevertheless, it is important to capitalise on this moment, ensuring that students are given the time and the space to acknowledge each other. Within in-person settings the instructor could say: "Raise your hand if you are sitting/standing next to somebody you have not spoken to before" – generally, the great majority of students do. "These people all around you are going to be your colleagues, your study-buddies, and your friends. Please take five minutes to introduce yourself to somebody you don't know. Ask them where they are from and how they have decided to be here today". In virtual settings, students could:

- be invited to acknowledge the different names in the chat list;
- be tasked to access breakout rooms to introduce themselves and talk about their country or area of provenience;
- be invited to connect to a virtual map[3] to drop a pin indicating their name, the location they come from, and outlining the economic issues currently debated in their area of provenience. More targeted tasks could ask them to quickly search for information about GDP, unemployment, or any other macroeconomic aggregates, to be added to the map. The outcomes of these simple interventions can be powerful.

Supporting students in acknowledging diversity is only the first step. Induction sessions can also be exploited as the perfect opportunity to challenge stereotypes and establish a climate of mutual respect amongst students and staff. However, rather than adding yet another slide to an endless presentation of policies, procedures, and codes of conduct, we can engage students in more active ways to explore issues of inclusion. Aricò (2021) suggests implementing an experiential approach (Kolb, 1984) consisting of exposing students to blunt statements about gender, ethnicity, sexual orientation and identity, as well any other aspect characterising a diverse student population.[4] Students are then allowed to explore these statements and share their views prior to being guided to what constitutes inclusive, reasonable, or even acceptable behaviour on campus. This approach relies on class response systems, which allow students to interact with the lecturer anonymously even in large classroom environments, and the approach can be used in-person as well as in virtual or hybrid environments. The sequence of events is simple: (i) the facilitator presents students with a controversial statement and offers some multiple choice options to interpret it or frame it; (ii) students are invited to select the choice that better represents their view; (iii) once the opinion poll is closed, the distribution of choices is revealed and the facilitator explores the statement, the class responses, and the choices along with the students; challenging bias, identifying stereotypes and fostering an inclusive culture. Some examples of this practice are reported in Table 4.1.

This approach allows for personalising the inclusive induction experience of different students, as it simultaneously sends a welcoming and reassuring message to members of minority groups as well as to the wider community. The practice could be further enriched by allowing students to share their thoughts through textual interaction, rather than multiple choice, especially when facilitated online. While exploring statements and the opinions shared by students facilitators might want to consider:

- pointing at responses indicating bias, sharing surprise and challenging such bias immediately (i.e. citing the name of famous female economists and their work, mentioning statistics on attainment), or highlighting (i.e. for the LGBTQ+ example) when there is no correct choice, but just one correct way to address each other with respect;
- acknowledging and exploring different feelings, reflecting on the challenges experienced by members of minority groups, such as adapting to a different culture and/or experiencing language barriers;
- emphasising that offensive behaviour or statements, even if shared outside of the classroom, can generate significant consequences, not just for the victims but also for the perpetrators, no matter what the underlying intention.

Table 4.1   Experiential approach to inclusive induction

Statement	Possible Choices for Students
In the great majority of British universities, the number of male students in Economics is significantly higher than the number of female students. Why, in your opinion?	Females are not proficient in Economics, in general; Females do not like Economics as a discipline, in general; Females might not feel comfortable fitting within a male-dominated subject; None of the above or I do not know.
Mark observes Paul studying his notes and says: "Highlighting your notes with different colours is so gay!" What does Mark mean?	Paul is doing something silly; Paul is probably gay; Paul is a weak and/or effeminate person; None of the above, or I do not know.
You will be studying, working, engaging in team-activities with people from different countries/religions/cultures and whose native language is not the same as yours. That makes you feel...	perplexed; interested/engaged; excited/energised; indifferent; worried/suspicious; open-minded.
A student is found or reported pronouncing some racist slurs or innuendos (even as a joke) or posting them in an online chat/forum. What is the most likely action that will be pushed by our department or by the University?	A formal reproach letter from the Teaching Director; A disciplinary meeting with the Head of School; A formal hearing in front of the University Senate; Expulsion from the University.

This approach can be tailored to designing scenarios that are suited for specific learning environments and their members, either online or in person. To this extent, it is important to emphasise that the examples presented above might not be suited to all audiences and that their application might backfire if minority groups in the classroom feel triggered, rather than empowered, by an overly blunt provocation to discuss diversity issues. The importance of a safe learning environment for all is critical. The implementation of this experiential approach should be considerate of the background of the student population and the social and political context within which we facilitate the learning. Nevertheless, the idea can be adapted to different environments and fine-tuning its applications is up to a lecturer's discretion. For instance, students could be more gently encouraged to discuss what they perceive as barriers to inclusion in economics education with their own eyes. They could then be invited to establish rules that should be agreed upon to develop a productive and welcoming learning environment for all.

The underpinning general principle is the same: students can internal-ise good practice and an inclusive code of conduct if they are involved in discussion and co-production, rather than being passively instructed about regulations. The anonymisation offered by class-response technologies allows for active participation in the debate as well as an open and direct way to acknowledge that living in such a diverse environment as a university commu-nity is a wonderful opportunity, which should be embraced with acceptance, compassion, and mutual respect. Facilitators considering experimenting with this direct approach should feel comfortable in acknowledging different views in the classroom, yet prepared to challenge stereotypes and prejudice at their core.

Directing students towards sources of information and support remains essential, along with offering guidance about the channels available to report instances involving bullying, harassment and discrimination experienced directly or from others.

Active Learning as a Means to Inclusion

Active learning is a powerful pedagogy whether in the physical or the online space, and it has been proven to be particularly effective for students who are not performing at the top of the grade distribution (Freeman et al., 2014; Yannier et al., 2021). The result is unsurprising, as socialisation of learning and the facilitation of a climate of mutual support in the classroom can level the playing field. Recent research in economics education has highlighted how active learning can also facilitate inclusion in the classroom. Cagliesi and Ghanei (2022) demonstrate how Team-Based Learning contributed to the closure of attainment gaps between students belonging to BAME (British Black, Asian, and minority ethnic) groups and white groups. Student narratives highlight that collaboration towards the achievement of a common goal can be a driver for this result. In his evaluation of Student Response Systems to facilitate peer-instruction, Aricò (2019) finds that peer instruction that makes use of class polling through technology allows students from all backgrounds to have a voice and participate confidently in learning activities in the class-room thanks to the anonymity of digitally-mediated interaction. In particular, the evaluation highlights that international students feel empowered with a voice and feel re-assured by the opportunity to discuss economic problems in small-group settings even within a large class environment. Indeed, Cheng and Selvaretnam (2022) find that the working together of students in multinational groups to complete an economics project led to significant positive externali-ties in common cultural understanding, leading to a more inclusive and more satisfactory learning environment.

This powerful nature of active learning and its ability to bring *all* students together in the same space to engage places even greater importance on the instructor's design stage. Not only is active learning beneficial pedagogically, it acts as a magnet to draw people together and share their diverse thoughts and experiences.

DIVERSITY

Where inclusivity concerns itself with ensuring all are equally welcome and valued, diversity can be thought of as specifically promoting different voices, experiences, backgrounds, and identities. Economics has long had a diversity problem in its profession (Bayer & Rouse, 2016) which is also evident in its student population (Advani et al., 2020). The instructors, students, and syllabus are often dominated by white, male, and privileged perspectives, and whilst it is out of the control of the instructor to address systematic issues, the online space often provides important and unique opportunities to promote diversity.

Critical Thinking, Pluralism and Decolonisation

Differently from other social sciences, economics is characterised by the dominance of a mainstream paradigm. Articulated through a mathematical jargon, this peculiar characteristic poses a challenge to the development of a critical mindset and an openness to social and cultural backgrounds and ways of thinking that do not align with the tradition of the industrialised West. Recent developments in economics education have seen the rise of movements that criticise the monist approach established by the mainstream, such as the pluralist approach embraced by Rethinking Economics (https://www.rethinkeconomics.org/), or the decolonisation agenda set by D-Econ (https://d-econ.org/). From the perspective of promoting diversity, the importance of these movements becomes even more relevant to empower students from different backgrounds with representation and a voice. Increased access to digital resources and platforms for debate could be seen as a means to facilitate the creation of a more diverse environment for economics education. Nevertheless, there are challenges. For instance, the introduction of language models relying on generative artificial intelligence could pose a false sense of security that relevant and critical information is ready at hand. Nevertheless, there is a debate on whether artificial intelligence reduces or amplifies bias. For instance, Bjork (2023) highlights how ChatGPT represents a threat to language diversity and inclusivity by replicating and amplifying the loudest voice, especially in disciplines that have been traditionally dominated by white men. At the same time, Hemsley et al. (2023) observe how artificial intelligence can improve inclusion for people with communication disabilities. Especially at these early stages of what is perceived as a paradigm shift in education, the first response is an urgent call for the development of critical thinking, with the aim of teaching our students how to question the information they are exposed to and how to identify and challenge bias. Creative assessment tasks could address this issue. For instance, instructors could task students to prompt artificial intelligence platforms to generate an analysis of contemporary economic issues around the globe. In a second stage, they could encourage students to challenge the analysis that has been generated and to identify alternative points of view, counterarguments, and evidence.

Fostering Diversity in Economics Education

We acknowledge the challenges faced by economics as a discipline dominated by a mainstream approach. Although the promotion of diversity in economics education is arguably still in its infancy, instructors should see this as an opportunity. Whilst there is significant scope for decolonising a primarily western, white, male, and privileged discipline (Kvangraven & Kesar, 2023) with little self-criticism in this regard, a powerful first step would be to simply promote and celebrate the diversity in our classrooms. If diversity is lacking, this should be highlighted to promote self-critical awareness of other cultures, perspectives, and the other side of the privileged coin, and an opportunity to bring such perspectives and experiences into the conversation. A few pedagogical principles and interventions that could support instructors in their quest to implement a more diverse curriculum could be the following:

- be mindful of the whole global economy, and acknowledge the relative importance of different objectives in different parts of the world; disentangle priorities and trade-offs, as well as tensions; ensure that multiple perspectives and points of view are reflected in the material discussed with students;
- do not underestimate the power of examples: students attending learning events or engaging with learning material can be trained to embrace diversity if exposed to diverse examples;
- allow for more freedom in designing the syllabus: once students master the essential tools to analyse economic problems, allow space for debate, interaction, student-driven or co-created lectures and seminars, where students can see themselves represented by suggesting topics that are close to their heart;
- allow for more freedom in assessment: encourage students to choose topics for their assignment, such as essays, empirical projects, presentations, also providing a list of potential issues that explicitly celebrates a variety of

different economic problems and acknowledges different social groups, ethnicities, as well as identities.

CONCLUSIONS

We introduced this chapter emphasising how instructors could approach their teaching with a sincere approach to the value of equality of learning opportunity and a commitment to celebrating student diversity. Efforts to transform the economics discipline and economics education into a significantly more inclusive and diverse space for all have been mixed, but they are steadily and notably intensifying. For instance, in the UK, the QAA Subject Benchmark for economics explicitly outlines inclusivity principles in setting the standards for the teaching of economics in British universities (Quality Assurance Agency for Higher Education, 2023). Interestingly, developments in behavioural economics, such as the work of Thaler and Kahneman underpin the principles of unconscious bias training (Kahneman, 2011) and offer valuable insights in the quest against discrimination, promoting accessibility, inclusivity and diversity in modern societies. When instructors design their learning and teaching curriculum, slow thinking can facilitate mindfulness and applications of inclusive education principles, as well as develop awareness of those principles that are most suited for the peer population students will interact with. Nevertheless, mindfulness alone is not sufficient, and it should always be complemented by effective communication. The power of dialogue was a recurring theme in our brief excursus on inclusive practice for economics education. Dialogue between staff and students can facilitate better understanding of students' needs. Our suggestion is for instructors to invite their students to discuss with them openly about their learning needs, explore course evaluation feedback, and engage with student representation bodies, rather than limiting themselves to consulting a list of reasonable adjustments or relying on their ability to second-guess what students might need. Similarly, facilitating dialogue amongst students can ensure that issues of accessibility and inclusion, as well as a celebration of diversity, are surfaced and acknowledged through classroom dynamics and through curricular design that emphasises how economics can play a fundamental role for social justice and a better society for all.

NOTES

1. The Digital Poverty Alliance defines digital poverty as the inability to interact with the online world fully, when, where, and how an individual needs to (Digital Poverty Alliance, 2023; see also Barrantes, 2007).
2. 'A threshold concept can be considered as akin to a portal, opening up a new and previously inaccessible way of thinking about something. It represents

a transformed way of understanding, or interpreting, or viewing something without which the learner cannot progress' (Meyer & Land, 2003, p.1; see also Meyer & Land, 2006). For a practical guide to threshold concepts in economics, we refer the interested reader to Davis and Mangan (2009).

3.   Padlet ® integrates with Google Maps to facilitate map annotation.
4.   Aricò (2021) mainly focuses on gender, but the practice can be extended to any aspect of diversity in the classroom.

REFERENCES

Advani, A., Sen, S., and Warwick, R. 2020. *Ethnic Diversity in UK Economics.* Institute for Fiscal Studies, https:// ifs .org .uk/ publications/ ethnic -diversity -uk -economics, accessed 20 March 2024.

Al-Bahrani, A. 2022. Classroom Management and Student Interaction Interventions: Fostering Diversity, Inclusion, and Belonging in the Undergraduate Economics Classroom, Journal of Economic Education, 53, 3, 259–272, DOI: 10.1080/00220485.2022.2075507

American Economic Association (AEA). 2023. Best Practices for Economists – Building a More Diverse, Inclusive, and Productive Profession, https://www.aeaweb .org/resources/best-practices, accessed 12 November 2023.

Aricò, F. 2019. Technology-enhanced Pathways to Active Learning: Student Response Systems Facilitating Peer-instruction and Self-assessment in Large Classrooms, All Ireland Journal of Higher Education, 11, 2, 1–14.

Aricò, F. 2021. Evaluative Conversations: unlocking the power of viva voce assessment for undergraduate students. In P. Baughan (Ed.), *Assessment and Feedback in a Post-Pandemic Era: A Time for Learning and Inclusion*, 47–56, AdvanceHE.

Aricò, F., and Lancaster, S. 2018. Facilitating Active Learning and Enhancing Student Self-assessment Skills, International Review of Economics Education, 29, 6–13, DOI: https://doi.org/10.1016/j.iree.2018.06.002

Bansak, C., and Starr, M. 2010. Gender Differences in Predispositions towards Economics, Eastern Economic Journal, 36, 33–57, DOI: doi.org/10.1057/eej.2008 .50

Barrantes, R. 2007. Analysis of ICT Demand: What is Digital Poverty and How to Measure it? In H. Galperin & J. Mariscal (Eds.), *Digital Poverty: Latin American and Caribbean Perspectives*, 29–53, Practical Action Publishing.

Bayer, A., Bhanot, S., Todd Bronchetti, E., and O'Connell, S.A. 2020. Diagnosing The Learning Environment for Diverse Students in Introductory Economics: An Analysis of Relevance, Belonging, and Growth Mindsets. AEA Papers And Proceedings, 110, 294–298. DOI: doi.org/10.1257/pandp.20201051

Bayer, A., Bruich, G., Chetty, R., and Housiaux, A. 2020. Expanding and Diversifying the Pool of Undergraduates Who Study Economics: insights from a new introductory course at Harvard, *Journal of Economic Education*, 51, 3–4, 364–379, DOI: 10.1080/00220485.2020.1804511

Bayer, A., and Rouse, C.E. 2016. Diversity in the Economics Profession: a new attack on an old problem, *Journal of Economics Perspectives*, 30, 4, 221–242, DOI: 10.1257/jep.30.4.221

Bayer, A., and Wilcox, D.W. 2019. The Unequal Distribution of Economic Education: a report on the race, ethnicity, and gender of economics majors at U.S. colleges and universities, *Journal of Economic Education*, 50, 3, 299–320, DOI: 10.1080/00220485.2019.1618766

Bjork, C. 2023. ChatGPT Threatens Language Diversity. More Needs to be Done to Protect Our Differences in the Age of AI, *The Conversation*, 9 February, https:// theconversation.com/chatgpt-threatens-language-diversity-more-needs-to-be-done -to-protect-our-differences-in-the-age-of-ai-198878

Burgstahler, S., and Cory, R. (Eds). 2008. *Universal Design in Higher Education: From Principles to Practice*. Harvard Education Press.

Cagliesi, G., and Ghanei, M. 2022. Team-based learning in economics: Promoting group collaboration, diversity and inclusion, *Journal of Economic Education*, 53, 1, 11–30, DOI: 10.1080/00220485.2021.2004276

Cheng, W., and Selvaretnam, G. (2022). Effects of mixed groups on multicultural inter-action and student experience, *Learning and Teaching*, 15, 2, 1–28. DOI: https://doi .org/10.3167/latiss.2022.150202

Coxon, A., Aricò, F., and Schildt, J. 2020. Accessibility and Inclusivity in Online Teaching. In S. McKenzie, F. Garivaldis and K.R. Dyer (Eds.), *Tertiary Online Teaching and Learning: TOTAL Perspectives and Resources for Digital Education*, 169–175, Springer.

Davis, P., and Mangan, J. 2009. Threshold Concepts in Economics: implications for teaching, learning and assessment, *The Economics Network*, https:// doi .org/ 10 .53593/n35a

Digital Poverty Alliance. 2023. *How We Define Digital Poverty*, https://digitalpover tyalliance.org, accessed 12 November 2023.

Dynan, K.E., and Rouse, C.E. 1997. The Underrepresentation of Women in Economics: A Study of Undergraduate Economics Students, *Journal of Economic Education*, 28, 4, 350–368, DOI: 10.1080/00220489709597939

Edgecombe Robb, R., and Robb, L. 1999. Gender and the Study of Economics: The Role of Gender of the Instructor, *Journal of Economic Education*, 30, 1, 3–19, DOI: 10.1080/00220489909595933

Espey, M. 2018. Diversity, effort, and cooperation in team-based learning, *Journal of Economic Education*, 49, 1, 8–21, DOI: 10.1080/00220485.2017.1397571

Ferber, M.A. 1984. Suggestions for Improving the Classroom Climate for Women in the Introductory Economics Course: A Review Article, *Journal of Economic Education*, 15, 2, 160–168, DOI: 10.1080/00220485.1984.10845065

Freeman, S., Eddy, S.L., McDonough, M., Smith, M.K, Okoroafor, N., Jordt, H., and Wenderoth, M.P. 2014. Active Learning Increases Student Performance in Science, Engineering, and Mathematics. Proceedings of the National Academy of Sciences of the United States of America, 111, 23, 8410–8415, DOI: 10.1073/pnas.1319030111

Hemsley, B., Power, E., and Given, F. 2023. Will AI Tech Like ChatGPT Improve Inclusion For People With Communication Disability? The Conversation, 19 January, https://theconversation.com/will-ai-tech-like-chatgpt-improve-inclusion -for-people-with-communication-disability-196481

Iosad, A. 2020. *Digital at the core: A 2030 strategy framework for university leaders*. https://www.salesforce.org/wp-content/uploads/2020/11/2030-strategy-framework -for-university-leaders-1.pdf, accessed 20 March 2024.

Jensen, E.J., and Owen, A.L. 2001. Pedagogy, Gender, and Interest in Economics, *Journal of Economic Education*, 32, 4, 323–343, DOI: 10.1080/00220480109596112

Kahneman, D. (2011). *Thinking, fast and slow*. Macmillan.

Kolb, D.A. 1984. *Experiential learning: Experience as the source of learning and development*. Prentice-Hall.

Kulkarni, M. 2019. Digital Accessibility: challenges and opportunities. *IIMB Management Review*, 31, 1, 91–98, DOI: https://doi.org/10.1016/j.iimb.2018.05.009

Kvangraven, I.H., and Kesar, S. 2023. Standing in the way of rigor? Economics' meeting with the decolonization agenda, *Review of International Political Economy*, 30, 5, 1723–1748, DOI: 10.1080/09692290.2022.2131597

Lage, M.J, Platt, G.J., and Treglia, M. 2000. Inverting the Classroom: A Gateway to Creating an Inclusive Learning Environment, *Journal of Economic Education*, 31, 1, 30–43, DOI: 10.1080/00220480009596759

Lage, M.J, and Treglia, M. 1996. The Impact of Integrating Scholarship on Women into Introductory Economics: Evidence from One Institution, *Journal of Economic Education*, 27, 1, 26–36, DOI: 10.1080/00220485.1996.10844891

MacCullagh, L., Bosanquet, A., and Badcock, N.A. (2017). University students with dyslexia: A qualitative exploratory study of learning practices, challenges and strategies. *Dyslexia*, 23(1), 3–23.

Meyer, J.H.F., and Land, R. 2003. Threshold Concepts and Troublesome Knowledge: linkages to ways of thinking and practising within the disciplines. In C. Rust (Ed.), *Improving Student Learning: Improving Student Learning Theory and Practice – Ten Years On*, Oxford Centre for Staff and Learning Development.

Meyer, J.H.F., and Land, R. 2006. Threshold concepts: an introduction. In J.H.F. Meyer and R. Land, *Overcoming barriers to student understanding: threshold concepts and troublesome knowledge*, Routledge.

Naples, M.I. 2017. Teaching Macroeconomics to the Visually Impaired: new tactile methods, verbal precision, and small groups, *Journal of Economic Education*, 48, 3, 193–197, DOI: 10.1080/00220485.2017.1320604

Quality Assurance Agency for Higher Education (QAA). 2023. *Subject Benchmark Statement – Economics*, https://www.qaa.ac.uk/the-quality-code/subject-benchmark-statements/subject-benchmark-statement-economics, accessed 12 November 2023.

Russ, S., and Hamidi, F. 2021. Online Learning Accessibility During the COVID-19 Pandemic. *W4A '21: Proceedings of the 18th International Web for All Conference*, 8, 1-7. https://doi.org/10.1145/3430263.3452445

Yannier, N., Hudson, S.E., Koedinger, K.R., Hirsh-Pasek, K., Michnick Golinkoff, R., Munakata, Y., Doebel, S., Schwartz, D.L., Deslauriers, L., McCarty, L., Cllaghan, K., Theobald, E.J., Freeman, S., Cooper, K.M., and Brownell, S.E. 2021. Active learning: "Hands-on" meets "minds-on", *Science*, 374, 6563, 26–30, DOI: 10.1126/science.abj9957

PART II

CREATING AN ADAPTABLE LEARNING
ENVIRONMENT

5. Using an online multimedia group project to introduce students to economics and their learning community

Parama Chaudhury and Cloda Jenkins

Having a sense of belonging is important for a successful learning experience (Yorke, 2014). In the context of higher education, we interpret belonging to mean feeling part of a peer learning community, faced with similar academic opportunities and challenges; engaging confidently with the staff that teach and support students; and understanding the content and approach to learning in the programme. It can be difficult to establish this sense of belonging in an undergraduate Economics programme, online or on campus, because Economics programmes tend to involve large cohorts of heterogeneous learners. Some will have a passing interest, perhaps unsure what the subject is about, and others will be very passionate about the topics being studied. Some will have chosen to take the course and others will only be there because they are required to. There will also be learners with different academic backgrounds: some will have a stronger mathematics background than others, and a portion of the class will potentially have a background in Economics from high school. This diversity is in addition to diversity of life experiences before and during the programme. There are also a wide range of different approaches to teaching and learning in Economics, for example in terms of the mode of delivery, mix of assessment types, the balance of directed learning and independent learning and the mix of individual work and group work (Allgood et al., 2015). There is a lot for any student to get their head around, whether they are online or on campus.

Navigating the nature of learning and who you are learning with is a challenge for any student and it can take time to establish the sense of belonging. We see this whether students move up to a higher level in education or they are moving across from another subject area to Economics. It is relevant whether they are doing a short (e.g., one semester) course in Economics, are embarking from (high) school to a degree programme in Economics or are moving into postgraduate learning. As course designers and leaders, we have a role to play in helping create opportunities to belong to the learning community.

To achieve each student's potential, we need to establish mechanisms from the outset to help students have a secure starting point for their belonging journey. Induction at the start of the academic year or term is often seen as a time to bring people together physically, with a mix of talks from staff about what will happen during the programme and social events. The premise is that belonging will come naturally once the mechanisms to meet, speak with and hear from others are put in place. This form of induction has a place in any course, particularly those that are longer-term and on campus, but it is not enough to securely establish the process of belonging to a learning community (Tice et al., 2021). This is why in our large undergraduate programme at a research-focused British university with highly competitive entry, we introduced an induction group project that requires students to get straight into thinking like an economist alongside peers and staff, even before they arrive on campus. The project is designed to help students work out what Economics is and what approach they will be taking to learning in their programme.

Prior to the Covid-19 pandemic, we ran this project in-person with great success, and this format has now been emulated by others and short-listed for an education award (Chaudhury and Spielmann, 2016). Like others in the education sector across the world, we had to come up with a new approach for the start of the 2020/21 academic year when learning was online for a high proportion of our students and staff. We describe the approach we took to pivoting the existing project to an online format in this paper. We explain the details of this reformatting and why retaining the project online continues to be an appropriate move, even when students are back on campus. We also provide advice on how to effectively design and deliver an online induction project like ours to help students improve their sense of belonging. Our biggest takeaway from the experience is that the project works better online, even when students are on campus, and it can provide the basis for induction to both online and in-person courses. The pandemic shock forced our hands and showed us a better way of doing something that has broad application.

WHAT IS THE FIRST YEAR CHALLENGE?

The First Year Challenge (FYC) was introduced into the first-year undergraduate Economics programme in 2014 to introduce students to the university, to Economics as a field and to a "research-based" learning model. In the UK, students choose a specialisation or major when they apply. However, for a subject like Economics, which not many have studied in high school, there is a mismatch between what students think Economics is and what it really looks like at the university level (Reimann, 2004; Allgood and McGoldrick, 2020).

In addition, the programme's focus on research-based education means that students are taught cutting-edge research from their first year (starting with VoxEU type blog articles and progressing to journal articles) and are expected to produce a minimum level of research themselves in the form of essays, term papers and dissertations. This expectation is also new to many students who do not often encounter this kind of independent work in high school. The FYC was an attempt to give students a window into both these aspects of their university lives, starting before their arrival at university.

The final issue that the FYC was introduced to address was the fact that as a very large university in a major metropolis, building a sense of community among students was difficult. This hurdle led to adverse outcomes for students, with many feeling lonely and unsupported, and low student satisfaction across the board. The FYC establishes connections with both first-year lecturers and peers, helping students to start to develop a sense of belonging to a learning community before they embark on university life. Students are divided into small groups, assigned a carefully chosen location close to campus, and asked to produce a brief video or audio output linking the location to the topic "growth and inequality", the overarching theme of the required first-year introductory Economics course. They receive detailed guidance before arriving and start on the project on their first day of induction week at university, completing it within the first two weeks of the academic year. Once the FYC ends, students continue to work in their assigned groups throughout the first year for small group tutorials in each of their required Economics courses. This connection leverages the peer-to-peer connections built during the FYC. The best FYC submissions receive a certificate and a small prize, but it is neither assessed formally nor a mandatory part of the curriculum. Despite this, the majority of students fully participate.

Over the past few years, several other universities have adopted the FYC and adapted it to their own contexts. These variations include assessing the FYC process and output which then counts towards the final grade in the first year, expanding the remit of the FYC to include additional follow-on activities over the course of the entire first year, and changing the theme of the FYC to reflect current events and the local context such as the Black Lives Matter movement. In addition, a version of the FYC has been used as a school-wide participation initiative to make studying Economics more attractive to a diverse student body. All these adaptations of the FYC share the same fundamental objectives of creating a learning community, introducing students new to the subject to the vast diversity within Economics, and developing their research, teamwork and exposition skills. An early evaluation of the original FYC initiative is discussed in Chaudhury and Spielmann (2016). In the next section, we provide an updated evaluation of the project since it was moved to an online format in

2020 and in the section that follows, we discuss how to design and deliver the FYC in different contexts.

The Value of Running the First Year Challenge Online

The FYC has provided a successful start to the learning journey of our students since 2014. We retained the value of the project when moving to an online format in 2020/21, when most of our students were learning online across the world. More importantly, adapting to an online format allowed us to enhance the experience by broadening our options for the design of the project and provided greater flexibility in how, when and where students met to work on the project. Going online also made the project set-up logistics easier from a staff and student perspective. Beginning the journey to belong to a learning community was, to our surprise, easier with the use of an online platform (Box 1.1).

Students work in groups of 5–7, in the original campus-based version and the online format, ensuring they immediately have a peer community that they know at the start of the course. The groups are allocated so that students are with peers that they continue to learn with in the same weekly tutorial groups in the first-year introductory Economics course. In 2020/21 we also connected the project groups to the same personal tutor (a staff member focusing on pastoral care and general academic advice) and upper year mentor, enhancing the connection with the wider support community. The creation of small groups within a large cohort, whether on campus or online, helps students enter an unfamiliar situation before getting to know a wider group over time.

BOX 1.1   STUDENT FEEDBACK ON THE VALUE OF DEVELOPING LEARNING COMMUNITY FOR THE YEAR

Great experience, sped up the interaction between us.

The high point was that I got to know people in my tutorial group. We still text and discuss class material.

We have now made a study group to help each other on content we are unsure of and just to talk in general.

An advantage of the online platform, relative to running the project solely on campus, is the flexibility that it offers students. Even if studying on campus, students can still choose to engage online through the platform. They can meet in person or do a mix of the two. Student groups figure out the best option for them; a one-size-fits-all approach is not imposed. At the start of the year, even with an on-campus degree, not everyone may be able to make it to the physical location for induction week due to immigration, other transportation issues or illness. This blended approach makes the experience more inclusive, allowing those with caring, work, or other commitments or constraints on their ability to come to campus to devise a personalised approach with their group (Box 1.2).

BOX 1.2   STUDENT FEEDBACK ON THE VALUE OF THE PROJECT BEING ONLINE

As someone who is studying remotely from home I found the challenge very helpful to make some friends, as I have found this the hardest to do this term.

A good connection with my teammates through Teams, we discuss and post our thoughts on Teams, it helps a lot from the remote disconnection.

There was a potential concern that not all students would have access to reliable technology (Lai and Widmar, 2020). In addition, there was a risk that the platform for the initial group connections, and where the FYC materials were posted, or the mapping software with assigned locations, would not work in all countries where our students were. In the summer of 2020, student interns helped to resolve this issue by piloting all the technology, making sure it worked by testing it with peers all around the world. It was a great relief to know that it was working at varying bandwidths in all countries covered by our global cohort. Ensuring the project was spread over a couple of weeks also meant that any temporary problems with connectivity could be worked around.

A related concern was that students would not know how to engage through online platforms, bearing in mind they had never met each other (Box 1.3). At this point, instructors as well as students were also very new to working fully online. Staff and students were learning together, and the ingenuity of the students throughout the whole process of meeting each other and creating great outputs was quite impressive. Of course, there were challenges getting students familiar with the platform, but it was worth investing the effort as the FYC introduced staff and students to the technologies they would be using throughout their programme. They remained on the same platform for all their courses over the year and the FYC helped them become comfortable online, for example engaging through the chat and online meeting functionality. Staff also got experience setting things up on the online platform that helped with their later courses.

BOX 1.3 STUDENT FEEDBACK ON USING ONLINE TECHNOLOGIES

Even though not everyone was on campus at the time, we were still able to work effectively using zoom calls. However, wi-fi problems sometimes did slow progress.

Since the FYC started in 2014, it has always been a challenge to manage the logistics of setting up project groups and ensuring they met each other in the assigned physical location. We selected Microsoft Teams as the online platform for the FYC, which allowed us to enrol groups into private channels ahead of the course starting and provided them with an easy way to meet for the first time, either through video call or discussion chat. In the past we had prepared detailed documents with information on who was in each group and where to meet, but students often struggled to follow the large volume of written information. Providing a structured platform for students to engage with interactive instructional materials, and to connect with their classmates, took away much of the confusion and uncertainty about what to do, where and when (Dhilla, 2017).

We struggled in the past to update the FYC groups, for example when new students enrolled in the course and others left. This difficulty often delayed the start of the project as we waited until we were confident that enrolment was relatively fixed. On Teams, we were able to set up the platform, and groups, earlier because it was easier for staff to change things live online.

We could move students onto or off the platform and move them across groups, right up until the project started, without the need to send lots of emails or updated documents. This was a significant time-saver for staff and made it easier for students to see what groups they were in and if their group had changed. We were of course concerned that students were missing out by not being able to meet socially in person. Student feedback on the FYC in prior years often emphasised the value of being able to find a new coffee shop together, work out how to get from A to B on campus or simply get to know people informally on the walk to the project meeting location. This was not an option in the height of the pandemic restrictions in September 2020, but for September 2021 we considered this aspect in our decision about whether to move it back to an on-campus experience.

The feedback from the 2020/21 students taught us that being online for the project, wherever they were for the university induction week, allows a flexibility of approach that does not reduce the experience of those who want to meet in person but enhances the experience for those who cannot. Being online did not take away the value of being able to learn about places in London and to make connections between the real world and the Economics they were learning. The benefits of starting the project online, with the option of meeting on campus if feasible, outweighed the downsides. In our case, that was in the context of expecting students to meet on campus after induction week. In other contexts, for example in a distance learning course, the advantages of harnessing the value of technology to enable collaboration and creation of community learning also come into their own. Thus, the use of the online platform facilitates peer interaction in different settings.

Staff-Student Communication and Engagement

As the FYC project is linked to the compulsory Introductory Economics course in our degree, it is an opportunity for the staff teaching that course, and those responsible for the pastoral care of first-year students, to meet them early in the academic year. When the project was purely on-campus, lecturers gave a one-off briefing to the whole cohort but then had to answer many emails on project logistics. Teaching assistants, who run the tutorials for the first-year course, met the students about the project in the first week of term. Personal tutors were also encouraged to talk to students about the project in their first meeting with the students. Channels to communicate with the students existed but they were disparate and sporadic. Moreover, students who were delayed arriving to campus essentially missed the opportunities to engage early-on with teaching staff.

The online platform changed the nature of our engagement, opening up additional, different ways for students to communicate with staff. It provided the structure that students always need when transitioning to a new course and particularly the jump from school to university (Briggs et al., 2012). It also allowed us to scaffold their learning by communicating with them in one space; that is, a unified virtual classroom. We continued to host a briefing session, but it was held online, so students could attend even if they were not yet on campus, and the recording was available so that groups could check back on what was said. The chat facility in the online platform was a game changer. Students, whether they were on campus or online, could post questions and staff could respond in a timely fashion so that initial problems were dealt with relatively quickly. This system was also relatively efficient as all students could see the answer to a question, and therefore multiple messages with the same queries were not required. All staff, including lecturers, teaching assistants, administrative assistants, and personal tutors, were also able to communicate through the platform, which meant that there was a common understanding of what was being asked and what the appropriate responses were. Communication between staff and students, and across students, opened up in a way that was never feasible – given the scale of the cohort and the limited hours of face-to-face interaction – with only campus-based methods.

An interesting and unexpected development was that we were able to observe how project groups were progressing over the course of the FYC. A quick glance through the Teams channels showed the chat within the groups, when video meetings had occurred and so on. The objective of such an audit was not to monitor the specifics of the group's activity, but it enabled us to spot inactivity and provide a nudge where appropriate. Students of course did not always stay on the platform provided for all their interactions, moving to their preferred mode of communication very quickly. It was a lesson in what "remote but not distant" could mean in terms of the future of higher education, with students spread around the world meeting to discuss the assigned landmarks in London and their connection to the theme of growth and inequality.

The real-time nature of staff-student engagement on the platform also meant that staff were able to obtain and respond to student feedback quickly. For example, if there was an issue with a particular location then an adaptation could be made. In the past students may have visited a location and found that the building was covered in scaffolding and was not visible. They would likely have felt discouraged and maybe even disengaged with the project. Online when situations like this arose, such as a website being down, the group could immediately ask for support in the chat and staff could encourage them to think through ways forward, highlighting for example, that the location link was a prompt, and the lack of access should therefore not be an impediment but rather a spur to creative thinking. The immediacy and ease of communication helped both students and staff.

Understanding What Economics Is and the Nature of Learning in the Course

In the FYC we ask students to connect the London location which their group has been assigned to the theme of growth and inequality across the world over the last couple of centuries. They are immediately immersed in the content of their Economics degree, and in the way that we use Economics to analyse big questions relevant to society. The place-based nature of the project also requires them to think creatively about the city they are studying in and its relevance to Economics and economists (Box 1.4). Using locations spread through the city identified on an interactive map, rather than just physical ones near campus, allowed us to broaden the scope of the project and be more adventurous with our choice of locations. This opened new lines of investigation for the students and more variety in approaches and outputs for a growing number of project groups.

The project provides students with a hands-on opportunity to work collaboratively and to undertake independent research, skills required throughout the research-based degree that they have enrolled in. Most of our students have little experience of independent research and will generally have worked on their own at school, often with more of a competitive than a collaborative mindset (Hibbert, 2012). They learn to think creatively about how to approach their research and produce a multi-media output. Study skills of time management, meeting deadlines and submitting work online are all developed.

BOX 1.4   STUDENT FEEDBACK ON LEARNING ABOUT ECONOMICS THROUGH THE PROJECT

The challenge was a great opportunity to work as a team with everyone and helped us learn about our chosen location's connection to Economics.

When I worked through this project, I had a good understanding of using Moodle, got used to the university life, the cooperation with my friends, and contributed the academic knowledge from unit 1 to build a connection with 'Museum' topic.

It is a good activity for the new entrants of University since we could learn the teamwork and knowing new friends of our course.

It was nice being thrown straight into work within a group.

Doing the project remotely meant that many of us were exposed to new challenges that we would not encounter if we could do it in-person. However, I think this made us more innovative in coming out with new methods for completing the task.

The approach also acclimated students to the teaching model we designed for 2020/21 and continue to use, with a mix of asynchronous, online learning and on-campus lessons. They were immersed in this approach from the outset and hence were able to transition to it across all their Economics courses with relative ease. This was also true for the teaching assistants and other staff engaging with students through technology for the first time. The project gave them a safe space to get used to the online side of teaching.

The evaluation of the students' projects and the dissemination of the top three entries also allows students to get a better sense of what good quality work looks like in our course. For example, they learn how accurate referencing of sources and evidencing of interesting ideas are more important than the quality of the video production. The students are also introduced to the idea that feedback comes in different ways in university, as they don't get individual comments on their own video but they are encouraged to reflect on how they did by comparing their work to the exemplars. This is a common approach to feedback across the Economics programme as well, with reflection interspersed with more traditional forms of feedback (Walstad, 2001). The winners of the FYC competition are awarded their prizes (and their video showcased) at the annual undergraduate conference, Explore Econ, where upper-year students present their independent research. This through line connection, from the start of their first year to the end of the degree, provides a reminder to students of the importance of research-based learning in their degree. For the first-years enthused by Economics, it also cements their interest and reminds them of opportunities to come.

HOW TO RUN THE FYC IN THE MOST EFFECTIVE AND FEASIBLE WAY

These benefits of running an induction project like the FYC of course come with a large amount of work behind the scenes. We have learned a lot about how to design and implement the project from years of trial and error, including with the move to online. The more care is taken with set-up, instructions, support and connectivity to wider learning on the course before and during the project experience, the more benefits are seen. Like with most things, choices about the specifics of the implementation of the project determine its value. We discuss what we have done to help ensure effective implementation and summarise our Top Tips on how to build on these lessons learned (Box 1.5).

BOX 1.5   TOP TIPS FOR RUNNING A PROJECT TO FACILITATE BELONGING TO A LEARNING COMMUNITY

- Get input/insights from upper year students who have already participated in the project.
- Don't be afraid to blend – having the online resource for organising a project and making first connections does not mean students can never meet on campus if that is what they prefer to do.
- Connect the induction project groups to a course that goes beyond the project itself, enhancing the learning community impact.
- Use an online platform you are comfortable with and that is part of the student learning environment for other purposes.
- Be on the platform with students. Seeing staff engage through the platform encourages them to do the same.
- Make use of pre-existing open access resources rather than re-inventing the wheel – e.g., Google Maps.

- Make sure instructions to students give clear actionable advice in interactive formats, with specific tasks and mini-deadlines made clear – getting upper year students to write these helps.
- Whilst this is a way for them to transition to more independent learning, do ensure transparent support structures are available to help students with any teething problems.
- Connect project groups to wider learning community interactions, such as seminar groups, personal tutor groups or mentor schemes.
- Celebrate what they achieve – even if for credit but especially if not.

As the FYC is designed for first-year students in Economics, a sizable group in most universities, running it in an effective and feasible manner involves significant pre-planning and coordination with different parts of the programme or department. Many of these challenges arise whether the FYC is run largely on campus, mostly online or in a blended fashion. In our case, the smallest cohort we have run this initiative for was 350 students, and the largest was 800 students. Even when it is possible to run it entirely in-person, the use of technology can facilitate making the process much more feasible for the largest groups.

The structure and timeline of the FYC is a key part of what makes it effective. Students get all the information and guidance about the project before they arrive at university for induction and before classes start. The benefit of this is that even though the FYC is an academic initiative, it is integrated into the usual induction activities such as campus and library tours, and therefore feels less like an add-on to either the first-year induction or the course. To make this structure work, however, a great deal of work involving administrative staff is required to set up the FYC groups, get in touch with students potentially before they have registered at university and have university email addresses and other accounts, which limits their access to key online portals and resources. Originally, the FYC was set up entirely on campus with students receiving the FYC guide and group information via email and then connecting with their groups on the day they arrived. As university registration has largely moved online, and often starts prior to the first day of induction, this initial connection with first-year students even post-pandemic is now made through the dedicated Microsoft Teams site where each FYC group has its own private channel. Students are asked, as the first task of the FYC, to introduce themselves to their groupmates online and set up their first in-person or online meeting. This can also be done through a Virtual Learning Environment (VLE), e.g. Moodle, and in fact, most of the students choose to move their group interactions to a social media outlet such as WhatsApp or WeChat. Having a one-stop online area to save work files, ask the professors for help, and connect with their peers (rather than emailing) is appreciated by students who are otherwise flooded with emails and other missives at this busy time at the start of the year. Running the FYC through Microsoft Teams also means that students can upload their FYC submission to their Teams channel, so that the process from the setup and initial communications with students to the final downloading of submissions is also one-stop for lecturers and programme administrators.

The FYC guide which students are provided with before they arrive used to be a PDF file, but is now set up as a Sway, Microsoft's storytelling app. This makes the guide much more interesting and easier to interact with as there are embedded videos and other multimedia, links to an interactive map where students can find their assigned location and, where possible, a video of their location in case they are not able to go there in person, as well as an index which makes it easy for students to navigate through the guide (Chaudhury, 2023). As the guide is an editable website, it is easy for those organising the FYC to make changes in real-time, rather than having to send out an edited PDF each time such changes are required. Again, a VLE's "pages" option is a way of doing something similar.

The final key element of running the FYC smoothly and efficiently is the guidance for and oversight of how students interact with the rest of their group. As these are first-year students, they are likely to be nervous and shy and have a different group dynamic than more experienced students or ones who know each other already. As a main intended outcome of the FYC is building community, failure of the initiative to deliver on this front is a major issue (Arslan, 2021). Starting off on the right foot is important as it sets the tone for the rest of the interaction, and for this reason, designing a set of initial, well-defined tasks (introducing themselves, making an appointment to meet, posting one interesting thing they learned about their assigned location, posting a team photo) is important. In addition, having a setup where tutors and lecturers can ask the group to report on how their work is going in an informal chat makes the importance of the initiative and working together clear and inserts an element of accountability despite the FYC in its original format not being part of the overall grade (Qiu and MacDougall, 2013).

CONCLUSION

Starting a new course, in person or online, is daunting whatever your background and experience. This is true for those transitioning to higher education from school, those embarking on short-term online courses without any connection to the cohort and those taking a course outside their main area of study or taking a course in an unfamiliar subject as a requirement. Whatever the situation, feeling part of a learning community from the outset can make the experience more fruitful for individuals and improve outcomes. This was particularly apparent during the Covid-19 pandemic when so many learners around the world who signed-up for a campus-based experience found themselves learning partially or wholly online. In a less constrained world, the need to provide structure and scaffolding from the start of a course to enable students to develop their sense of belonging to a learning community remains as strong as ever. What has changed is that we are more experienced in harnessing the benefit of technology, whether the course is formally online or on campus.

We have highlighted the value of running an induction project, like the FYC, to provide the starting point. When care is taken to design the project to suit the context in which it is taking place, the online platform provides a flexible space for communicating and meeting (Stone, 2017). Students in an online course connect through the platform and those in a campus-based course can choose to connect in person or online, adapting through the project. The platform provides a standard online classroom environment whether students are all studying Economics or come from a mix of specialisms, and it is less likely to exclude students with specific needs. In this way it can be one mechanism to make Economics learning more inclusive and engaging for those unsure about the subject, perhaps attracting students who are still deciding to continue with the subject in later courses.

It is important to emphasise that no matter what you do, not all students will engage with a project like this or even when they do not all will value the experience. What we found was that where students expressed doubts about the value of the FYC when run online, they were very similar to what prior cohorts had said when the activity was on campus. The concerns raised related to not wanting to work with people they did not know, pressures of being asked to work on a project so early in the course and concerns about free riding. These are common challenges of collaborative work, and ones that cannot be easily designed out of a group project. The challenges, and linked dissatisfaction amongst some students, was no worse when online and was offset to a large extent by many more students expressing satisfaction with the flexibility of the mode of delivery.

The value and success of our FYC initiative is demonstrated by the number of other universities who have adopted and adapted the idea, and the creation of a new Second Year Challenge (SYC). The project, at the start of the Second Year of a three-year degree, is an attempt to continue community building at a time when many of the official first-year support structures have expired. The idea of the SYC, at least in part, arose from student feedback of how the learning community falls away after the first year and at a time when many students are feeling overburdened by job and internship expectations. The re-connecting opportunity is particularly important for vulnerable students such as those from under-represented backgrounds. The SYC, building on the success of the FYC, is a reminder that belonging to a learning community does not come easily, particularly with large and diverse cohorts in Economics. Embedding structures to provide support to students to help them belong to the learning community is important for the student experience and student outcomes. This can be done effectively by harnessing the value of technology and learning lessons from projects such as ours.

ACKNOWLEDGEMENTS

As with all things in education, many people were involved with the design and implementation of this project since 2014. We would like to thank Christian Spielmann and Frank Witte for helping create the FYC and supporting its initial implementation. We could not have moved online without the dedication of the UCL Economics Undergraduate Administrators and IT support and Aoife Horan, Course Manager 2020/21. We would also like to thank the undergraduate assistants who helped us test the online model, Jingyan Sun and Shama Riddhi. Finally, we would like to thank the hundreds of students who have given the project a go over the years, showing us what is working well and where improvements can be made. It is always a highlight of the year judging the outputs that they produce.

REFERENCES

Allgood, S. and K. McGoldrick. (2020). How can economists use the cognitive challenges framework to enhance economic education? *Journal of Economic Education, 52*(1), 41–52. doi:10.1080/00220485.2020.1845267

Allgood, S., W. Walstad and J. Siegfried. (2015). *Journal of Economic Literature, 53*(2), 285–325. Retrieved from https://www.jstor.org/stable/24433983

Arslan, G. (2021). Loneliness, college belongingness, subjective vitality, and psychological adjustment during coronavirus pandemic: Development of the College Belongingness Questionnaire. *Journal of Positive School Psychology, 5*(1), 17–31. doi:10.47602/jpsp.v5i1.240

Briggs, A., J. Clark and I. Hall. (2012). Building bridges: understanding student transition to university. *Quality in Higher Education, 18*(1), 3–21. doi:10.1080/135383 22.2011.614468

Chaudhury, P. (2023). Asynchronous learning design—Lessons for the post-pandemic world of higher education. *The Journal of Economic Education, 54*(2). Research on Teaching Economics to Undergraduates. doi:10.1080/00220485.2023.2174233

Chaudhury, P. and C. Spielmann. (2016). Let's Make a Movie – Introducing Economics with a Multimedia Research Project. *Journal of Economics Teaching.* Retrieved from https://journalofeconomicsteaching.org/lets-make-a-movie-introducing-economics -with-a-multimedia-project/

Crooks, T. (1988). The Impact of Classroom Evaluation Practices on Students. *Review of Educational Research, 58*(4), 438. doi:10.2307/1170281

Dhilla, S. (2017). The Role of Online Faculty in Supporting Successful Online Learning Enterprises: A Literature Review. *Higher Education Politics & Economics, 3*(1), xx. Retrieved from https://digitalcommons.odu.edu/aphe/vol3/iss1/3/

Hibbert, B. (2012). Thinking about … transition from sixth form to university. *Teaching History, 148*, 4–7. Retrieved from https://www.proquest.com/scholarly -journals/thinking-about-transition-sixth-form-university/docview/1076717540/se -2?accountid=145

Lai, J. and N. Widmar. (2020). Revisiting the digital divide in the COVID-19 era. *Applied Economic Perspectives and Policy, 43*(1), 458–464. doi:https://doi.org/10 .1002/aepp.13104

Qiu, M. and D. McDougall. (2013). Foster strengths and circumvent weaknesses: Advantages and disadvantages of online versus face-to-face subgroup discourse. *Computers & Education, 67*, 1–11. doi:10.1016/j.compedu.2013.02.005

Reimann, N. (2004). First-year Teaching-Learning Environments in Economics. *International Review of Economics Education, 3*(1), 9–38. doi:10.1016/ s1477–3880(15)30147-x

Stone, C. (2017). *Opportunity through online learning: improving student access, participation and success in higher education.* Retrieved from https://apo.org.au/ node/94591

Tice, D., R. Baumeister, J. Crawford, K. Allen and A. Percy. (2021). Student belongingness in higher education: Lessons for professors from the COVID-19 pandemic. *Journal of University Teaching & Learning Practice, 18*(4). doi:https://doi.org/10 .53761/1.18.4.2

Walstad, W. (2001). Improving Assessment in University Economics. *The Journal of Economic Education, 32*(3), 281–294. doi:10.1080/00220480109596109

Yorke, M. (2014). The development and initial use of a survey of student 'belongingness', engagement and self-confidence in UK higher education. Assessment & Evaluation in Higher Education, 41(1), 154–166. doi:10.1080/02602938.2014.990 415

6. Moving metrics online: challenges, solutions, and practical advice

Alice Louise Kassens

INTRODUCTION

The COVID-19 pandemic pushed classrooms traditionally taught in person to the virtual world midway through the spring academic semester of 2020 and generally accelerated online courses available to post-secondary learners. The National Center for Education Statistics (NCES) noted that 75% of all post-secondary students in the United States took online courses in the fall of 2020 during the height of pandemic in-person learning restrictions, compared to 36% in the fall of 2019 (Hamilton, 2023). The move from an in-person class to online was relatively seamless for some for a variety of reasons, including that some courses were already hybrid or at institutions with a long-standing, healthy online course catalog and with needed expertise and technology on hand; for others, like small liberal arts institutions with courses taught in the traditional setting, it required a quick pivot into unchartered waters.

Some courses might more easily lend themselves to the online space from the instructional perspective. For example, those courses requiring significant reading and reflection are perhaps more adaptable to an online format. Regardless of format, other courses are more challenging to teach online, including those requiring considerable one-on-one interaction between the instructor and students.[1] Quantitative courses, such as econometrics, fit into the latter category, particularly when there is a wide range or low level of student data literacy and coding experience.

This chapter describes a small, traditionally in-person econometrics course taught at a small liberal arts college and the modifications made when the same course moved online for a semester during the COVID-19 pandemic. This chapter focuses on changes made to shift the course online and their pedagogical reasoning. Specifics of the day-to-day format, including a discussion of materials, are included for those considering teaching econometrics online for the first time or looking to modify an existing course. After an overview of the traditional in-person version most often taught at the author's institution, this chapter outlines the changes made to shift the class to an online format, why those changes were made, and how the modifications worked in this case. The latter is not guided by statistical evidence, as the one class was too small for any such analysis, but rather by professor observation.

IN-PERSON APPROACH

The econometrics course that is the focus of this chapter is a required course in the economics major at a small liberal arts college. Typical enrollment is less than twenty students, primarily juniors and seniors. The prerequisites for the course are a lower-level math course, an introductory statistics course, and either intermediate macroeconomics or intermediate microeconomics. In addition to economics majors (and minors), students in the course frequently come from the Actuarial Science major, where the course can be used as a quantitative requirement. Finally, it is common for the economics majors in the course to be double majors in mathematics and business. Thus, each semester, students in the course have a wide range of data literacy and coding experience. For some, it has been 2–3 years since they took the prerequisite math and statistics courses; others regularly take classes that rely on the data literacy skills leaned heavily upon in econometrics and are experienced in one or more coding languages, including R and Python. The discussed econometrics course uses SAS Studio, which most students have never used. Familiarity with one coding syntax, logic, and semantics makes it much easier to learn another that is similar, thus giving an advantage to those with prior coding experience. Care is taken each semester to reach the entire spectrum of student experience and background.

In 2017, the in-person econometrics course pivoted away from the traditional introductory econometrics course, heavy on econometric theory, to one focused on the doing of econometrics, following the call to action by Angrist and Pischke (2017). The setup vastly differs from most econometrics courses that focus on traditional lectures with a textbook (Harter & Asarta, 2022). The course begins with a two-week boot camp in which students go through the SAS Programming I e-course,[2] earning a certificate from SAS noting their programming skills and reviewing the statistical and mathematical tools from the prerequisite courses needed for econometrics. For the rest of the semester, the course sets aside 2–3 weeks for each of the five empirical tools used by empirical economic researchers today: 1) randomized control trials, 2) regression, 3) instrumental variables, 4) regression discontinuity design, and 5) difference-in-differences. Rather than following a traditional textbook, the course uses *Mastering 'Metrics* (Angrist & Pischke, 2014) as a complement to the lecture and has a heavy focus on learning proper research design and how to implement the five tools, accurately interpret the results, and understand what the generated results are and are not telling us (Kassens, 2019a). The class meets in a computer lab so students can work on their coding skills daily as we work through the empirical tools; it is an active learning environment.

One of the benefits of teaching a small group of students in person is the ability to wander around the classroom while students are working and spend intentional time with those who have questions. In econometrics, these one-on-one conversations in the classroom often involve students' issues getting their code to "work." I often sit in the seat next to them and ask them to talk me through their script's logic and help them discover where and why their problem occurs. These opportunities are also possible with traditional office hours, but working with students "in the moment" effectively teaches the material. Additionally, their classroom neighbor likely has the same or similar problem and can join the conversation.

Assessment in the course is through attendance (5%), five homework sets, one on each empirical tool (20%), portions of an original empirical paper (prospectus [5%], literature review [10%], and data and methods [15%]), the final empirical paper (15%), a midterm (15%) and final exam (15%).[3] Students can work in groups on the homework sets. Homework sets are often started in class to ensure students understand the instructions and expectations. The midterm and final are closed book and taken in class, although students can access SAS online help as that is standard practice in the "real world." We utilized SAS OnDemand, which allows the professor to load any needed data sets and materials into a shared library for homework and tests and the students to upload their data and save their files (SAS, 2023).

ONLINE MODIFICATIONS

Econometrics was taught online for the first time after the pivot to online courses during the pandemic in the fall of 2020.[4] Some aspects of the course were changed to better suit the online and pandemic environment, but others remained the same.[5] This section outlines the modifications to my in-person delivery and why these changes were made. I also note what stayed the same and why. The online version of the course was only taught once, as by the following fall semester, when the course was next scheduled to be taught, classes were all returned to in-person.

With the move online, the course continued on its usual Tuesday/Thursday schedule, but the Tuesday class was synchronous (Zoom), while the Thursday class was asynchronous. Most courses taught at the College that semester were hybrid in this way. Hence, the mixed format for econometrics kept some consistency across all courses for the students and offered them flexibility in a strange and stressful environment. The hybrid structure can also capitalize on both asynchronous and synchronous learning benefits. Synchronous learning allows for easy engagement and in-time interactivity, while asynchronous learning allows flexibility and convenience (for both the professor and students) (Bennett, 2020).

On Monday morning of each week, a plan was posted on the course LMS page outlining the specifics covered that week, including any assignments. The material typically covered via traditional lecture was moved to the synchronous days, coupled with think/pair/share exercises utilizing assigned Zoom meeting rooms for smaller group discussion and sharing. Coding practice and applications of the empirical tools were the focus of the asynchronous days and were reviewed on the following synchronous day (the next week). The delay allowed students ample time to dedicate to learning SAS and how to apply and interpret results.

The topics covered in the online version, including the two-week boot camp, remained the same with the move online. Since there was less time together as a group, some details of the empirical tools were left out, making the course less rigorous. The loss in rigor was aimed at those students with the least data literacy and coding experience so that they could be successful with adequate effort given the loss of valuable in-person instruction. The one-week gap between group meetings required me to spend more time at the start of the synchronous sessions reviewing material covered in the previous week and how it connected to the overall course. Still, the asynchronous day was a more efficient way for the students to go through and practice the software and applications.

Due to losing the traditional classroom, walking around the room was impossible. While I could ask students to share their screens as they worked (if they were using SAS on the same device as their Zoom connection), that seemed a bit invasive. Those uncomfortable sharing their screen might be reluctant to ask for help. Instead, in addition to traditional office hours (held remotely), a period each week was set aside for a session to work with econometrics students on software and applications, like a virtual lab. Typically, 2–4 students would attend and express gratitude for the special session before leaving. If no students had questions at the start of the special session, I walked students through prepared helpful coding tips and application of the empirical tool currently being covered. Then, I posted the notes and exercises on the LMS after the lab for those unable to attend. Based on my experience with the course, with this sample of one class, the special session was an effective method of helping students with a data literacy and coding gap. Still, it did not replace the effectiveness of walking through the classroom and helping students in need.

Assessment of the online course was similar to the in-person version, with modifications to incentivize asynchronous work: Attendance (synchronous sessions, 4%), Asynchronous work (weekly, due Mondays at 5:00 pm and reviewed the following day in the synchronous session, 20%), Homework (15%), portions of an original empirical paper (prospectus [5%], literature review [10%], and data and methods [10%]), the final empirical paper (10%), a midterm (13%) and final exam (13%.) Adding the asynchronous work required adjusting the weights of the other assessments relative to the traditional, in-person course.

Extra credit recall quizzes were employed to incentivize preparation for the synchronous classes and dedication to the asynchronous work. The quizzes were not difficult. A simple review of the previous class period's notes and a basic understanding of the concepts earned high marks. The quizzes primarily tested a mixture of SAS knowledge or general concepts about the empirical tool currently being covered and were given at the start of the synchronous class via a Google form set up as a quiz. The professor sent the quiz via Zoom chat and gave students 2–3 minutes to complete it before closing it. The quiz was set up such that students saw their scores, the correct answers, and the reasoning for the correct answers after submission for immediate feedback. Quiz scores were accumulated over the semester and applied as a modest bump to the final exam grade. These quizzes were not previously employed in the in-person version of the course but were so effective that they were maintained when classes resumed their traditional format in later semesters. Students noted that they appreciated the carrot and were motivated by the incentive to study course material more carefully than if they did not have the quizzes. Literature supports using recall quizzes to incentivize review and promote student success (Agarwal & Bain, 2019).

OUTCOMES

While I cannot statistically test for differences between the online course and the in-person version for various reasons, including the important one of small sample (class) size, I can offer observations. I have taught this course for nearly twenty years and can provide informed anecdotal evidence. Of course, I may have different strengths, weaknesses, and preferences than the reader, which should be kept in mind.

In terms of grades, while not an optimal measurement of student learning, they are comparable over time, given assignments are relatively consistent and provide some evidence of student progress and success. Overall, grades were considerably higher online than in the typical semester. I attribute this to several things: 1) some of the more detailed, challenging material was omitted due to the above-discussed constraints; 2) the midterm and final, two areas where grades were much higher than usual in the online format, were open book, which, when combined with the lessened rigor, contributed the most to the higher scores; 3) the midterm and final grades in the typical in-person course are typically lower and weighted more than in the virtual version due to adding the asynchronous work; and 4) I graded assignments with a softer touch than usual due to the observed stress students appeared to be under navigating a global pandemic as young adults. Put together, these reasons put upward pressure on grades in the online econometrics course.

The grade distribution was also tighter on the left-hand side than in the traditional course: the average student earned a higher grade (see above), and the worst students earned a higher grade than the in-person course. The share of students earning A's was similar to the typical semester, so the higher average was primarily from pulling up the lower end of the distribution. I do not believe this shift is driven mainly by students who typically perform poorly in this type of course, excelling in an online environment; instead, I think that the altered spread of the grade distribution is driven by the aforementioned reasons, namely reduced rigor and softer grading.

One measure of student learning in econometrics is the final paper, a capstone to the course. Students develop an original research question, craft their research design, go through the steps of building an appropriate data set, and apply the appropriate empirical tools acquired throughout the semester. The quality of the paper components and the final paper were slightly below that of the traditional semester, primarily due to missing empirical details mentioned above that were no fault of the students. Given the material we covered in class, the students did a commendable job. Still, the typical student left the online course with less knowledge, as evidenced by the final paper, than students in the in-person course.[6]

CONCLUSION

Econometrics can be taught online, but this professor believes it is best taught in-person if the goal is student learning, particularly when there is a data literacy and coding skills gap. The data literacy and coding gap at the institution covered in this chapter, likely common across many institutions, is more easily accommodated and student learning maximized by a traditional in-person setting, particularly with the professor walking around the room, deliberately interacting with students.

However, suppose one is tasked with teaching the course online. In that case, the online course layout described in this chapter will adequately teach students how to use the five common empirical tools used by economists today, when each is appropriate, and the requirements and assumptions behind each. These are powerful skills to bring into the labor market. The capstone for the course, the individual paper, showcases individual student learning.

It should be noted that this course was taught online in 2020, before the proliferation of large language models like ChatGPT. If an instructor wants to limit the use of ChatGPT, modifications to the online format provided above are necessary. This is also true of an in-person course.

NOTES

1. There is also evidence that online education disparately harms less proficient students (Dynarski, 2018). This chapter, however, focuses on the instructor's side of the classroom and modifications made to bring an in-person course to the online space.
2. SAS Programming I: Essentials is an excellent, free e-course covering the basics of coding using SAS (https://learn.sas.com/course/view.php?id=118).
3. See Appendix 6.1 for the fall 2022 syllabus, which is representative of the in-person version of the course since the modifications to the course in 2017.
4. See Appendix 6.2 for the fall 2020 syllabus.
5. I relied on various resources to develop the online structure, including recommended best practices from Harvard University (Harvard University, n.d.).
6. It is acknowledged that the online course was only taught once and is being compared to nineteen editions of the in-person version, which is perhaps "unfair."
7. The instructor's personal information (phone, address, etc.) has been removed, as have policies unrelated to the topic of this chapter.

REFERENCES

Agarwal, P. K., & Bain, P. M. (2019). *Powerful Teaching: Unleash the Science of Learning.* Jossey-Bass.

Angrist, J. D., & Pischke, J.-S. (2014). *Mastering 'Metrics: The Path from Cause to Effect.* Princeton University Press.

Angrist, J. D., & Pischke, J.-S. (2017). Undergraduate Econometrics Instruction: Through Our Classes, Darkly. *Journal of Economic Perspectives, 31*(2), 125–144.

Bennett, L. (2020, September 3). 9 Benefits of Synchronous and Asynchronous E-learning. *kaltura blog.* Retrieved November 5, 2023, from https://corp.kaltura.com/blog/9-benefits-of-synchronous-and-asynchronous-e-learning/

Dynarski, S. (2018, January 19). Online Courses Are Harming the Students Who Need the Most Help. *The New York Times.* Retrieved July 17, 2023, from https://www.nytimes.com/2018/01/19/business/online-courses-are-harming-the-students-who-need-the-most-help.html

Hamilton, I. (2023, May 24). By the Numbers: The Rise of Online Learning In The U.S. *Forbes.* Retrieved November 5, 2023, from https://www.forbes.com/advisor/education/online-learning-stats/

Harter, C., & Asarta, C. (2022). Teaching Methods in Undergraduate Intermediate Theory, Statistics and Econometrics, and Other Upper-Division Economics Courses: Results from a Sixth National Quinquennial Survey. *The American Economist, 67*(1), 132–146.

Harvard University. (n.d.). *Pedagogical Best Practices: Residential, Blended, and Online*. Retrieved from Harvard University: Teach Remotely, https://teachremotely .harvard.edu/best-practices

Kassens, A. L. (2019a). Taking a Path Less Travelled: Mastering 'Metrics without a Textbook. In J. Hall & K. Lawson, *Teaching Economics: Perspectives on Innovative Economics Education* (pp. 137–153). Springer.

Kassens, A. L. (2019b). Theory vs. Practice: Teaching Undergraduate Econometrics. *Journal of Economic Education, 50*(4), 367–370.

SAS. (2023). *SAS OnDemand for Academics*. Retrieved July 14, 2023, from https:// www.sas.com/en_us/software/on-demand-for-academics.html

APPENDICES

Portions of the Typical In-person Econometrics Syllabus[7]

Table 6A.1   *Course outline for in-person econometrics syllabus*

Class Dates	Topic	Reading	Assignments
September 2	The Big Picture	MM Introduction Lecture Note 1	Create SAS OnDemand account (use email from Kassens) Programming I Lessons 1–3
September 7–16	SAS BOOT CAMP Statistics Review	Lecture Note 2	Programming I Lessons 4–7 Prospectus (Sunday September 19, 5:00 pm, Turnitin)
September 21–23	Analysis and Interpretation of Randomized Trials	MM Chapter 1 Lecture Note 3	Homework #1
September 28–October 14	Regression Basics	MM Chapter 2 Lecture Note 4	Homework #2 Literature Review (Sunday October 10, 5:00 pm, Turnitin)
October 26–November 11	Instrumental Variables (IV)	MM Chapter 3 Lecture Note 5	Homework #3 MIDTERM November 11
November 16–23	Regression Discontinuity Design (RDD)	MM Chapter 4 Lecture Notes 6	Homework #4 Data and Methods (Tuesday November 23, 5:00 pm, Turnitin)
November 30-December 9	Differences-in-Differences	MM Chapter 5 Lecture Note 7	Homework #5 Final Paper (Friday December 10, 5:00 pm, Turnitin)
December 16	-	-	FINAL EXAM, 8:30 am

Note: Several online resources exist to help in your learning of the material including these SAS tutorials found here.

Grade Determination and Details

Attendance (5%) – Students are expected to be in every class and follow all College public health guidelines, including those pertaining to masks. If you cannot make it to class you must alert me prior to the start of class for you to be considered excused. Students will be marked present any day that I take attendance and they are either present or excused. More than three unexcused absences will result in a *full course letter grade reduction.*

Homework (20%) – Homework sets are submitted via Inquire. Emailed assignments will not be accepted. Late assignments will be accepted with a 10% deduction per hour it is late starting at the deadline. If you have a conflict with the due date you must notify Dr. Kassens at least a week in advance. The associated program file must be included for each SAS assignment, or the work will suffer a 10% grade penalty. The results for SAS problems must be neatly presented. You will be graded on your presentation. Specific details on presentation will be provided. You may work together on homework assignments, but each student must submit a homework.

Prospectus (5%) – A 2–3 page prospectus is due Sunday, September 19th by 5:00 pm via Turnitin. The homework late penalty will be used. Emailed papers will not be accepted. Your prospectus must include a clear motivation, research question, and hypothesis. Additionally, you must include a developing literature review linking the selected papers to your project. APA guidelines should be followed. Additional details will be given at a later date.

Literature Review (10%) – A 3–5 page literature review is due Sunday, October 10th by 5:00 pm via Turnitin. The homework late penalty will be used. Emailed papers will not be accepted. APA guidelines should be followed. Additional details will be given at a later date.

Data and Methods (15%) – A 3–5 page write-up is due Tuesday, November 23rd by 5:00 pm via Turnitin. The homework late penalty will be used. Emailed papers will not be accepted. Your write-up must describe your hypothesis and economic and econometric models. Additionally, you must carefully describe the variables needed and data sources. A screen shot of the first page of your data spreadsheet must be attached, but not included in the page count.

Final Paper (15%) – A 10–15 page final paper is due Friday, December 10th by 5:00 pm via Turnitin. The homework late penalty will be used. Emailed papers will not be accepted. The program file showing all SAS commands for your project must be included as an attachment, but not included in the page count. APA guidelines should be followed. Additional details will be given at a later date.

Midterm and Final Exam (15% each [30%]) – If you have a conflict with the test(s), you must notify me at least a week in advance and make other arrangements. Late tests for unexcused absences are not given and a zero will be recorded in these cases. The midterm is currently scheduled for November 11th. This date is technically past the middle of the semester, but is in the middle of our course material when accounting for the weeks spent in the Boot Camp. The final exam date is set by the College and cannot be changed. The final exam is December 16th, 8:30 am–11:30 am.

*You must turn in (email) a certificate for the SAS Programming I e-course to demonstrate completion. Failure to do so by SEPTEMBER 17th at 5:00 pm will result in a *5-point reduction in your course grade.**

Portions of the Online Econometrics Course Syllabus

Table 6A.2   Course outline for online econometrics syllabus

Dates	Topic/*subtopic*	Reading	Assignments
August 20	The Big Picture	MM Introduction Lecture Note 1	Create SAS OnDemand account (use email from Kassens) Programming I Lessons 1–3
August 25– September 3	SAS BOOTCAMP Statistics Review	Lecture Note 2	Programming I Lessons 4–7 Asynchronous Work 1–2
September 8–17	Analysis and Interpretation of Randomized Trials	MM Chapter 1 Lecture Note 3	Asynchronous Work 3–4 Homework #1 Prospectus (Sunday September 20, 5:00 pm, Turnitin)
September 22– October 15	Regression Basics	MM Chapter 2 Lecture Note 4	Asynchronous Work 5–8 Homework #2 Literature Review (Sunday October 11, 5:00 pm, Turnitin)
October 20–29	Instrumental Variables (IV)	MM Chapter 3 Lecture Note 5	Asynchronous Work 9–10 Homework #3 MIDTERM November 1
November 3–5	Regression Discontinuity Design (RDD)	MM Chapter 4 Lecture Notes 6	Asynchronous Work 11 Homework #4 Data and Methods (Sunday November 8, 5:00 pm, Turnitin)
November 10–17	Differences-in-Differences	MM Chapter 5 Lecture Note 7	Asynchronous Work 12 Homework #5 Final Paper (Wednesday November 18, 5:00 pm, Turnitin)
November 23	-	-	FINAL EXAM, 8:00 am

Note: Several online resources exist to help in your learning of the material, including this video series by Ben Lambert. SAS tutorials can be found here.

Grade Determination and Details

Attendance (4%) – Students are expected to be in all synchronous classes. If you cannot make it to class you must alert me prior to the start of class for you to be considered excused. Students will be marked present any day that I take attendance and they are either present or excused. More than three unexcused absences will result in a *full course letter grade reduction.* If you have a temperature of 100.4 or higher or other coronavirus symptoms, don't come to the classroom. Call Health Services IMMEDIATELY. Do not come to class or go to any public area on campus. Do keep up with all readings, assignments, and deadlines. In order for your absence to be excused, you must give Health Services permission to notify me that you have consulted them about coronavirus symptoms. If Health Services informs you that you should isolate and not attend class for multiple days or weeks, inform me so that we can make a plan to keep you current in the course. All absences caused by consultation with Health Services about coronavirus symptoms or isolation ordered by Health Services will be excused.

Asynchronous Work (20%) – Weekly asynchronous assignments practicing concepts covered in readings and the synchronous class meetings. Students are permitted to work on assignments together and use class notes, Angrist & Pischke, and online SAS resources. Other resources are not permitted unless explicitly noted in the assignment. Assignments are found on Inquire and are due Mondays at 5:00 pm.

Homework (15%) – Homework sets are submitted via Inquire. Emailed assignments will not be accepted. Late assignments will be accepted with a 10% deduction per hour it is late starting at the deadline. If you have a conflict with the due date you must notify Dr. Kassens at least a week in advance. The associated program file must be included for each SAS assignment, or the work will suffer a 10% grade penalty. The results for SAS problems must be neatly presented. You will be graded on your presentation. Specific details on presentation will be provided. You may work together on homework assignments, but each student must submit a homework.

Prospectus (5%) – A 2–3 page prospectus is due Sunday, September 20th by 5:00 pm via Turnitin. The homework late penalty will be used. Emailed papers will not be accepted. Your prospectus must include a clear motivation, research question, and hypothesis. Additionally, you must include a developing literature review linking the selected papers to your project. APA guidelines should be followed. Additional details will be given at a later date.

Literature Review (10%) – A 3–5 page literature review is due Sunday, October 11th by 5:00 pm via Turnitin. The homework late penalty will be used. Emailed papers will not be accepted. APA guidelines should be followed. Additional details will be given at a later date.

Data and Methods (10%) – A 3–5 page write-up is due Sunday, November 8th by 5:00 pm via Turnitin. The homework late penalty will be used. Emailed papers will not be accepted. Your write-up must describe your hypothesis and economic and econometric models. Additionally, you must carefully describe the variables needed and data sources. A screen shot of the first page of your data spreadsheet must be attached, but not included in the page count.

Final Paper (10%) – A 10–15 page final paper is due Wednesday, November 18th by 5:00 pm via Turnitin. The homework late penalty will be used. Emailed papers will not be accepted. The program file showing all SAS commands for your project must be included as an attachment, but not included in the page count. APA guidelines should be followed. Additional details will be given at a later date.

Midterm and Final Exam (13% each [26%]) – If you have a conflict with the test(s), you must notify me at least a week in advance and make other arrangements. Late tests for unexcused absences are not given and a zero will be recorded in these cases. Tests will be reviewed, but will be collected by the professor afterwards. All tests are property of the professor. You may come to review your test during office hours. The midterm is currently scheduled for November 1st. The final exam date is set by the College and cannot be changed. The final exam is November 23rd, 8:00 am–12:00 pm.

*You must turn in (email) a certificate for the SAS Programming I e-course to demonstrate completion. Failure to do so by SEPTEMBER 7th at 5:00 pm will result in a *5-point reduction in your course grade*.*

7. Liberal arts education and the online context

Rebecca L. Moryl

INTRODUCTION

Liberal arts[1] (LA) education has been expanding (Pippins et al., 2019), and so has demand for online courses. However, LA institutions have been slow to move into the online learning environment (Hollis, 2016). One benefit of the emergency remote learning of the 2020 Covid-19 pandemic may be an opportunity to explore how online teaching rooted in sound pedagogical theory could uniquely serve the learning goals of the LA (Geng & McGinley, 2021). The potential benefits could also accrue to learning contexts that may not identify as traditionally LA but have a focus on learning across the curriculum, a strong co-curricular community, and experiential learning. These institutions should consider the potential benefits from online education, including new and expanded geographic markets and partnerships, improved economic returns, growth opportunities for faculty, and increased student satisfaction (Appana, 2008).

In consideration of the role of economics as a discipline in this opportunity, this chapter explores student, faculty and institutional expectations of the LA education and of online learning; what is required for success in online instruction, particularly in the liberal arts context; and how economics instructors can deliver online courses serving LA values. I focus on high yield strategies and specific examples drawn from the economic education literature and my own experience.

STUDENT EXPECTATIONS OF LA

According to Gonyea et al.'s (2006) comparison of the experiences of LA college students to those attending other types of institutions, LA students experience more frequent discussions with faculty outside of class, more frequent participation in classroom discussions, spend more time preparing for class, and do more collaborative out-of-class work. While students at both types of institutions work during the school year, LA students are more often working on campus. As further evidence for this increased campus community interaction, more LA students engage in co-curricular activities than their counterparts. LA students report that their institutions place a strong emphasis on "academics, academic support, attending campus events, and interacting with students from different backgrounds" (p. 14).

IMPLICATIONS FOR LA ONLINE EDUCATION

Among undergraduate students, online courses have a reputation for poor design, lack of community, and lack of communication with and feedback from the instructor. Students particularly perceive one-sided expectations of active engagement for students, but not for instructors (Konrady, 2015). Students complain about community engagement efforts, such as threaded discussions and synchronous classroom sessions, that are too instructor driven. They also dislike project-based work that is not structured to support shared contribution and connection. Students defined a "good" instructor as accessible, flexible, and one who provides individual feedback (Konrady, 2015).

FACULTY EXPECTATIONS OF TEACHING ONLINE

LA faculty express concerns about online education around lack of institutional support, particularly with technology, and recognition of the workload involved. They are also concerned about the quality of online instruction, particularly with assessment and providing complex learning tasks. Some also report fearing the format or change more generally (Bolliger et al., 2019; Borup & Evmenova, 2019; Herrington et al., 2005).

Faculty report concerns regarding student engagement, worrying that it won't be of the same quality they experience in in-person courses (Bolliger et al., 2019), which will diminish their enjoyment of teaching (Borup & Evmenova, 2019). Faculty express uncertainty about using class time to facilitate connection (Berry, 2019), though those with more online experience are both more open to this use of class time and to its benefits (Bolliger et al., 2019). Faculty also express concern about a lack of connection among instructors resulting in a failure of opportunities for networking to share teaching and course development ideas (Boling et al., 2012).

LA INSTITUTION EXPECTATIONS OF ONLINE LEARNING

Hollis (2016) finds LA college presidents lack exposure to online education modalities and have limited understanding of the scope of online education.

LA institutions have been slower to consider and adopt online education, perhaps because of concerns about whether and how it aligns with LA mission, culture, and community. Further, LA presidents expressed concerns about faculty resistance to online education, echoing the faculty concerns outlined above that online instruction doesn't align with LA values.

Many LA presidents haven't considered that students might take hybrid or online courses simultaneously with in-person courses and so have opportunities to interact in a traditional way with faculty and their peers. This may be due to leaders' own conventional experiences in the classroom and on campus, and a biased perception of online learning as inferior to that traditional experience. Despite evidence that online education is "at least as effective as traditional classroom instruction …online education has faced scrutiny in terms of quality, effectiveness, and legitimacy from various stakeholders, yet the same stakeholders do not scrutinize conventional education methods in the same way" (Hollis, 2016, p. 200).

WHAT IS REQUIRED FOR SUCCESS IN ONLINE INSTRUCTION

Broadly, the principles of effective instruction are the same regardless of modality, but the details and practices of delivery, structure, engagement, and assessment should change. Research suggests that a constructivist approach to online education will support both learning and student engagement outcomes. In a constructivist approach, the classroom community works to construct knowledge and meaning, becoming the "vehicle through which learning occurs" (Palloff & Pratt, 2007, p. 18) This type of active, applied, project-based learning can thrive in the online environment (Carrasco, 2022; Jankowski & Bheda, 2022). Further, the social foundation of this constructivist approach necessitates a focus on the engagement so critical to successful online learning in the LA context. This focus on engagement enhances the "social presence" necessary for quality relationships online. Short et al. (1976) defined social presence as the degree to which a person is perceived by others as "real" in mediated communication, such as an online classroom. Social presence is taken for granted in an in-person classroom but must be fostered online through structure and opportunities to facilitate meaningful connection and shared learning (Palloff & Pratt, 2007).

For a constructivist approach, the norms and expectations to support community should be set out purposefully for all interactions – from asynchronous discussion boards to synchronous video class meetings (Palloff & Pratt, 2007). The instructor must remind students of and assess them on the expectation of shared learning (Beaudoin, 2001).

Effective instruction requires students actively engage with their own learning, being "facilitated to learn" rather than "being taught" (Herrington et al., 2005). Enabling self-directed learning lends itself to the LA context, where students report spending more time preparing for class (Gonyea et al., 2006). It begins with clear, engaging course structure and continues through instructor facilitation that explains the rationale and provides a clear guide to students. When instructors demonstrate the "courage" to establish course structure and facilitation to support self-directed learning rather than "content delivery," the result is courses that are "more clear, engaging and less sterile" (Herrington et al., 2005, p. 363). It is important that the full course content be posted at the start of the semester with a consistent layout, with assignments due on the same day each week (Groarke et al., 2020).

WHAT IS REQUIRED FOR ONLINE INSTRUCTION IN AN LA CONTEXT

As noted above, LA students identify prioritizing academics, academic support, campus events, and, most importantly, community engagement as important for successful online education.

Community Engagement

Gonyea et al. (2006) point out that the higher community engagement level of LA education is itself a mechanism through which increased learning and development outcomes occur. The risk of lack of connection and a resultant sense of isolation online (Palloff & Pratt, 2007) increases the importance of intentionally building community to motivate students and support learning (Chakraborty & Nafukho, 2014). For instructors, building community and connections with and among students may make the online teaching experience more rewarding (Glazier, 2016).

To foster this community engagement necessary for self-directed learning, instructors must provide structures for engagement between faculty and student, student and student, student and content (Shackleford & Maxwell, 2012), and student and self (McBrien et al., 2009). An additional consideration for the LA context is engagement with students of diverse backgrounds. Instructors can foster and assess the level of engagement in a course using observable evidence, including: (a) active interaction with both course content and individuals, (b) collaborative learning that is more student-to-student than student-to-instructor, (c) communication of agreement and questioning of course content and one another to develop socially constructed meaning, (d) resource sharing among students, and (e) a willingness of students to critically evaluate the work of others as well as expressions of support among students (Palloff & Pratt, 2007).

Academics, Academic Support, Campus Events

Alongside fostering community engagement, the strengths of academics, academic support and campus events and activities are key expectations of LA education that must be incorporated online. In terms of academics, in the LA online context an important consideration is what students need to know and be able to do in a world where "information" is at their fingertips. Instructors and academic disciplines should consider what to teach and help students learn, as well as how to assess that in the online context. For example, perhaps assessment with open books and demonstration of applied learning skills – hopefully developed in a collaborative and applied learning context of the course – is a better strategy online (Jankowski & Bheda, 2022). Similarly, to support student-driven learning, it is useful to incorporate formative assessment strategies and regular check-ins to help students understand learning expectations and their progress (Jankowski & Bheda, 2022).

During the pandemic learning experience, students identified the importance of academic support both inside and outside the classroom, including access to technology and tech support, as well as instructional resources (Jankowski & Bheda, 2022). Courses can integrate academic support by bringing campus staff into class through asynchronous video introductions or synchronous class meetings, or assignments that require engagement with such staff or offices (Gonyea et al., 2006).

Academic support is not only for students. The most common request of faculty during the pandemic experience was for professional development training to build capacity for effective, meaningful and robust technology use. Faculty may be experts in the learning outcomes and skillsets of their discipline, but need assistance identifying delivery and assessment opportunities to achieve those outcomes (Jankowski & Bheda, 2022).

HOW ECONOMICS INSTRUCTORS CAN DELIVER ONLINE COURSES IN THE LA CONTEXT

Let's first consider how to foster community as the foundation of LA education and how in particular economics instructors can support this. Shackelford & Maxwell (2012) have identified "high-yield interactions" that contribute the most to building a sense of community in online learning. The top five, in decreasing order of contribution to community building are (1) introductions, (2) collaborative group projects, (3) the sharing of personal experiences, (4) class-wide discussions, and (5) student exchange of learning resources.

Economics instructors in the LA context should prioritize these strategies. As I present each, I will identify economic-education-specific examples from the literature and my own online teaching experiences.

Introductions

Introductions early in the class establish social presence (Palloff & Pratt, 2007), a foundation for community building, and increased satisfaction with online learning (Gunawardena & Zittle, 1997). It is important that online introductions be followed with engagement from the instructor and fellow students. Students can feel unrecognized and disengage if they post an introduction with no response (Palloff & Pratt, 2007). Instructors can engage in additional relationship fostering activities, such as, remembering names, smiling, listening, demonstrating a personal interest in students – asking about weekend plans or college activities –, and being available (Kearney & Plax, 1992). To build classroom community online, faculty must make space for personal and even "mundane" interactions of everyday life (Palloff & Pratt, 2007).

In an upper-level economics class, I have students work in small discussion groups for about six weeks. Their first assignment is to record a three-minute introduction video including five elements: (1) their full name and what they prefer to be called, (2) their expected year of graduation, (3) their major or area of interest, (4) a brief explanation of why they chose to take this course, and finally (5) one question for their group members to answer. The question could be about the topic of the course, about their first week's readings, or something they would like to know about the group members that "might help to build a learning community and a sense of shared experience going forward." Three days after the introductory videos are due, students are required to submit a reply – by video or text – to at least two of the questions asked by their group members. Viewing the videos supports social presence by putting faces, voices, and personality to names, and builds student-to-student engagement. Each student receives at least two responses, providing critical acknowledgement. Reviewing the posts, I observed that students participated in resource exchanges without prompting, sharing supplemental content relevant to the first week's readings; and similar as well as diverse interests and experiences within the group. Another effective way to foster student-to-student interaction from week one is to hold a student mixer where students meet their peers and identify potential group members for collaborative learning activities (Wooten et al., 2020). Even providing some space for social interaction or ice-breaker activities among established class groups early in their work together can be an effective way to foster peer engagement (Gonyea et al., 2006).

Collaborative Group Projects

Collaborative group projects provide opportunities for student-to-student interaction and a foundation for the development of community (Baturay & Bay, 2010; Conrad, 2005; Gallagher-Lepak et al., 2009; Rovai, 2001). In the pandemic remote learning context, problem solving skills were among those learning outcomes most positively impacted. Some students may resist group work due to expectations of free riders or challenges with coordination and communication. However, instructor transparency and communication about the goals and rationale behind the project (Palloff & Pratt, 2007) as well as, in my experience, sharing the research evidence supporting how the work will contribute to learning objectives, can reduce resistance and improve outcomes.

It is important to scaffold group projects (Gillett-Swan, 2017), particularly in the economics context (Green et al., 2013). Synchronous meeting tools such as Zoom or Google Communities can facilitate planning, collaboration, and practice. In parallel, students can use asynchronous technologies – such as Learning Management System (LMS) shared documents or Google documents – to advance project development between synchronous meetings. Many of these tools also provide techniques for faculty to review student contributions and interactions in meetings (recorded Zoom sessions) or in shared documents (Google docs). This can increase opportunities for instructors to provide immediate feedback and identify and remediate technical issues that might otherwise linger and cause frustration or disengagement. (Gillet-Swan, 2017)

Experience with online collaborative tools is required professional development in an increasingly digital and remote-work friendly environment. This may be of particular value in the context of economic education, where many students go on to a business setting that expects proficiency in communication through various media (Gillett-Swan, 2017). Collaborative group projects allow students to develop problem-solving skills important in business environments, the pattern intelligence skills useful in an economic context, and the creativity to meet challenges that employers seek (Tapia & Ekigwe, 2021).

I have found group project contracts an effective foundation for scaffolding assignments. The act of determining expectations for the group, articulating how those will be assessed, and how the group will deal with group members not meeting expectations, etc., can itself build community as well as setting "ground-rules" and establishing the expectation that it is the group and not the instructor who should mediate teamwork challenges. The act of engaging with student peers to make meaning and sense of the course content, assignment objectives, and group working strategies are all part of the process (Gillett-Swan, 2017)

Gillet-Swan (2017) suggests providing resources to support self-directed learning including step-by-step instructions for scaffolded assignment elements, overview of various collaboration tools available to students, and tips for developing teamwork skills. Utilizing LMS tools to present collaboration resources can also establish the expectations that the group members should work to develop these skills and the instructor will serve as a facilitator and guide. Research shows that increased student-to-student interaction in groups and a class design that facilitates development of these interactions and the related skills enhances a sense of community in online learning (Dawson, 2006; Rovai, 2001; Yang & Liu, 2008)

To support development of collaborative skills, I require that group members assess one another's contribution to the project and to the effectiveness of the team as part of their grade. I use two check-ins where members reflect on and evaluate themselves and their peers on the group-project learning outcomes, such as responsibility to the team, effective communication, provision of feedback and critical thinking, and development as a team member. Group members complete an ungraded mid-project check-in, where I collate and share the anonymous feedback to each team member, providing a "360-review" to help each student understand how their work is perceived and provide an opportunity to grow. Group members then evaluate one another after the completion of the project, which contributes to their project grade. Anecdotally I have observed a decrease in poor evaluations and an increase in recognition and development of collaboration skills through this exercise.

Contributing Personal Experiences

Something long recognized in the economic education literature that is of critical importance to building community online is the act of students articulating how course content and concepts relate to their personal experiences. Not only does this enhance understanding and application of abstract economic concepts, it also develops social presence (Shackelford & Maxwell, 2012). Students who share their experiences in the class context report the highest measures of classroom community and that sharing improved both their learning and their ability to connect concepts to the world (Baab, 2004).

For the instructor, sharing personal experiences also increases "teaching presence," which is itself an important foundation for community and learning outcomes (Ke, 2010). Teaching presence is built on course instruction, facilitation of communication within the class, and the design and structure of the course itself (Garrison, 2007). Instructors can incorporate video or audio through overviews at the start of each week or module, weekly wrap-ups, or connections to current events, all of which can serve to reinforce learning objectives, while building teaching presence and fostering community (Boling et al., 2012; Glazier, 2016).

To build teaching presence and community, my LMS course sites are structured to provide clear, intentional, and consistent components week to week; transparent, research-based rationale for assignments and activities; as well as thorough assignment descriptions, rubrics, and due dates all set out for the entire course semester at the start of the term. I use weekly welcome videos in each week's module, as well as wrap-ups to build teaching presence and community. Students report this approach makes them quickly feel secure in the course structure and in my skills as an instructor.

The economic education literature provides numerous assignments and activities that give students opportunities to connect their personal experiences with course concepts, enhancing concept understanding for individuals and the group (Lee et al., 2008) and fostering community. For example, EconSelfies (Al-Bahrani et al., 2016) or student-created economic podcasts (Moryl, 2016) could be assigned across the semester and selected submissions shared at the start of class as a visual or audio welcome, or as a discussion prompt. This would foster not only the recognized benefit of connecting economics concepts to the "real world," but also to the shared experience of peers, while enhancing social presence (Groarke et al., 2020). Such assignments could also be scaffolded to include peer-review components, which expand that application of personal experience to their peers, while fostering social presence and awareness of the personalities and uniqueness of others in the course, to build community.

The exchange of personal experiences can be purposefully designed to support the LA value of engagement with students from different backgrounds (Gonyea et al., 2006). Al-Bahrani (2022) provides specific strategies economics instructors can use to increase diversity and a sense of inclusion, particularly in introductory level courses, which could further support the recommendations provided here for economics instruction in an LA context.

Entire Class Discussions

Entire class discussions are a common component of in-person instruction and research indicates that they are also important in the online learning context to foster community. Shackelford & Maxwell (2012) note that opportunities for the group to ask clarifying questions about assignments, or to expand their understanding of course concepts through follow-up questions, provide insights about other students in the course which foster social presence and build community. Rather than a one-way flow of information that might come from a lecture, the instructor-mediated interaction with peers through class-wide discussion helps students both to make sense of complex content (Wallace, 2003) and to experience that sense-making in a shared community environment.

For effective learning and community building through discussions in an online context, instructors must use their expertise to identify the technology tools and activities that will best foster engagement (Vrasidas, 2000). Class-wide discussions can be asynchronous discussion boards, with thoughtful moderation and engagement, or synchronous class-wide discussions in video class meetings. In my experience, techniques such as utilizing breakout rooms in Zoom to discuss content questions and problems in smaller groups, then share back is an effective activity to achieve these goals and one that students find beneficial. Anecdotally students report feeling more comfortable exploring new ideas in smaller groups, particularly if those groups are consistent across multiple weeks of the semester, and then sharing with the broader group. This process helps individuals build connection with their peers through collaborative work in small groups, while providing opportunities to engage with the entire class. I make a point to call each student by name when asking them to share their findings, and to make connections by name among observations, fostering that sense of shared meaning making and a learning community. Sessions can be constructed to incorporate the exchange of personal experiences and connections to concepts, which would combine three of those highest-yield activities for building community (exchanging personal experiences, collaborative learning, and then full-class discussions).

Exchanging Resources

The last of the highest-yield activities for fostering community in an online course is when students exchange resources, such as techniques they use for success in a course, or documents and articles they find useful or interesting. These activities reinforce self-directed learning, while providing insights into what others are doing to engage with the course, thus boosting social presence. This exchange of ideas also develops the idea of peers in the course as a resource for learning strategies, enhancing the mutuality and reciprocity of the learning community (Haythornthwaite et al., 2006; Stepich & Ertmer, 2003).

Instructors can build opportunities for such exchanges into the course architecture through small group discussions, asynchronous discussion boards specific to exchanging tips and resources, or through class-related social media. In an introductory economics course, I use an anonymous survey at the second and fifth weeks, where students share what has been working for them in the course, what they find challenging, and what strategies they plan to try in the coming week. Each time I review and summarize the most common and most useful tips to share as highlights in an LMS announcement. I often find students referencing ideas they took from the first survey as strategies they've since tried in the second one. I also make a point to suggest strategies from the responses in synchronous class meetings, or in weekly wrap-up videos to enhance the connection from the asynchronous online survey responses to other class interactions. Students report finding comfort and support in hearing common struggles, as well as inspiration and ideas from the experiences of their peers. In a senior seminar economics course, I have students engage in periodic asynchronous metacognition discussions where they similarly share the challenges they've been facing and the strategies they've used, or areas where they would like input and ideas. Students are required to respond to at least one peer, but often share messages of support and ideas with multiple peers. I also make a point to recognize and acknowledge common challenges and use suggestions from peers to support and build connections among the group.

Using Social Media to Connect

Beyond implementing these five high-yield actions, it is important for instructors to select the right communication platform (Chakraborty & Nafukho, 2014). Social media may be particularly well suited as an engagement platform for online education (Barczyk and Duncan, 2013; Stern & Willits, 2011), while also supporting academic outcomes (Ellison et al., 2011; Junco, 2013). Some social media platforms, such as Pronto, can be integrated into an LMS, or institutions may construct a "social network" experience within the LMS itself (Barbour & Plough, 2009). The benefit of "social" networking within the LMS is that it retains the "walled garden" experience and privacy of a traditional LMS while providing both academic and social benefits. Alternatively, institutions might consider social media platforms external to the LMS, which may reduce faculty-student power imbalances and bring discipline content beyond the "ivory tower" (Stern & Willits, 2011). Introduction to collaboration tools, such as Slack, could provide students with skillsets to bring to the professional realm. Al-Bahrani & Patel (2015) explore the use of popular platforms X (formerly Twitter), Instagram and Facebook in the economics curriculum.

I have experience using WhatsApp for secure messaging while teaching in Rwanda. Students created a class chat and used it to ask for clarifying instructions, or to exchange resources. I could also share documents directly with students or make announcements. I used Instagram to foster broader connection with students and faculty across our economics program during the pandemic (Al-Bahrani & Moryl, 2020). I utilized the platform in a new way to support the "whole" student, which is important in an LA context. While continuing to use @ProfMoryl to share course-specific content, I also posted program and campus-wide virtual activities; highlighted support opportunities from campus resources; posted internship and job opportunities; highlighted student success stories; and shared virtual lectures and events both within economics and across disciplines, supporting the interdisciplinary LA context. I was even able to engage students and enhance a sense of social presence beyond the classroom unit by utilizing polls, quizzes and open-ended questions within the Instagram platform.

Other Instructor Strategies that Are Important for Effective Online Learning

While techniques that create and support a constructivist online learning environment focus on those that foster communication and engagement foremost, approaches that support the student-driven learning environment, to explore and create shared meaning, are also important. These include clear and transparent rules and expectations, and feedback that fosters student-driven learning and the role of faculty as facilitator (Bryant & Bates, 2015; Palloff & Pratt, 2007).

Communicating the policies and learning objectives of a course provides a foundation for development of a learning community (Palloff & Pratt, 2007). In the case of economics, what might otherwise be a dry review of course rules and expectations can connect economics to the "real world" from day one (Burdina & Sasser, 2018). In introductory courses, I introduce concepts such as incentives, opportunity cost, externalities, human capital and specialization on the first day as I explain course policies in the context of "economics is everywhere."

Instructors can model collaboration by opening a discussion, either synchronous or asynchronous, of the learning objectives of the course and what students require from one another and from their instructor to support moving toward those goals. Depending on the course level, I may have students discuss this in small groups and report back to the class or hold an entire-class discussion. We use these discussions to set the rules and expectations for student and faculty engagement in the course in the first week of class.

Instructors can also explain how assignments support the course learning goals, providing the transparency required for online learning (Carrasco, 2022) and alleviating resistance to and frustration with challenging assignments (Palloff & Pratt, 2007). On the homepage for each course, I post a chart aligning course assignments to learning goals. I also integrate the learning goals into course assignment rubrics.

Research indicates that consistent, timely feedback to students is among the most effective strategies for promoting learning in the online context (Boling et al., 2012; Bryant & Bates, 2015; Chakraborty & Nafukho, 2014), as well as building rapport (Glazier, 2016). Individual feedback can be assignment specific, or student specific to course performance. Detailed, personalized feedback can help students face challenges in the online course setting (Glazier, 2016), and produce higher student satisfaction (Konstantinou & Epps, 2017).

Taking particular care to use students' names and credit their ideas in discussion board feedback can foster social presence and connection. Iraj et al. (2020) explore using technology-mediated customized messages to streamline provision of individualized feedback in larger classes and in the face of increasing time demands on faculty. They find that personalized engagement with students early in the semester is strongly associated with course completion.

The online teaching format also lends itself to alternative ways of delivering feedback, including recorded audio or video feedback. To enhance student-faculty connection in a senior seminar, I periodically provide an audio recording overview of my written comments on individual student thesis drafts (Lunt & Curran, 2010). Anecdotally students commented positively on this in class and wrote more responses to my feedback in the LMS.

Finally, in the context of feedback, instructors should provide opportunities for students to give as well as to receive feedback. Just as discussions about rules and expectations and explanation of policy and assignment rationales help to foster community connection, so can faculty request for feedback and implementation of responses do the same. It is particularly useful for students to see their feedback informing real-time course delivery and instructional practice both to reinforce the idea of a collaborative learning environment, and also to demonstrate the way that end of semester evaluations are utilized (and valued) by instructors and programs.

In addition to summarizing and sharing the most common responses to the anonymous feedback surveys mentioned above, I also adjust the course delivery where appropriate. Further, I explain my rationale when I am not going to make an adjustment, such as when there are differing views on the same assignment. This openness enhances student-faculty communication, acknowledges student experiences, and provides further transparency and rationale to course structure. Modeling this performance feedback process for students can also introduce the expectations and experience of the workplace (Glazier, 2016) and model the sort of constructive feedback they might give their peers in collaborative projects in the academic (discussed above) or professional setting.

CONCLUSION

The economic education literature has produced research and numerous innovations that can inform the design of online economics courses for the liberal arts context. Beginning with the strategies of effective pedagogy in any context, such as establishing rules and expectations and providing feedback, economics instructors can incorporate high-yield interactions and online tools to build community in a course, building a foundation to serve the values and expectations of the LA. This chapter provides specific examples drawn from personal experience and the economic education literature to implement each in a variety of course levels and economic topics. By utilizing these strategies, economics instructors can lead the way to effective online instruction in the LA context.

NOTE

1. For a definition and learning goals of liberal arts see American Association of Colleges and Universities (2024).

REFERENCES

Al-Bahrani, A. (2022). Classroom management and student interaction interventions: Fostering diversity, inclusion, and belonging in the undergraduate economics classroom. *The Journal of Economic Education*, 1–12.

Al-Bahrani, A., Holder, K., Moryl, R. L., Murphy, P. R., & Patel, D. (2016). Putting yourself in the picture with an 'ECONSelfie': Using student-generated photos to enhance introductory economics courses. *International Review of Economics Education*, *22*, 16–22.

Al-Bahrani, A. & Moryl, R. (2020). Using Social Media to retain and connect with students in the shift to online education. *Faculty Focus*. Available from: https://www.facultyfocus.com/articles/online-education/online-student-engagement/using-social-media-to-retain-and-connect-with-students-in-the-shift-to-online-education/

Al-Bahrani, A., & Patel, D. (2015). Incorporating Twitter, Instagram, and Facebook in economics classrooms. *The Journal of Economic Education*, *46*(1), 56–67.

American Association of Colleges and Universities. (2024). https://www.aacu.org/

Appana, S. (2008). A review of benefits and limitations of online learning in the context of the student, the instructor and the tenured faculty. *International Journal on E-learning*, *7*(1), 5–22.

Baab, L. (2004). Effect of selected factors on students' sense of classroom community in distance learning courses. Doctoral dissertation. Pepperdine University.

Balboni, G., Perrucci, V., Cacciamani, S., & Zumbo, B.D. (2018). Development of a scale of sense of community in university online courses. *Distance Education*, *39*(3), 317–333.

Barbour, M., & Plough, C. (2009). Helping to make online learning less isolating. *TechTrends*, *53*(4), 57.

Barczyk, C. C., & Duncan, D. G. (2013). Facebook in higher education courses: An analysis of students' attitudes, community of practice, and classroom community. *International Business and Management*, *6*(1), 1–11.

Baturay, M. H., & Bay, O. F. (2010). The effects of problem-based learning on the classroom community perceptions and achievement of web-based education students. *Computers & Education*, 55(1), 43–52.

Beaudoin, M. (2001). Learning or lurking? Tracking the 'invisible' online student. Orlando, FL. Paper delivered at the 7th Sloan. In *International Conference on Asynchronous Learning Networks*.

Berry, S. (2019). Faculty perspectives on online learning: The instructor's role in creating community. *Online Learning, 23*(4), 181–191.

Birch, D., & Burnett, B. (2009). Bringing academics on board: Encouraging institution-wide diffusion of e-learning environments. *Australasian Journal of Educational Technology, 25*(1).

Blackley, S., & Sheffield, R. (2015). Digital andragogy: A richer blend of initial teacher education in the 21st century. *Issues in Educational Research, 25*(4), 397–414.

Boling, E. C., Hough, M., Krinsky, H., Saleem, H., & Stevens, M. (2012). Cutting the distance in distance education: Perspectives on what promotes positive, online learning experiences. *The Internet and Higher Education, 15*(2), 118–126.

Bolliger, D. U., Shepherd, C. E. & Bryant, H. V. (2019). Faculty members' perceptions of online program community and their efforts to sustain it. *British Journal of Educational Technology, 50*(6), 3283–3299.

Borup, J., & Evmenova, A. S. (2019). The effectiveness of professional development in overcoming obstacles to effective online instruction in a college of education. *Online Learning, 23*(2), 1–20.

Boyles, P. C. (2011). Maximising learning using online student assessment. *Online Journal of Distance Learning Administration, 14*(3).

Brooks, J. G., & Brooks, M. G. (2001). *In search of understanding the case for constructivist classrooms.* Merrill/Prentice Hall.

Bryant, J., & Bates, A. J. (2015). Creating a constructivist online instructional environment. *TechTrends, 59*(2), 17–22.

Burdina, M., & Sasser, S. L. (2018). Syllabus and economics: Reasoning with Generation "Why". *The Journal of Economic Education, 49*(1), 38–45.

Cameron, B. A., Morgan, K., Williams, K. C., & Kostelecky, K. L. (2009). Group projects: Student perceptions of the relationship between social tasks and a sense of community in online group work. *American Journal of Distance Education, 23*(1), 20–33.

Carrasco, M. (2022). Assessing pandemic learning. *Inside Higher Ed.* Available from: https://www.insidehighered.com/news/2022/03/23/survey-views-pandemic-learning-overwhelmingly-negative

Chakraborty, M., & Nafukho, F. M. (2014). Strengthening student engagement: what do students want in online courses? *European Journal of Training and Development, 38*(9), 782–802.

Conrad, D. (2005). Building and maintaining community in cohort-based online learning. *Journal of Distance Education, 20*(1), 1–20.

Dawson, S. (2006). A study of the relationship between student communication interaction and sense of community. *Internet and Higher Education, 9*, 153–162.

Ellison, N. B., Steinfield, C., & Lampe, C. (2011). Connection strategies: Social capital implications of Facebook-enabled communication practices. *New Media & Society, 13*(6), 873–892.

Gallagher-Lepak, S., Reilly, J., & Killion, C. (2009). Nursing student perceptions of community in online learning. *Contemporary Nurse: A Journal for the Australian Nursing Profession, 32*, 133–146.

Garrison, D. R. (2007). Online community of inquiry review: Social, cognitive, and teaching presence issues. *Journal of Asynchronous Learning Networks, 11*(1), 61–72.

Geng, H., & McGinley, M. (2021). Comparing Student Performance and Satisfaction Between Face-to-Face and Online Education of a Science Course in a Liberal Arts University. *Journal of College Science Teaching, 51*(2).

Gillett-Swan, J. (2017). The challenges of online learning: Supporting and engaging the isolated learner. *Journal of Learning Design, 10*(1), 20–30.

Glazier, R. A. (2016). Building rapport to improve retention and success in online classes. *Journal of Political Science Education, 12(4), 437–456.*

Gonyea, R., Kuh, G., Kinzie, J., Cruce, T., & Nelson-Laird, T. (2006). Expectations and engagement: How liberal arts college students compare with counterparts elsewhere. *National Survey of Student Engagement Center for Postsecondary Research.*

Green, G. P., Bean, J. C., & Peterson, D. J. 2013. Deep learning in intermediate micro-economics: Using scaffolding assignments to teach theory and promote transfer. *Journal of Economic Education, 44*(2), 142–57.

Groarke, J. M., Berry, E., Graham-Wisener, L., McKenna-Plumley, P. E., McGlinchey, E., & Armour, C. (2020). Loneliness in the UK during the COVID-19 pandemic: Cross-sectional results from the COVID-19 Psychological Wellbeing Study. *PloS one, 15*(9).

Gunawardena, C. N., & Zittle, F. J. (1997). Social presence as a predictor of satisfaction within a computer-mediated conferencing environment. *The American Journal of Distance Education, 11*(3), 8–26.

Haythornthwaite, C., Kazmer, M. M., Robins, J., & Shoemaker, S. (2006). Community development among distance learners: Temporal and technological dimensions. *Journal of Computer-Mediated Communication, 6*(1).

Herrington, J., Reeves, T. C., & Oliver, R. (2005). Design research: A socially respon-sible approach to instructional technology research in higher education. *Journal of Computing in Higher Education, 16*(2), 96–115.

Hollis, E. T. (2016). Traditional liberal arts colleges' consideration and adoption of online education: A presidential perspective. *Theses and Dissertations–Education Sciences. 21.* University of Kentucky.

Iraj, H., Fudge, A., Faulkner, M., Pardo, A., & Kovanović, V. (2020, March). Understanding students' engagement with personalised feedback messages. In *Proceedings of the Tenth International Conference on Learning Analytics & Knowledge* (pp. 438–447).

Jankowski, N. A. & Bheda, D. (2022) *Pandemic insights to shape a better future: Assessment for teaching, learning, equity and student success.* Examsoft.

Junco, R. (2013). Inequalities in Facebook use. *Computers in Human Behavior, 29*(6), 2328–2336.

Ke, F. (2010). Examining online teaching, cognitive, and social presence for adult students. *Computers & Education, 55,* 808–820.

Kearney, P. & Plax, T. G. (1992). Student resistance to control. In V. P. Richmond & J. C. McCroskey (eds.), *Power in the classroom: Communication, control, and concern* (pp. 85–100). Routledge.

Konrady, D. M. (2015). *Choosing to Participate in E-Learning Education: A Study of Undergraduate Students' Diverse Perceptions, Attitudes, and Self-Identified Barriers To E-Learning.* Drexel University.

Konstantinou, G., & Epps, J. (2017). Facilitating online casual interactions and creat-ing a community of learning in a first-year electrical engineering course. In *2017 IEEE 6th International Conference on Teaching, Assessment, and Learning for Engineering (TALE)* (pp. 128–133). Institute of Electrical and Electronics Engineers.

Lee, M. J. W., McLoughlin, C., & Chan, A. (2008). Talk the talk: Learner-generated podcasts as catalysts for knowledge creation. *British Journal of Educational Technology, 39*(3), 501–21.

Lunt, T., & Curran, J. (2010). 'Are you listening please?'The advantages of electronic audio feedback compared to written feedback. *Assessment & evaluation in higher education, 35*(7), 759–769.

McBrien, J. L., Jones, P., & Cheng, R. (2009). Virtual spaces: Employing a synchronous online classroom to facilitate student engagement in online learning. *International Review of Research in Open and Online Learning, 10*(3), 1–17.

McClendon, C., Neugebauer, R. M., & King, A. (2017). Grit, growth mindset, and deliberate practice in online learning. *Journal of Instructional Research, 8*, 8–17.

Moryl, R. L. (2016). Pod learning: Student groups create podcasts to achieve economics learning goals. *The Journal of Economic Education, 47*(1), 64–70.

Palloff, R. M., & Pratt, K. (2007). *Building online learning communities: Effective strategies for the virtual classroom* (2nd ed.). Jossey-Bass.

Pippins, T., Belfield, C. R., & Bailey, T. (2019). *Humanities and Liberal Arts Education across America's Colleges: How Much Is There?* Community College Research Center, Teachers College, Columbia University.

Rovai, A. (2001). Building classroom community at a distance: A case study. *Educational Technology Research and Development, 49*(4), 33–48.

Shackelford, J. L., & Maxwell, M. (2012). Sense of community in graduate online education: Contribution of learner to learner interaction. *International Review of Research in Open and Distributed Learning, 13*(4), 228–249.

Short, J., Williams, E., & Christie, B. (1976). *The social psychology of telecommunications.* Wiley.

Stepich, D. A., & Ertmer, P. A. (2003). Building community as a critical element of online course design. *Educational Technology, 43*(5), 33–43.

Stern, D. M., & Willits, M. D. (2011). Social media killed the LMS: Re-imagining the traditional learning management system in the age of blogs and online social networks. In C. Wankel (ed.), *Educating educators with social media* (Vol. 1, pp. 347–373). Emerald Group Publishing Limited.

Tapia, R., Jr., & Ekigwe, E. (2021). First generation business students attitudes towards learning in small liberal arts colleges. *College Student Journal, 55*(1), 80+.

Vrasidas, C. (2000). Constructivism versus objectivism: Implications for interaction, course design, and evaluation in distance education. *International Journal of Educational Telecommunications, 6*, 339–362.

Wallace, R. M. (2003). Online learning in higher education: A review of research on interactions among teachers and students. *Education, Communication and Information, 3*, 241.

Wooten, J., Geerling, W., & Thomas, N. (2020). Facilitating student connections and study partners during periods of remote and online learning. *Journal of Economics Teaching, 5*(2), 1–14.

Yang, H. H., & Liu, Y. (2008). Building a sense of community for text-based computer mediated communication courses. *Journal of Educational Technology Systems, 36*, 393–413.

8. Fostering inclusive excellence: designing effective assessments for online education

Stefania Paredes Fuentes

INTRODUCTION: THE EVOLVING LANDSCAPE OF ASSESSMENTS IN HIGHER EDUCATION

As lecturers, we all have encountered the question "Is this on the exam?" at least once. While this refrain might occasionally trigger some frustration, it underscores the significant role assessments play for students. Assessments can indeed influence student behaviour more than teaching, as students *study* to do well on the assessment.

Despite their undeniable importance, assessments in higher education have remained remarkably unchanged for decades. The fundamentals of assessment design seem to adhere to consolidated academic conventions (Bearman, Boud and Ajjawi, 2020) often without due consideration of their suitability for educational purposes. A case in point is the persistence in academia of high-stake assessments for evaluating student performance and progress. This, despite the association of these assessments with adverse outcomes such as increased mental health issues (Hamilton et al., 2021), reduced student learning and engagement (Kearney, 2013) and, regrettably, a failure to fulfill learning outcomes. Furthermore, they contribute to exacerbating *awarding* gaps[1] for disadvantaged students (Madaus and Clarke, 2001; Jones, 2007; Heissel, et al., 2021).

Before the pandemic, online education had begun recognising the need to adapt assessment methods to accommodate students' learning needs (Gaytan and McEwen, 2007). However, these changes were largely confined to specific courses. The abrupt shift to online or hybrid learning during the COVID-19 pandemic in 2020 compelled many academics to reimagine assessments, prompting considerations of inclusivity and effectiveness in promoting learning outcomes (Burnett and Paredes-Fuentes, 2020).

In the post-pandemic landscape, many higher education institutions are keen to retain some of the positive aspects of diverse assessment methods adopted during the pandemic. Assessment design is now taking centre stage in teaching and learning, rather than an afterthought for lecturers (Slade et al., 2021). The advent of new technological tools has ushered in an era of flexibility and creativity in assessment design aiming to increase student engagement (Slack and Priestley, 2023). This shift has also prompted a reconsideration of the validity and effectiveness of traditional high-stakes assessments (Mottiar et al., 2022). There are also other considerations to make. The widespread adoption of Artificial Intelligence tools for content generation, coupled with the emergence of large language models like ChatGPT, has raised concerns about academic misconduct. Section 3 explores these challenges and offers recommendations to accommodate these technologies in the assessment design.

This chapter presents a comprehensive framework for assessment design that draws from lessons learnt in both pre- and post-pandemic online teaching. It aims to positively impact student engagement, create inclusive teaching environments, and facilitate deep learning experiences for *all* students while addressing recent challenges.

At the heart of this framework are three fundamental elements: *subject, students, and purpose.* Only through a holistic consideration of all relevant aspects can assessments be both effective and inclusive. In fact, we argue that effective assessments are inclusive. *Effective assessments* are designed to gauge students' comprehension, skills, or proficiencies in a specific subject or field of study. *Inclusive assessments* are intentionally crafted to be accessible, equitable, and fair to all students, irrespective of their personal attributes.

The consideration of these three aspects allows for the adaptability of the framework to any teaching delivery, including online teaching. This process involves questioning the *who, what, why, when,* and *how* of assessment design using an inquisitive problem-solving method that we will call "Five Ws + One H."

A FRAMEWORK FOR INCLUSIVE ASSESSMENT DESIGN

Reshaping assessments is a complex and time-consuming process due to the array of assessment options, timing considerations, and implementation methods. This framework is designed to address these challenges by encouraging critical reflection.

While not the first of its kind in higher education assessment design,[2] this framework stands out for its accessibility and adaptability to diverse teaching settings, including online education. It places a strong emphasis on inclusivity and a student-centred approach. By engaging with this framework, educators can create assessments that boost student engagement and enable learners from diverse backgrounds to demonstrate their understanding of learning outcomes without encountering assessment hurdles.

The framework considers three fundamental aspects of assessment design: subject, students, and purpose (see Figure 8.1). Many academics tend to, primarily or solely, focus on the *subject*. It is indeed important that assessments align with the intended learning outcomes for the module; however, it is equally crucial to acknowledge that students' backgrounds and prior experiences play a significant role in shaping their interest, engagement with the subject, and their overall approach to assessments.

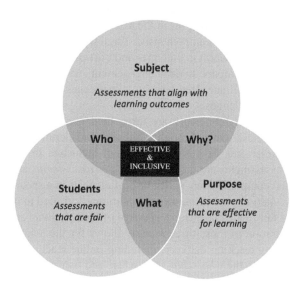

Figure 8.1   Key aspects of assessment design

Assessments serve a purpose that goes beyond merely evaluating learning; they can actively contribute to facilitating it by fostering positive engagement and nurturing students' passion for the subject matter. Negative feelings towards assessments can affect performance and engagement (Goetz et al., 2023). Consequently, assessments should encompass considerations related to who is being assessed, why we are conducting the assessment, and how the assessment impacts student learning. The effectiveness of assessments hinges on their ability to account for the synergies and interrelations among these three critical aspects.

Five W's + One H

To ensure that *subject, students,* and *purpose* are all comprehensively considered during the assessment design process, we can employ an inquisitive approach inspired by problem-solving methods. The "Five Ws + One H" approach involves reflecting on six primary macro-questions: *who, which, what, why, when,* and *how.* These questions help gain a deeper understanding of the intricate relationships among these three critical aspects. Table 8.1 offers some basic considerations and suggestions to initiate your engagement with this method.

This approach remains highly relevant for online teaching. Due to its inherent student-centred nature and its broader consideration of the role of assessment in engaging students, it can be instrumental in addressing some of the challenges commonly associated with online teaching, such as low student engagement, the need for support irrespective of students' personal situations, and the issue of high dropout rates (Bettinger et al., 2017).

Table 8.1   *Five W's + one H*

Questions	Considerations	Starting Points	Relevant Aspects
Who is being assessed?	Do I understand my students' background and needs? What challenges might students face in this module? Are external factors affecting student engagement?	Use *Universal Design for Assessments* principles. Identify student demographics. Beginning of the year/term survey exploring potential challenges.	Student background Subject
Which assumptions am I making about students?	Are there non-written pre-requisites expected for this module? Are certain skills assumed but not taught in the module? Are assessment criteria aligned with module content?	Determine expected knowledge. Examine skills and resources needed to complete each assessment. Create marking criteria that focus on the module's learning outcomes.	Student background Assessment purpose

Questions	Considerations	Starting Points	Relevant Aspects
Why are we assessing?	Is the assessment aiming to increase engagement? Is the assessment aimed to measure a specific learning outcome? Can the assessment scaffold learning effectively?	Write down *all* the potential aims for each assessment. Write down marking criteria for each assessment. Write down key feedback sentences for scaffolding.	Assessment purpose Subject
When does the assessment take place?	Is this assessment taking place during term time? Are other concurrent assessments (e.g., from other subjects) taking place at the same time? Is the assessment scheduled around important cultural or religious events?	Consider a timetable of assessments at programme level. Consider providing flexibility on assessment deadlines. Use a calendar of cultural events.	Assessment purpose Student background
What are we assessing?	Does the assessment align with specific learning outcomes? Is the same learning outcome assessed in other assessments? Are there aspects of the module that are not assessed at all?	Revise learning outcomes regularly. Communicate how assessments relate to learning objectives. Communicate the marking criteria for each assessment.	Subject Assessment purpose
How does the assessment contribute to learning?	What is the impact on learning by engaging with this assessment? How do students demonstrate their learning through the assessment? Are there alternative ways to demonstrate their learning?	Analyse student performance by assessment. Analyse whether different groups of students perform differently in each assessment. Consider a variety of assessment methods.	Subject Student background

Who Are We Assessing?

Research has identified strong correlations between factors such as gender, ethnicity, and socio-economic status, and student performance across different assessment formats (Linn, 2000; Townsend, 2002; Iriberri and Rey-Biel,

2021). Consequently, effective assessments cannot overlook the identity of our students.

Developing strategies to better understand the student population can aid in planning teaching and assessment designs that consider the specificities of our students. Educators can derive valuable insights from student demographic information (e.g., gender ratios, proportions of underrepresented groups, nationalities, and disclosed disabilities). Alternatively, or in addition, conducting an anonymous survey can provide information about students' backgrounds and experiences.

Unfortunately, it may not always be feasible to tailor teaching materials and assessments for every demographic shift. We can mitigate these challenges through the application of universal design principles for assessments. These principles involve considering the needs of all learners, including those with disabilities. At the core of these principles are *accessibility* and *flexibility* aiming to decrease the need for individual accommodations by minimising the impact of irrelevant aspects in engaging with the assessments.

Accessibility ensures that all students can understand the assessment instructions. For instance, avoiding unnecessary jargon or verbosity not relevant to the subject and learning objectives and maintaining consistent formatting throughout the assessment (e.g., same font and spacing) benefits all learners, especially those with reading difficulties or language barriers. Organising content logically, using headings and breaking up content aids students with cognitive or attention-related disabilities. *Flexibility* means offering alternatives. Offering assessments in various formats (e.g. text and audio) and providing descriptive alt-text for images can assist students who rely on screen readers to access content. Student disability services should be engaged in ensuring these provisions are available to all students.

The goal is not to make the assessment *easier* but to ensure that assessment results are not influenced by factors such as disability, economic situation, race, or any student's personal characteristic. These measures should align within a broader framework of universal design for teaching (to learn more see Dinmore, 2014; Guptill, 2015; Keeler and Horney, 2007; Rao et al., 2015).

Which Assumptions Are Made About Students?

Educators must engage in introspective inquiry to examine how their own backgrounds and experiences influence their teaching approaches. When designing assessments, it is essential to consider the assumed knowledge of students. Educators often draw on personal experiences to shape their teaching and assessment strategies: "this method worked well for me." However, we often lack information about those for whom these methods were not effective and who might have been systematically excluded by certain practices.

During the assessment design process, it is important to consider the skills not explicitly taught within the module but required for assessment success. Do you require students to make a video? Do you explain how to make a video? Is a key outcome of the assessment to show good communication with a specific audience? Do you explain how to address the specific audience?

Providing opportunities for scaffolding these skills may become crucial. Additionally, offering alternative assessment methods allows students to focus on demonstrating the module-required skills.

Furthermore, educators must remain aware of implicit biases and their impact on behaviours. Implicit biases are unconscious stereotypes that affect our understanding, actions, and decisions. They can inadvertently lead to decisions incongruent with explicit intentions, potentially creating barriers to opportunity and achievement for some students. This point is particularly relevant when marking assessments, as biases may affect how students' work is evaluated, with weight given to aspects unrelated to learning outcomes (e.g., ways of expressing ideas, format choice).

To mitigate these biases, educators can engage in a process of self-assessment. Tools like *Project Implicit* offer a series of tests on implicit associations that can assist in identifying and addressing implicit biases in decision-making processes.[3] In the case of assessments, writing clear marking criteria and feedback notes before starting the marking process can help maintain focus on the relevant aspects of the submitted work.

Why Are We Assessing?

Assessments serve multiple roles in education. Historically, assessments in higher education have primarily focused on measuring learning, enabling a "reliable" comparison of students within and across cohorts and institutions. However, contemporary educational research emphasises the importance of striking a balance between quantitative metrics and assessments that actively contribute to the learning process.

Assessments can serve multiple purposes, all of which should be considered in the assessment design. Ideally, we should aim for a variety of assessment purposes, including those that foster engagement, scaffold knowledge, and help students to acquire skills needed for future assessments, in addition to assessments that measure learning. Conversely, if we find that multiple assessments assess the same skills and learning outcomes, it may be necessary to re-evaluate the actual value of these assessments.

A deep understanding of the purposes of each assessment can guide the design of marking criteria. Furthermore, it facilitates the provision of feedback that is both constructive and relevant to students, enhancing their engagement with the subject. Clearly communicating these aspects—assessment purpose, marking criteria, and the feedback process—to students is instrumental. This not only helps them understand the assessment but also encourages active engagement with the provided feedback.

When Are Assessments Taking Place?

The timing of the assessment plays a pivotal role in their effectiveness, and this consideration is closely tied to the purpose of the assessment itself. If the objective of the assessment is to actively engage students with the subject matter or provide opportunities for scaffolding learning, these cannot be clustered at the end of the course.

In a broader context, various factors influence the timing of assessments, some of which relate to the diverse personal experiences of students. Despite universities taking great pride in the diversity of cultures and backgrounds among their student bodies, there is still work to be done in enhancing awareness and respect for this cultural diversity. A growing body of research highlights the connection between student performance and cultural festivities, emphasising the need for inclusive assessment designs that take these considerations into account (see, for instance, Oosterbeek and van der Klaauw, 2013; Hornung et al., 2023). This point also underscores the importance of understanding our students and their backgrounds.

Timing considerations extend beyond cultural aspects. In online education, for example, there is often a more mature student demographic. These students may juggle an array of responsibilities alongside their academic commitments, including parenting or caregiving duties. These responsibilities inevitably impact student engagement and assessment performance (Hovdhaugen et al., 2013).

In the context of a highly diverse student body, accommodating all these different calendars can be challenging. However, introducing flexibility in assessment deadlines may help. For instance, varying deadlines for different types of assessment can be established, enabling students to choose deadlines that align with their unique schedules. This approach preserves the essential element of deadlines while providing students with the autonomy to organise their assessment timelines according to their specific needs.

It is worth noting that the autonomy to set assessment deadlines may not always rest with individual educators. In such cases, it is important for educators to be aware of these limitations and avoid imposing unrealistic expectations on students. While educators might not have direct control over assessment deadlines, they should advocate for reasonable timelines that promote effective learning and accommodate students' diverse needs.

What Are We Assessing?

It may be surprising to some that this question does not come first. While it is undeniable that the choice of assessment must align with the subject being taught and its corresponding learning objectives, it is equally easy to become overly fixated on the "what" (the subject) and inadvertently neglect the other equally critical aspects: the "who" (students) and "why" (purpose).

Assessments must be intrinsically linked to the module's learning outcomes, and periodic updates to learning outcomes should reflect syllabus changes. Furthermore, emphasising the transferable skills that students are expected to acquire through engagement with assessments can significantly contribute to maintaining focus on what we are assessing and reflecting on how our teaching contributes to the development of these skills.

How Does the Assessment Contribute to Student Learning?

When exploring the various "levels" of student learning, assessment literature commonly relies on *learning taxonomies* (Moseley et al., 2005). One of the most widely used is Bloom's taxonomy, which categorises learning into six stages: remembering, understanding, applying, analysing, evaluating, and creating (Krathwohl, 2002).

We can leverage these stages to think about how a specific assessment contributes to student learning. What are our desired learning outcomes for students? A valuable perspective highlights that *understanding* a concept requires *remembering* it, while *application* relies on prior *understanding*. These stages form the foundation of learning. However, to achieve deeper learning, characterised by higher-order thinking, we need to go beyond these foundational stages. *Evaluating* a process demands thorough analysis, and formulating accurate conclusions requires a comprehensive *evaluation* (Shabatura, 2018). Early-stage assessments can aid students in grasping concepts and applying them to basic scenarios, serving as the foundational building blocks for deeper comprehension and higher-order thinking, enabling analysis, evaluation, and ultimately, creation.

For each assessment, we want to consider its impact on learning, which stage we aim to achieve, how students can demonstrate their learning, and whether there are more ways to achieve this. Post-assessment, it may be useful to analyse student performance and check whether it is consistent across different groups and how the variety of assessments offered may impact any observed differences.

Ideas for Application and Basic Considerations

Table 8.2 demonstrates how to apply the framework, addressing the "Ws + H" questions and providing marking criteria and feedback examples.

Table 8.2   *Examples of how to use the framework for a variety of assessments*

Assessment	Five Ws + One H considerations	Marking Criteria (marks)	Feedback notes/Other Considerations
Sociology *Final year project*: Write a policy report on how to tackle the rise in mental health disorders among university students. This assessment: *"Write 750 words on how different schools of thought in psychology may explain the rise of mental health issues among students."*	*Who? Which assumptions?* Students' prior knowledge of policy reports Students' personal situations Understanding of "policy reports" *Why?* Prepare for the final year project's literature review Enhance referencing skills Early engagement with the main assessment *When?* Early in the term to allow time for feedback *What?* Mastery of diverse schools of thought Effective communication for a wider audience (transferable skills) *How?* Develop evaluation skills Compare different perspectives Apply these skills to a specific topic	Contrasting schools of thought are considered (2/3) Citations and references need to follow appropriate style (1/3)	Ensure the discussion covers multiple schools of thought and highlights contrasting aspects among them. Follow the Harvard referencing style. Provide alternative topic choices for students. Large Language Models (LLMs) can assist students in writing. Use LLM-generated responses as discussion points in class for students to critically engage with and improve in their submissions.

Assessment	Five Ws + One H considerations	Marking Criteria (marks)	Feedback notes/Other Considerations
Monetary Economics This assessment: *"Create a 3-min video for a general audience explaining how an increase in interest rates affects mortgage rates."*	*Who? Which assumptions?* Video creation skills Creative content skills Proficiency in English for diverse audiences *Why?* Enhance communication skills of subject-related knowledge *When?* During term-time if university equipment is needed *What?* Understanding the impact of interest rates on the economy Recognising variations among mortgage holders *How?* Refining communication skills Summarising complex information for a broad audience	Demonstrate understanding of changes in interest rate on the mortgages rates (4/10) No use of economics jargon (2/10) No use of modelling (2/10) Video shorter than 3 minutes (2/10)	The video aims to explain intricate economic concepts to a general audience unacquainted with economics terminology. Avoid using complex models (e.g., AD/MP) that might confuse the general audience. Keep the video concise; lengthy ones will receive lower scores. Allow alternative submission formats (e.g., podcasts, blog entries). Consider how other assessment aspects (e.g., video graphics quality, specialised software use) will affect grading.

Assessment	Five Ws + One H considerations	Marking Criteria (marks)	Feedback notes/Other Considerations
Data Analysis Group work based on cleaning a database and providing basic statistical analysis. This assessment: *"Compose a self-reflection on the key lessons learned while cleaning the dataset and what you would do differently in the future." (500 words max)*	*Who? Which assumptions?* Willingness to share vulnerabilities Considering this an "easy" assessment *Why?* Enhancing self-awareness of strengths and weaknesses Improving group dynamics for final submission *What?* Data-related tasks like management and manipulation Working collaborative *How?* Engaging with how knowledge is created and how we engage with this process	Explain how collaboration with others helps you to learn something new. This is an ungraded assessment, and upon satisfactory completion, students get +5 marks in the final assessment.	Consider integrating key lessons into your next submission and leveraging your strengths. Think about the support you need to overcome weaknesses and enhance your next submission. Reflect on how you can contribute to improving group dynamics. Provide effective feedback considering students' vulnerabilities. Clarify how the activity connects to the broader assessment and how students should integrate it into their overall work.

The answer to the "Who" question depends on the student cohort taking the assessment. This variation should be reflected in the marking criteria and feedback. For instance, in the case of assessment 1, not all students might be familiar with policy reports. If this document has not been explained anywhere else in the programme, it must be clearly outlined in the assessment instructions, and the marking should reflect this. Including examples of policy reports can also help to address this. Moreover, this is a topic that may be very close to some students (e.g., those with a diagnosis of mental health issues) and working on this assessment may trigger negative experiences. Considering offering two or three alternative topics can help address these issues.

Each marking criterion is weighted based on its relevance and is linked to specific learning outcomes. These weights are indicative and can be adapted to any marking scale (e.g., 1–100). Assessment 1 aims for students to master how to reference, while marking criteria for assessment 2 highlight the importance of developing communication skills.

Sharing feedback notes with students before submission can further support their understanding of the assessment task and how their work will be evaluated against the marking criteria. Clear communication of marking criteria and feedback is beneficial not only to students but also facilitates the grading process, making it more focused on what is relevant for the assessment.

There are other considerations when setting assessments. One is how to select the type of assessment. A skill now widely requested in the job market is working collaboratively (Jenkins and Lane, 2019), and this is included in undergraduate and postgraduate programmes as a transferable skill to develop during studies. However, collaborative assessments ("group work") are not always favoured by students. Student perceptions of group work are closely correlated with the benefits of group work experience; if students perceive group work as beneficial, they are more likely to be engaged and motivated (Butt, 2018).

The impact of group work on student learning and engagement will be influenced by the assessment design. As with any other assessment, when setting group work, it is essential to provide clear guidance of the task and how it relates to the learning outcomes of the module. Opportunities for scaffolding and fostering a positive attitude towards the benefits of group work seem to positively influence student perceptions (Butt, 2018). Effective design of group work can create opportunities for peer learning and social support (Healy et al., 2018, offer an example for Accounting).

Another consideration is how to grade assessments. It has already been mentioned the importance of clear assessment criteria for students. It is also important to notice that there are alternatives. Ungraded assessments can help students to engage with the subject without the pressure of making mistakes, allowing them to focus on their own learning process. These assessments need to be carefully crafted and students need to understand their validity. They can be used for scaffolding knowledge or helping students to develop skills required for higher-stakes assessments. Rapchak et al. (2022) describe some teacher experiences with this practice. See also Stommel's blog entry (2020).

Assessment 3 provides an example of an ungraded assessment, a self-reflection on the main learnings of working in groups. Another peculiarity of this assessment is the task. This assessment requires writing a self-reflection, a task that can be quite challenging for students, as it may highlight their vulnerabilities. Of course, there is not a single correct way to engage with this assessment, which further highlights the importance of providing clear instructions on what is expected from the assessment and an explanation of how this assessment links to learning outcomes and how it can be used in future submissions. This example also highlights the importance of creating safe learning environments for all students to allow for meaningful engagement with this type of assessment.

Further considerations are linked to potential engagement with academic misconduct, which we develop in the next section.

CHALLENGES OF ONLINE ASSESSMENTS

The Rise of AI

The emergence of Large Language Models (LLM) based on Artificial Intelligence (AI), such as ChatGPT and Google Bard, has raised significant concerns within academia regarding academic integrity due to their impressive dialogue-based task-processing capabilities. These platforms perform satisfactorily in generating answers that require open responses. The growing body of literature on the use of these tools in writing assessments indicates that they have the potential to pass assessments, although not always with excellent results (for examples, see Choi et al., 2023, for Law; Clark, 2023, for Chemistry; Geerling et al., 2023, for Economics; Kortemeyer, 2023, for Physics). However, various trials have demonstrated that when questions require multi-step reasoning, the answers can be less satisfactory and even prone to errors (Paredes-Fuentes, 2023).

While the concerns regarding academic misconduct must be addressed, it is essential not to see AI as a threat to education. These technologies are going to revolutionise work practices across all sectors, and there is little doubt they will become valuable educational tools. Indeed, there are already good examples of how the use of LLM technologies can support educators with teaching and assessment design (Finley, 2023; Heaven, 2023; Wilichowski and Cobo, 2023).

When specifically considering online assessments, it becomes even more critical to contemplate the skills we aim to evaluate. These tools excel at providing rapid and basic answers to questions requiring memorisation and basic understanding. However, they are less adept at assessing critical thinking and problem-solving—skills highly valued in academia. Consequently, the rise of LLMs underscores the need to re-evaluate assessment design.

Figure 8.2 uses Bloom's taxonomy to illustrate the impact of LLM models on assessments and some considerations. Assessments that merely require the reproduction of memorised information (e.g. providing definitions or describing basic facts) can be easily handled by ChatGPT. Arguably, these assessments were not particularly effective even before ChatGPT, as they could be answered with the aid of basic resources such as textbooks. More importantly, if assessments solely involve regurgitating memorised information, students are unlikely to be motivated to engage fully with the material (Berliner, 2011). This does not diminish the importance of remembering and understanding but suggests that these activities could primarily occur in the classroom.

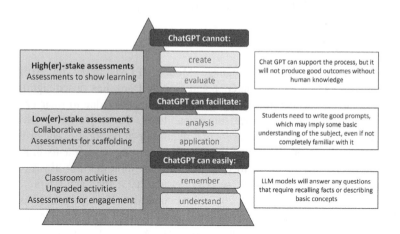

Figure 8.2   ChatGPT, assessments and Bloom's taxonomy

The heart of what we desire from students lies in *application* and *analysis*. ChatGPT can facilitate these aspects. We expect students to employ the concepts and tools acquired in the classroom across various scenarios, examining alternatives, comparing and contrasting concepts, recognising trends, and more. While ChatGPT and similar technologies can assist in these tasks, they require well-crafted prompts to provide better answers. Effective prompts necessitate precise wording and instructions to optimise output, enhancing relevance and accuracy. While not overly complex, it requires developing skills in using these models and, in many cases, creating context-specific prompts that furnish LLMs with domain-specific terms or background information for contextually relevant outputs. This may require some familiarity with the subject material.

Even more relevant for assessments, LLMs lack the ability to reason or think like humans. Current affairs, referencing, and critical analysis are in fact the main limitations of these models. Assessments demanding students make decisions based on evaluation, weighing different views supported by provided evidence, or using information to create something novel and relevant within specific contexts cannot be easily accomplished solely with these models. Such tasks require students to possess a strong grasp of the subject matter, with greater familiarity resulting in better outcomes. While students may use these models to support their work, they necessitate the skill of crafting effective prompts and the ability to evaluate the validity and potential application of provided outputs—a valuable skill in itself.

Academic Misconduct: Beyond AI

Academic misconduct existed even before LLM technologies, and these concerns are generally amplified in remote assessments. Before ChatGPT, students could access cheating services such as essay mills, and cheating in exam rooms is more common than what we like to admit (Bengtsson, 2019; Bretag et al., 2019; Burnett, 2020). Assessment design can help mitigate academic misconduct, whether derived from using LLMs, essay mills, or other behaviours.

A good predictor of student ability and effort is student's previous ability and effort. Breaking up the assessment into various steps not only contributes to scaffolding learning, but also provides a good idea of student work while at the same time supporting their progress. The marking criteria can also include some aspects on how students incorporated the feedback provided into the final assessment.

We can also use ChatGPT answers as a starting point for discussions of strengths and weaknesses of the arguments presented. This can help students to overcome the initial fears of tackling the assessment, and contribute to provide more in-depth responses, in which the baseline goes beyond of what LLM technologies can offer.

Creating more innovative and "authentic" assessments can also minimise academic misconduct. Sharing learning through alternative formats, closer to tasks students will have to do after graduation, increases student engagement, and provides opportunities to diversify assessments. Assessments that require self-reflection regarding specific activities and student learning journeys are also more difficult to plagiarise or contract, and LLMs may not perform well at these.

Moreover, assessment tasks that require analysis, evaluation, and creation are less likely to be externally contracted, especially when these are based on ongoing assessments that students develop during the module.

Of course, plagiarism software such as Turnitin can help to detect poor academic practices, and tools to detect AI writing from human writing are in development. However, these provide only technical solutions to behavioural issues, addressing symptoms without addressing the root cause: why students cheat? Lack of motivation, engagement with the course, and interest are all aspects that increase academic misconduct, and good teaching and assessment design should try to deal with these issues first.

FINAL REMARKS: THE FUTURE OF ASSESSMENTS

Throughout this chapter, assessments are considered a crucial aspect of teaching and learning, on par with content and teaching methods. However, it is important to recognise that very few academics possess expertise in education pedagogy. They often rely on personal experience or traditional institutional practices to set assessments. We aim for the framework introduced in Section 2 to change this.

In Section 3, we discussed the challenges of online vs. remote assessments. Yet, the primary challenge in higher education does not arise from Artificial Intelligence, but rather from a lack of understanding and engagement with educational and pedagogical research among academics. This gap hampers the development of assessments that allow all students to demonstrate their alignment with learning objectives and provide equal opportunities for success, regardless of their backgrounds.

While online education experts have grappled with these issues for some time, the recent shift to hybrid teaching formats, triggered by the COVID-19 pandemic, has opened new avenues for teaching delivery. This may have a positive impact on students by offering additional alternative ways to learn content, and assessments must evolve accordingly to engage this diverse student body.

After all, universities have embraced diversity and inclusion goals as strategic objectives, and internationalisation and widening participation strategies translate into even more diverse student cohorts. Effective assessments should immerse students in the subject matter, developing skills relevant to their field of study, irrespective of their backgrounds. Hence, to be effective, assessments must be inclusive, otherwise embedded biases in the system will systematically discriminate against under-represented groups, and negatively impact the strategic diversity goals of universities.

While this chapter aims to support keen educators aiming to improve their assessments, change cannot happen without institutional support. Changing assessments requires time and resources. If institutions are truly committed to embracing diversity and reducing disparities in academic outcomes, they must provide the necessary support, both financially and in terms of time and resources.

NOTES

1.   Awarding gaps refer to the difference in top degrees awarded to different groups of students in higher education institutions. This is often called "attainment gap," but we prefer the first term, as it emphasises that the gap is an outcome of structural institutional factors, rather than students' individual

characteristics. This distinction matters for the solutions to close these gaps. The former suggests the need for institutional changes in their administrative and pedagogical practices, rather than only on influencing students' behaviours.

2. For example, Bearman et al. (2023) present an organisational framework that incorporates digital tools into assessments to develop students' digital literacy and post-study human capabilities. Other studies offer tools for developing assessments with specific characteristics, such as designing "authentic assessments" (Villarroel et al., 2018), promoting "active learning" (Liu et al., 2021), and cultivating "critical reasoning" (Molerov et al., 2020).

3. Available at: https://implicit.harvard.edu/implicit/takeatest.html. It is important to note that these tests, and training in general, do not address systematic issues driving discrimination. People's actions are not just guided by the unconscious but are dictated by the social norms and constraints in the organisation. Without changing structural barriers at institutional level, we cannot fully address discriminatory behaviour.

REFERENCES

Ahn, M. Y., & Davis, H. H. (2020). Four Domains of Students' Sense of Belonging to University. *Studies in Higher Education, 45*(3), 622–634. DOI: 10.1080/03075079.2018.1564902

Alpert, W. T., Couch, K. A., & Harmon, O. R. (2016). A Randomized Assessment of Online Learning. *American Economic Review, 106*(5), 378–382.

Bearman, M., Boud, D., & Ajjawi, R. (2020). New Directions for Assessment in a Digital World. In M. Bearman, P. Dawson, R. Ajjawi, J. Tai & D. Boud (eds.), *Re-imagining University Assessment in a Digital World. The Enabling Power of Assessment* (vol 7). Springer. https://doi.org/10.1007/978-3-030-41956-1_2

Bearman, M., Nieminen, J. H., & Ajjawi, R. (2020). New Directions for Assessment in a Digital World. In M. Bearman, P. Dawson, R. Ajjawi, J. Tai & D. Boud (eds.), *Re-Imagining University Assessment in a Digital World* (pp. 7–18). Springer.

Bearman, M., Nieminen, J. H., & Ajjawi, R. (2023). Designing assessment in a digital world: an organizing framework. *Assessment & Evaluation in Higher Education, 48*(3), 291–304. DOI: 10.1080/02602938.2022.2069674

Bengtsson, L. (2019). Take-home exams in higher education: A systematic review. *Education Sciences, 9*(4). DOI: https://doi.org/10.3390/educsci9040267

Berliner, D. (2011). Rational responses to high-stakes testing: the case of curriculum narrowing and the harm that follows. *Cambridge Journal of Education, 41*(3), 287–302.

Bettinger, E. P., Fox, L., Loeb, S., & Taylor, E. S. (2017). Virtual classrooms: How online college courses affect student success. *American Economic Review, 107*(9), 2855–2875.

Bretag, T., Harper, R., Burton, M., Ellis, C., Newton, P., Rozenberg, P., Saddiqui, S., & van Haeringen, K. (2019). Contract cheating: a survey of Australian university students. *Studies in Higher Education, 44*(11), 1837–1856. DOI: 10.1080/03075079.2018.1462788

Burnett, T. (2020). Understanding and developing implementable best practice in the design of academic integrity policies for international students studying in the UK. Technical report Jan 2020, UK Council for International Student Affairs. Retrieved from https:// www .ukcisa .org .uk/ Research - -Policy/ Resource -bank/ resources/196/Understanding-and-developing-implementable-best-practice-in-the -design-of-academic-integrity-policies-for-international-students-studying-in-the -UK

Burnett, T., & Paredes-Fuentes, S. (2020). Assessment in the Time of Pandemic: A Panic-free Guide. *Economics Network Case Study.* DOI: https:// doi .org/ 10 .53593/n3298a

Butt, A. (2018). Quantification of Influences on Student Perceptions of Group Work. *Journal of University Teaching & Learning Practice, 15*(5). Retrieved from https://ro.uow.edu.au/jutlp/vol15/iss5/8

Choi, J. H., Hickman, K. E., Monahan, A., & Schwarcz, D. B. (2023). ChatGPT Goes to Law School. *Journal of Legal Education.* DOI: http://dx.doi.org/10.2139/ssrn .4335905

Clark, T. M. (2023). Investigating the Use of an Artificial Intelligence Chatbot with General Chemistry Exam Questions. *Journal of Chemical Education, 100*(5), 1905–1916. DOI: 10.1021/acs.jchemed.3c00027

Cornelius-White, J. (2007). Learner-centered teacher-student relationships are effective: A meta-analysis. *Review of Educational Research, 77,* 113–143.

Dinmore, S. (2014). The Case for Universal Design for Learning in Technology Enhanced Environments. *International Journal of Cyber Ethics in Education, 3,* 29–38. DOI: https://doi.org/10.4018/ijcee.2014040103

Finley, T. (2023, March 13). 6 Ways to Use ChatGPT to Save Time. *Edutopia.* Retrieved from https:// www .edutopia .org/ article/ 6 -ways -chatgpt -save -teachers -time/

Gaytan, J., & McEwen, B. C. (2007). Effective Online Instructional and Assessment Strategies. *American Journal of Distance Education, 21*(3), 117–132. DOI: 10.1080/08923640701341653

Geerling, W., Mateer, G. D., Wooten, J., & Damodaran, N. (2023). ChatGPT has Aced the Test of Understanding in College Economics: Now What? *The American Economist, 68*(2). DOI: https://doi.org/10.1177/05694345231169654

Goetz, T., Bieleke, M., Yanagida, T., Krannich, M., Roos, A.-L., Frenzel, A. C., Lipnevich, A. A., & Pekrun, R. (2023). Test boredom: Exploring a neglected emotion. *Journal of Educational Psychology.* Advance. DOI: https:// doi .org/ 10 .1037/edu0000807

Guptill, A. (2015). Universal Design for Online Learning. In D. L. Edyburn (ed.), *Accessible Instructional Design* (Vol. 2, pp. 47–75). Emerald Group Publishing Limited. DOI: https://doi.org/10.1108/S2056–769320150000002003

Hamilton, N., Freche, R., Zhang, Y., Zeller, G., & Carroll I. (2021). Test Anxiety and Poor Sleep: A Vicious Cycle. *International Journal of Behavioral Medicine, 28,* 250–258. DOI: https://doi.org/10.1007/s12529–021–09973–1

Healy, M., Doran, J., & McCutcheon, M. (2018). Cooperative learning outcomes from cumulative experiences of group work: differences in student perceptions. *Accounting Education, 27*(3), 286–308.

Heaven, W. D. (2023, April 6). ChatGPT is going to change education, not destroy it. *MIT Technology Review.* Retrieved from https:// www.technologyreview.com/ 2023/04/06/1071059/chatgpt-change-not-destroy-education-openai/

Heissel, J. A., Adam, E. K., Doleac, J. L., Figlio, D. N., & Meer, J. (2021). Testing, Stress, and Performance: How Students Respond Physiologically to High-Stakes

Testing. *Education Finance and Policy, 16*(2), 183–208. DOI: https://doi.org/10.1162/edfp_a_00306

Hornung, E., Schwerdt, G., & Strazzeri, M. (2023). Religious practice and student performance: Evidence from Ramadan fasting. *Journal of Economic Behavior & Organization, 205*, 100–119. DOI: https://doi.org/10.1016/j.jebo.2022.10.025

Hovdhaugen, E. (2015). Working while studying: the impact of term-time employment on dropout rates. *Journal of Education and Work, 28*(6), 631–651. DOI: 10.1080/13639080.2013.869311

Hovdhaugen, E., Frølich, N., & Aamodt, P. O. (2013). Informing Institutional Management: institutional strategies and student retention. *European Journal of Education, 48*(1), 165–177.

Iriberri, N., & Rey-Biel, P. (2021). Brave boys and play-it-safe girls: Gender differences in willingness to guess in a large scale natural field experiment. *European Economic Review, 131*. DOI: https://doi.org/10.1016/j.euroecorev.2020.103603

Jenkins, C., & Lane, S. (2019). *Employability Skills in UK Economics Degrees*. Report for the Economics Network. Technical report, The Economics Network. Retrieved from https://www.economicsnetwork.ac.uk/sites/default/files/Ashley/Report for website - Final.pdf

Jones, B. D. (2007). The Unintended Outcomes of High-Stakes Testing. *Journal of Applied School Psychology, 23*(2), 65–86. DOI: 10.1300/J370v23n02_05

Kearney, S. (2013). Improving engagement: The use of 'Authentic self-and peer-assessment for learning' to enhance the student learning experience. *Assessment & Evaluation in Higher Education, 38*, 875–891. DOI: https://doi.org/10.1080/02602938.2012.751963

Keeler, C., & Horney, M. (2007). Online Course Designs: Are Special Needs Being Met? *American Journal of Distance Education, 21*, 61–75. DOI: https://doi.org/10.1080/08923640701298985

Ketterlin-Geller, L., & Johnstone, C. (2006). Accommodations and Universal Design: Supporting Access to Assessments in Higher Education. *The Journal of Postsecondary Education and Disability, 19*, 163–172.

Kortemeyer, G. (2023). Could an artificial intelligence agent pass an introductory physics course? *Physical Review Physics Education Research, 19*(1). DOI: https://doi.org/10.1103/PhysRevPhysEducRes.19.010132

Krathwohl, D. R. (2002). A Revision of Bloom's Taxonomy: An Overview. *Theory into Practice, 41*(4), 212–218. DOI: https://doi.org/10.1207/s15430421tip4104_2

Linn, R. L. (2000). Assessments and accountability. *Educational Researcher, 29*(2), 4–16. https://doi.org/10.3102/0013189X029002004

Liu, C., Zou, D., Chan, W. H., Xie, H., & Wang, F. L. (2021). An Assessment Framework for Online Active Learning Performance. In ICBL (Conference), *Blended Learning: Re-Thinking and Re-Defining the Learning Process* (pp. 338–350). Lecture Notes in Computer Science. Springer International Publishing. DOI: 10.1007/978-3-030-80504-3_28

Madaus, G. F., & Clarke, M. (2001). The adverse impact of high-stakes testing on minority students: Evidence from 100 years of test data. In *Raising standards or raising barriers? Inequality and high-stakes testing in public education*. The Century Foundation Press.

Molerov, D., Zlatkin-Troitschanskaia, O., Nagel, M.-T., Brückner, S., Schmidt, S., & Shavelson, R. J. (2020). Assessing University Students' Critical Online Reasoning Ability: A Conceptual and Assessment Framework with Preliminary Evidence. *Frontiers in Education, 5*. DOI: 10.3389/feduc.2020.577843

Moseley, D., Baumfield, V., Elliott, J., Gregson, M., Higgins, S., Miller, J., & Newton, D. P. (2005). *Frameworks for thinking: A handbook for teaching and learning.* Cambridge University Press.

Mottiar, Z., Byrne, G., Gorham, G., & Robinson, E. (2022). An examination of the impact of COVID-19 on assessment practices in higher education. *European Journal of Higher Education.* DOI: https:// doi .org/ 10 .1080/ 21568235 .2022 .2125422

Nasution, N. (2023). Using artificial intelligence to create biology multiple choice questions for higher education. *Agricultural and Environmental Education, 2,* em002. DOI: https://doi.org/10.29333/agrenvedu/13071

Oosterbeek, H., & Van der Klaauw, B. (2013). Ramadan, fasting and educational outcomes. *Economics of Education Review, 24,* 219–226. DOI: https://doi.org/10 .1016/j.econedurev.2012.12.005

Orfield, G., & Kornhaber, M. L. (Eds.). (n.d.). *Raising standards or raising barriers? Inequality and high-stakes testing in public education.* The Century Foundation Press.

Paredes-Fuentes, S. (2023). Some initial lessons from using ChatGPT and what I will tell my Macroeconomics students. *The Economics Network Case Study.* DOI: https://doi.org/10.53593/n3579a

Rao, K., Edelen-Smith, P., & Wailehua, C. (2015). Universal design for online courses: applying principles to pedagogy. *Open Learning: The Journal of Open, Distance and e-Learning, 30,* 35–52. DOI: https://doi.org/10.1080/02680513.2014 .991300

Rapchak, M., Hands, A. S., & Hensley, M. K. (2022). Moving Toward Equity: Experiences with Ungrading. *Journal of Education for Library and Information Science, e20210062.* DOI: https://doi.org/10.3138/jelis-2021–0062

Shabatura, J. (2018). Using Bloom's Taxonomy to Write Effective Learning Objectives. *University of Arkansas.* Retrieved from https:// tips .uark .edu/ using -blooms-taxonomy/

Slack, H. R., & Priestley, M. (2023). Online learning and assessment during the Covid-19 pandemic: exploring the impact on undergraduate student well-being. *Assessment & Evaluation in Higher Education, 48*(3), 333–349. DOI: 10.1080/02602938.2022.2076804

Slade, C., Lawrie, G., Taptamat, N., Browne, E., Sheppard, K., & Matthews, K. E. (2021). Insights into how academics reframed their assessment during a pandemic: Disciplinary variation and assessment as an afterthought. *Assessment & Evaluation in Higher Education,* 1–18. DOI: https://doi.org/10.1080/02602938.2021.1933379

Stommel, J. (2020). Ungrading: an FAQ. Blog entry. Retrieved from https://www .jessestommel.com/ungrading-an-faq/

Townsend, B. L. (2002). "Testing While Black" Standards-Based School Reform and African American Learners. *Remedial and Special Education, 23*(4), 222–230. DOI: https://doi.org/10.1177/07419325020230040501

Villarroel, V., Bloxham, S., Bruna, D., Bruna, C., & Herrera-Seda, C. (2018). Authentic assessment: creating a blueprint for course design. *Assessment & Evaluation in Higher Education, 43*(5), 840–854. DOI: 10.1080/02602938.2017.1412396

Wilichowski, T., & Cobo, C. (2023, May 2). How to Use ChatGPT to support teach-ers: the good, the bad, and the ugly. *World Bank Blogs.* Retrieved from https:// blogs.worldbank.org/education/how-use-chatgpt-support-teachers-good-bad-and

-ugly #: ~: text = Teachers %20can %20use %20ChatGPT %20to ,and %20proficiency %2C%20but%20not%20delivery

PART III

COLLABORATIVE LEARNING IN AN
ONLINE CLASSROOM

9. Experiments for teaching economics

Humberto Llavador

Tell me, and I forget.
Show me, and I may remember.
Involve me, and I understand.
From the Xunzi by Xun Kuang
Confucian philosopher
(314–235 B.C.)

Homines dum docent discunt
Seneca (4 B.C. – 65 A.C.)

INTRODUCTION

Classroom experiments are a particularly popular and powerful tool that make use of the advantages of learning from personal experience. Students who have just participated in an experiment and seen the resulting data are interested to discover for themselves how well (or poorly) the theory works to explain the reality that they have observed, instead of simply learning the theory as dogma to be memorized. They are also able to observe many aspects that are difficult to convey in a lecture, like how heterogeneous students act or the adjustment process to equilibrium. In addition, experiments foster "social and academic integration" (Braxton et al. 2000).

Classroom experiments have been successfully pursued for many decades now. At first, they were run with the use of pen-and-paper instructions and written contracts (e.g. Frank 1997; Emerson and Taylor 2004; Dickie 2006; Durham et al. 2007; Bergstrom and Miller 2000). Then, computers in lab rooms were used, prominently by Holt and his collaborators (Holt 1996; Anderson and Holt 1996; Holt and Laury 1997; Ball and Holt 1998; Goeree and Holt 1999; Holt and Sherman 1999; Holt and Capra 2000). More recently, new technologies have introduced online platforms that make use of handheld devices (smartphones and tablets), reducing the costs of running an experiment and collecting data, increasing the popularity of experiments as a teaching tool, and allowing for both in-class and online implementation.

As outlined in the next section, there is wide evidence showing that experiments have a positive impact on students' performance and increase both the teachers' and the students' enjoyment of the class. They also foster an environment where students engage with the material more comprehensively and ask more advanced questions. In my experience, most instructors get excited when introduced to the use of experiments as a teaching tool. However, the use of experiments, though growing, is not as widely spread as all this evidence and enthusiasm would suggest. The main reason deterring instructors from adopting experiments is the perception that transitioning to a different teaching methodology will be costly in preparation time and/or installations and material.[1] However, technology and newly available material have drastically reduced these costs and made running experiments in the classroom or online an easy way to engage students and facilitate the understanding of "difficult" concepts without sacrificing, and most likely improving, student performance, while helping making teaching a more enjoyable experience.

The next section discusses the main findings related to the impacts of using experiments as a teaching tool. Section 3 focuses on the new available technologies and materials, and addresses several of the frequently asked questions raised by instructors considering the use of experiments. Section 4 shows that the differences between running experiments in-class or online are fading out. Section 5 concludes.

WHY USE EXPERIMENTS AS A TEACHING TOOL? THE IMPACT OF EXPERIMENTS IN STUDENTS' PERFORMANCE, ENGAGEMENT, AND ENJOYMENT

The use of active learning techniques such as experiments is now widespread in economics and other social sciences. The motivation for these techniques is "creating memorable experiential learning events that tap into multiple senses and emotions" (Lantis et al. 2010, p.6). But beyond the obvious arguments for using experiments to engage students, it is also important to know whether they have a real impact on students' performance. Since the popularization of experiments in the classroom in the 1990s, the economic education literature has tried to study the impact of introducing experiments in the classroom, with a particular focus on their effect on students' achievements. The standard analysis uses an experimental design with a control group that receives more traditional chalk-and-talk lectures, and a treated group exposed to the experimental treatment. Performance is measured by grades and, more commonly, test scores, usually based on multiple-choice questions. Several controls are used to control for a number of student characteristics.

Emerson and Taylor (2004) is a representative example. They collected data in a sample of 9 sections of micro principles, two of which used extensive experimentation (11 experiments from the well-known Bergstrom and Miller [2000] textbook) and tested students using the Test of Understanding in

College Economics (TUCE). They find that the two sections using experiments performed better than the control group in the TUCE scores, showing evidence that experiments improve student achievement and retention in economics principles classes. These findings are corroborated by several other studies, like Dickie (2006), Durham et al. (2007), Emerson and English (2016a) and, more recently, Tila (2021).[2] Tila (2021) finds that not only did students obtain higher scores but they also recognized improvements in understanding the material and boosted their attitudes towards the subject. Similar results show up in more advanced courses: Frank (1997) tested the impact of using an experiment in explaining the tragedy of the commons for environmental economics and public finance courses. And they are also common to other disciplines and other active learning methodologies. For instance, in a meta-analysis of 225 published papers, Freeman et al. (2014) study the effects of introducing active learning and interactive classrooms in science, technology, engineering, and mathematics (STEM) courses. They find that students' scores increased by 6%, on average, in active learning sections, while students in more traditional sections were 1.5 times more likely to fail.[3]

The literature has also studied the drivers behind these general positive impacts. Durham et al. (2007) used a similar control-and-treated-groups design, but created their own specific multiple-choice questions to test the students' understanding of the specific concepts associated with each experiment. They discovered that making several decisions in a series of rounds, compared to making just one decision, and participation, compared to observing the actions of a few volunteers, are more effective and had a larger positive impact. Experiments are also more effective when students are required to perform follow-up work, such as homework after the experiment (Cartwright and Stepanova 2012), and when students participate in more than one experiment. Emerson and English (2016b) find that additional experiments during a course have a positive, but diminishing, marginal benefit, with the maximum benefit being obtained between the fifth and seventh experiment. So, "more is more," but up to a limit. Finally, experiments have also been shown to be beneficial in large principles courses, even when the technology for a proper implementation was not yet widely available (Ball et al. 2006).

Other important questions are how the benefits are distributed among different groups of students and if the benefits are higher for low-performing students, since active learning techniques may engage different types of learners and help some students more than others. The general view is that while the overall effect is neutral or beneficial, classroom experiments may help to bridge some achievement gaps. Positive impacts tend to be higher for low achievement groups, females (Emerson and Taylor 2004) and freshmen (Ball et al. 2006).

Other than the cognitive impacts of experiments in teaching, it is also important, as for any other pedagogical approach, to study their effectiveness on a wide variety of outcomes (Becker and Powers 2001). First, a direct side-effect of participating in experiments in the classroom is that students may learn about conducting experiments and testing theories. Secondly, educational psychology and gamification research highlight that games activate motivation which improves learning outcomes, including cognition, creative problem solving, teamwork, and social-emotional abilities (Dichev and Dicheva 2017). Thirdly, students also seem to enjoy participating and recognize the learning impact, improving their attitudes toward the subject and towards economics in general (Dickie 2006; Durham et al. 2007; Tila 2021). Increased motivation is perhaps the most robust of all impacts (Gremmen and van den Brekel 2012). Finally, in a recent paper, Bartels et al. (2022) ran a case study in India and found some evidence that participating in the experimental game induced real-world changes, opening the possibility that participation in experimental games may change real life behavior (a transfer from in-game to out-game behavior as a learning outcome).

Studying the effectiveness of different teaching methods faces several difficulties: attaining sufficient instruction time to make a difference, selection bias, measurement of outcomes, institutions and instructor's differences, students' strategic reactions, and barriers to data collection by IRBs (Allgood et al. 2015). The empirical studies in this section have been carefully designed to overcome many of these obstacles, and they show that game experiments in the classroom have a robust and positive effect on student learning achievement, on retention of economic material in the course, and on a more favorable impression of economics, as compared with the traditional chalk-and-talk pedagogy. Finally, experiments also have a positive impact on students' evaluations and motivation, and on instructors' satisfaction.

RUNNING EXPERIMENTS IN THE CLASSROOM

Economics is especially well suited for the use of experiments since it studies the behavior and interactions of people in economic situations. Students, acting as economic agents, are able to experience first-hand the problems faced by such agents, making economic ideas come to life in the classroom.

To address concerns frequently raised by instructors considering experiments, this section begins by describing available resources, and more specifically the advantages of online platforms and their companion material.

Online Platforms

Running classroom experiments with pen-and-paper is a time- and resource-consuming approach. Many instructors who are intrigued by the idea of running classroom experiments are deterred by the organizational burden of running them. Running experiments in a lab is also possible but it requires expensive installations and a reduced number of students. These drawbacks disappear when experiments are run in the classroom or online using a web-based platform and mobile devices such as smartphones, tablets and personal computers.

There are several web-based online tools for running classroom experiments.[4] Currently, the dominant platforms are classEx, MobLab, and veconLab.[5] All three offer a broad range of pre-programmed games for teaching microeconomics, macroeconomics, game theory, public economics, environmental economics, psychology, and other subjects (Table 9.1). classEx and veconLab are available free of charge to any lecturer and participant (unlike MobLab that requires a subscription fee). classEx and MobLab are platform-independent and are optimized for the use of mobile devices (smartphones, tablets, notebooks, and personal computers). classEx and MobLab are friendlier to use than veconLab. And classEx also offers the possibility to create your own games and modify existing ones, providing the flexibility to adapt any game to your needs, or use existing games as a starting point for the design of new ones. Instructors may also share their games and outcomes. Because it is free, user-friendly, and flexible, I have been using and collaborating with classEx for over a decade now. Hence, I will refer to its features when describing specific details about the platforms. Nevertheless, most of what I have to say, if not all, is common to all three platforms.

classEx (Giamattei and Lambsdorff 2015, 2019) runs as a centralized application and only requires an internet connection and a standard (up-to-date) browser.[6] Instructions, any public information, and the output from running the experiment can be projected to the entire classroom, while private information and decisions are displayed on the students' mobile devices. Experiments may be run completely anonymously or may require an identifying code or alias in case you want to keep personal records. The graphical output and the data obtained in previous sessions is easily accessible within a game and can also be downloaded prior to the session. This feature provides an insight into the expected results prior to running the experiment, facilitating the preparation of the lecture, and can be used as a backup in case of unusual outcomes or unexpected problems, for example the loss of internet connection. Experiments can be run online as well as in-class with face-to-face interaction, even with very large groups.

Finally, the number of resources with instructions on how to run the most common experiments in these platforms is rapidly growing. They include fully detailed student's and instructor's manuals, exercises that help test students' understanding of the rules, and questions and problem sets to reflect on the outcome of the experiment. Some examples include the e-book *Experiencing Economics* (The CORE Team 2023) with experiments linked to specific units of *The Economy* (The CORE Team 2017) and *Economy, Society, and Public Policy* (The CORE Team 2019), yet self-contained and hence usable alongside other textbooks; Lambsdorff and Giamattei (2020), a macroeconomic textbook with an extensive use of experiments; or the webpage Econ Class Experiments: Experiments with Economics Principles (Bergstrom et al. 2020), which implements several market experiments from Bergstrom and Miller (2000).

Table 9.1   *Representative experiments available in online platforms*

Experiments	Online platforms
Markets and competition	Pit market†§ Taxation†§ Entry and exit† Cournot Bertrand Stackelberg Monopoly and Cartels† Price discrimination
Standard games	2x2 games Prisoners' dilemma Stag-Hunt Dictator game Ultimatum Trust game (Camerer 2003) Coordination and Focal points (Mehta et al. 1994) Gift-exchange (Falk and Kosfeld 2006)
Macro and finance	Comparative advantage Beauty contest Phillips curve and Fisher effect Bubbles and crashes Calvo pricing Life cycle consumption (Carbone and Duffy 2014) Keynesian multiplier Coordination game§ Gains from trade Exchange rate and PPP (Lambsdorff and Giamattei 2020) Interest rate parity (Lambsdorff and Giamattei 2020)

Experiments	Online platforms
Cognition and decision making	Nudging Anchoring effects‡ Halo effect‡ Linda problem‡ Framing effect‡ Money illusion
Externalities and public goods	Pollution game†§ Tragedy of the commons Public good contributions (Herrmann et al. 2008)§ Network economies of scale§ Competing standards§
Auctions	Dutch English (Private value) English (Common value) Sealed bid (Private value) Sealed bid (Common value)
Experimental ethics	Trolley experiment (Hauser et al. 2007) Ambiguity (Dana et al. 2007) Gneezy game (Gneezy 2005)

Note: All experiments are implemented in either classEx, MobLab or veconLab, with many of them available in more than one platform. References indicate the source for the experiment, as reported in the platform.
† Bergstrom and Miller (2000)
‡ Kahneman (2011)
§ Companion material in *Experiencing Economics* (The CORE Team 2023)

How to Incorporate Experiments in the Classroom

As seen in Section 2, there is ample evidence that running experiments engages students and improves performance. But running an experiment and showing the outcomes is not sufficient to make experiments a meaningful part of the learning experience. Students must be actors, and not mere spectators, reflect on the experiment and analyze the data.

I favor a common approach that combines elements of a flipped-classroom and of experiential learning. The approach emphasizes the importance of complementing classroom experiments with constructive homework, making students reflect on the experiment and analyze the data. This is, for example, the structure built in the well-known book by Bergstrom and Miller (2000).[7]

Each experiment is structured in three stages.

First, students prepare for the experiment by reading the instructions and working on some warm-up questions that should get them thinking about how to behave in the experiment for all possible roles (like sellers and buyers or proposers and responders). Students can work on this preparation before coming to the classroom or at the beginning of the session, depending on the complexity of the experiment and the time available during the session. Then, the instructor runs the experiment with a discussion during and after the process, inviting students to come up with possible explanations for the observed results and to work on their economic intuitions.

Next, a series of questions and tasks help them reflect on their experience and understand their and others' behavior in the experiment. Many resources (like Bergstrom and Miller [2000] or The CORE Team [2023]) provide questions and constructive homework that uses the data from your session; and most online platforms let you download the data from your experiment in a format that can be read by popular spreadsheets.[8]

Later, during the lecture, the instructor generalizes the results by presenting the mathematical, more abstract analysis, provides applications, and solves the doubts that students had while working on the questions and tasks.

Finally, students test/practice their recently acquired knowledge in assignments.

Observe the similarities with the four stages in Kolb's (1984) experiential learning theory: Concrete experience → Observation and reflection on that experience → Abstract conceptualization → Active experimentation and testing the new concepts. You may have to adapt this general structure to your study plans, schedule, size of the class, and the particular characteristics of the experiment.

Time required

The use of online platforms leaves enough time for a fruitful discussion in a regular session. Many of the most popular experiments can be run in 15–20 minutes or less, plus instructions, which could also be sent to students before the class if necessary. In a trading-pit market where participants need to find a buyer or seller and negotiate a price, we find that students quickly understand the dynamics of the experiment and each round requires no more than four minutes to be completed (Giamattei and Llavador 2020). A more involved experiment of voluntary contributions to a public good with penalties can be easily run in less than 15 minutes (see Chapter 1 in *Experiencing Economics* [Giamattei and Llavador 2022]). Simple games, like the prisoner's dilemma, the dictator game, or the beauty contest, require as little as 5–10 minutes for the whole activity.

Number of participants

Another advantage introduced by online platforms is that experiments can be run with groups of many different sizes, though some experiments work better than others. Very small groups with few students are more susceptible to outliers and, in market experiments, to collusion among roles who benefit from reducing competition. When students do not need to interact directly (e.g. in the beauty contest, auction games, or the Keynsian multiplier) or when they are matched in pairs or groups (e.g. in any standard 2x2 game, the public good, or the tragedy of the commons), experiments can be conducted synchronously even with large groups of hundreds of students with live streaming (Giamattei and Lambdorff 2019; Li et al. 2021). Nevertheless, it is always possible to run several parallel sessions or to get students to make their decisions in groups. This last option may have key advantages, even in smaller classes: It allows students to discuss the decisions as the game progresses, helping to obtain a better understanding of the issues involved; and may increase engagement with the game, reducing the risk of unmotivated students and their impact on the result of the game (Guest 2015).

Incentives and payoffs
Experimental economics have put much emphasis on the relevance of incentives when running experiments (Davis and Holt 1993). Monetary incentives improve outcomes (Bettinger 2012), as do reputational incentives (Filsecker and Hickey 2014) or external rewards (Madan 2013). And there is also evidence of no substantially different outcomes from field games with and without performance-based individual payoffs (Bartels et al. 2022).

In teaching, grade incentives help experimental outcomes to match theoretical predictions, making it easier to use experiments in the classroom, but there is the risk that "the effort students devote to earning grade credit crowds out the attention they would otherwise pay to the economic lessons conveyed by the experiments" (Dickie 2006). In my own experience, reputation is a powerful enough incentive for most students, while very small grade incentives are sufficient to enlist those who require extra motivation. It is important, when designing incentive rules, that they do not promote cunning behavior and that they are perceived as fair. Helpful tips include using simple normalizing formulas and choosing the payoffs from only some ex-post chosen rounds or sessions. You should be careful to make the choice non-foreseeable, treat different roles fairly, and consider eliminating outliers.

What if Something Goes Differently from Expected?

Another common concern among potential adopters of experiments is that the game may not work. This is, however, a fear easily overcome. Most teaching experiments have been widely tested and deviations from expected outcomes are clearly identified. In any case, unusual outcomes should not be automatically discarded, but transformed into teaching opportunities. Understanding what generated those results usually provides excellent opportunities for an enriched debate.

Online platforms usually provide outcomes from previously run sessions that can be used as an easy backup for the discussion. And additional material for the instructor, like in *Experiencing Economics* (The CORE Team 2023), explicitly addresses possible deviations, and offers tips on how to conduct the discussion.

Once again, it is important to ask students to reflect on why their session differed from the predicted results, not only because it is a good tool to discover the mechanisms working behind the economic theory, but also to avoid leading them to think that one or the other is false.

USING EXPERIMENTS IN ONLINE TEACHING: WHAT IS DIFFERENT? CHALLENGES AND BENEFITS

Most of what I wrote in the previous sections applies to both in-class and online teaching. On the other hand, there is little written on whether experiments work better in-class or online. Carter and Emerson (2012) compare students in sections with manually administered in-class experiments and those in sections with computerized online experiments and find no significant differences in student achievements or overall views of the course or the instructor. They find, however, that students report greater satisfaction with in-class experiments, more interactions with their classmates, and direct contact with a larger number of them. In my experience, these interactions may foster a greater sense of community and lead to out-of-class interactions, like study groups or even long-term friendships. One of the reasons why students come to class is (or should be) to relate with other students. Experiments work as a good instrument for this purpose. Sharing experiences while bargaining, making exchanges, or thinking together foster relationships that in some cases can extend beyond the classroom. This *disadvantage* is not specific to online experiments but shared with the broad concept of online teaching. Perhaps, avatar-based meeting platforms may soon allow for a smoother communication among students in online sessions, lowering some barriers to personal interactions among students.

Modern technology is blurring the differences between administering experiments face-to-face in the classroom and online. Thanks to online platforms and hand-held devices, in-class sessions can take advantage of computerized experiments and run experiments with very large groups. Hence, while sitting in the classroom, students can participate in experiments administered purely online (where students receive private information in and submit their responses from their personal devices, while public information is projected for the whole class), in a hybrid format (where students interact off-line and then submit their input through their handheld devices), or purely hand-held, with all the costs associated to distributing and collecting information. For example, in a market experiment, where buyers and sellers need to meet and negotiate a price, online trading lets students send buying and selling offers on their devices, and transactions result from accepting standing offers; while in a hybrid format, negotiations are done verbally, and transactions formalized once students input and submit the agreed price on their devices (Giamattei and Llavador 2022). Both approaches enjoy automatized data collection and immediately available output to use in the discussion. Online experiments may face a higher risk that less engaged students hold up the game, since peer pressure is reduced, and students can become more easily distracted and lose focus (Guest 2015). However, this runs contrary to my experience. The blogpost of Jenkins (2021) recounts a very successful implementation with a very large group of more than 350 students. In any case, more experiences and research are needed.

CONCLUSIONS

Experiments allow students to step into the roles of economic agents or decision-makers, providing a hands-on, experiential learning opportunity. Students get to exercise their economic intuition, and the discussion during and after experiments encourages economic reasoning. The data outcomes can be used to create homework and constructive problems, which get automatically renewed from year to year, challenging students to discover the main concepts by themselves. During the lecture, the instructor can more efficiently focus on generalizing the findings, presenting applications, and solving doubts, since students have already grasped the intricacies and the intuition.

In this chapter I have discussed the impacts of experiments in students' performance, motivation, and satisfaction, and elaborated on the general principles and guidelines on using experiments for teaching economics. If you are searching for a concrete example and step-by-step instructions on how to run an experiment, I recommend reading any of the chapters in *Experiencing Economics* (The CORE Team 2023). The first scenario of "An Excise Tax in the Apple Market," (Bergstrom et al. 2022) in essence a simple trading-pit experiment, is a good starting point.

In a closing reflection, it is important to consider not just the impact experiments may have on students but also on instructors. While designing a course, it is common to prioritize content relevance and material appeal for students. However, we often forget that the course must also be interesting to teach, even after having taught it several times. In my experience, instructors get excited about incorporating experiments in the classroom, resulting in increased motivation and more effective teaching.

NOTES

1. Other arguments are the quantity of material that will be covered in class-time, concerns that the game would not work or fear of losing control in the classroom (Guest 2015). In Section 3, I show how newly available material helps anticipate what might go differently and transform the situation into an opportunity for a better lecture. The argument about the optimal coverage of content has been taking place for a long time and will remain an issue independently of the teaching methodology. As a general principle, I believe that instructors should focus on what students learn rather than on what they have covered in their lectures (Hansen et al. 2002), but this topic is complex and falls outside our current scope.

2. Refer to Guest (2015) and Tila (2021) for a more exhaustive list of references.

3. They performed several tests to assess that the results did not suffer from publication bias.

4. A longer list includes, among others, Aplia, ARS, classEx, MobLab, VeconLab, LIONESS, oTree, and zTree. The last three programs are research-oriented, while classEx and, to a lesser extent, VeconLab can be used both for teaching and for research.

5. classEx: https://classex.de; MobLab https://moblab.com; VeconLab: https://veconlab.econ.virginia.edu.

6. A complete documentation of classEx can be found at https://classex-doc.readthedocs.io.

7. Several of their experiments have been updated and complemented with classEx packages, which can be found, as well as their companion material, on the webpage http://econclassexperiments.com (Bergstrom et al. 2020) and in the Experiencing Economics e-book (CORE Team 2023).

8. In addition, Bergstrom et al. (2020) provide Excel files that read the output files from classEx and automatically generate solutions to the exercises and report participation, profits and the number of correct answers to the warm-up quiz (in case you want to keep records).

REFERENCES

Allgood, S., W. B. Walstad, & J. J. Siegfried. 2015. "Research on Teaching Economics to Undergraduates." *Journal of Economic Literature* 53 (2): 285–325. https://doi.org/10.1257/jel.53.2.285

Anderson, L., & C. Holt. 1996. "Classroom games: Information cascades." *Journal of Economic Perspectives* 10: 187–193. https://doi.org/10.1257/jep.10.4.187

Ball, S. B., C. Eckel, & C. Rojas. 2006. "Technology Improves Learning in Large Principles of Economics Classes: Using Our WITS." *American Economic Review* 96 (2): 442–46. https://doi.org/10.1257/000282806777212215

Ball, S., & C. Holt. 1998. "Classroom games: Speculation and bubbles in an asset market." *Journal of Economic Perspectives* 12: 207–218. https://doi.org/10.1257/jep.12.1.207

Bartels, L., T. Falk, V. Duche, & B. Vollan. 2022. "Experimental Games in Transdisciplinary Research: The Potential Importance of Individual Payments." *Journal of Environmental Economics and Management* 113 (February): 102631. https://doi.org/10.1016/j.jeem.2022.102631

Becker, W. E., & J. R. Powers. 2001. "Student Performance, Attrition, and Class Size given Missing Student Data." *Economics of Education Review* 20 (4): 377–88. https://doi.org/10.1016/S0272–7757(00)00060–1

Bergstrom, T., M. Giamattei, H. Llavador, & J. Miller. 2020. *Econ Class Experiments: Experiments with Economics Principles*. Webpage [Accessed on 30 May 2022].

Bergstrom, T., M. Giamattei, H. Llavador, & J. Miller. 2022. "An Excise Tax in the Apple Market". Unit 4 in The CORE Team, *Experiencing Economics*. Available at https://www.core-econ.org. [Accessed on 30 May 2022].

Bergstrom, T. C., & J. H. Miller. 2000. *Experiments with Economic Principles: Microeconomics*. 2nd ed. McGraw-Hill Higher Education.

Bettinger, E. P. 2012. "Paying to learn: the effect of financial incentives on elementary school test scores." *Review of Economics and Statistics* 94: 686–698.

Braxton, J. M., J. F. Milem, & A. S. Sullivan. 2000. "The influence of active learning on the college student departure process: Toward a revision of Tinto's theory." *Journal of Higher Education* 71 (5): 569–90.

Camerer, C. 2003. *Behavioral Game Theory: Experiments in Strategic Interaction*. Princeton University Press.

Carbone, E., & J. Duffy. (2014). "Lifecycle consumption plans, social learning and external habits: Experimental evidence." *Journal of Economic Behavior & Organization* 106: 413–427

Carter, L. K., & T. L. N. Emerson. 2012. "In-class vs. Online experiments: Is there a difference?" *Journal of Economic Education* 43: 4–18. https://doi.org/10.1080/00220485.2011.636699

Cartwright, E., & A. Stepanova. 2012. "What Do Students Learn from a Classroom Experiment: Not Much, Unless They Write a Report on It." *Journal of Economic Education* 43 (1): 48–57. https://doi.org/10.1080/00220485.2012.636710

CORE Team, The. 2017. *The Economy*. E-book available at https://www.core-econ.org/the-economy [Accessed on 30 May 2022].

CORE Team, The. 2019. *Economy, Society, and Public Policy*. E-book available at https://www.core-econ.org/espp [Accessed on 30 May 2022].

CORE Team, The. 2023. *Experiencing Economics*. E-book available at https://www.core-econ.org/experiencing-economics [Accessed on 28 November 2023].

Dana, J., R. A. Weber, & J. X. Kuang. 2007. "Exploiting moral wiggle room: experiments demonstrating an illusory preference for fairness." *Economic Theory* 33 (1): 67–80.

Davis, D. D., & C. A. Holt. 1993. *Experimental economics*. Princeton University Press.

Dichev, C., & D. Dicheva. 2017. "Gamifying education: what is known, what is believed and what remains uncertain: a critical review." *International journal of educational technology in higher education* 14 (1): 1–36.

Dickie, M. 2006. "Do Classroom Experiments Increase Learning in Introductory Microeconomics?" *Journal of Economic Education* 37 (3): 267–88. https://doi.org/10.3200/JECE.37.3.267–288

Durham, Y., T. McKinnon, & C. Schulman. 2007. "Classroom Experiments: Not Just Fun and Games." *Economic Inquiry* 45 (1): 162–78. https://doi.org/10.1111/j.1465–7295.2006.00003.x

Emerson, T. L.N., & L. K. English. 2016a. "Classroom Experiments: Teaching Specific Topics or Promoting the Economic Way of Thinking?" *Journal of Economic Education* 47 (4): 288–99. https://doi.org/10.1080/00220485.2016.1213684

Emerson, T. L. N., & L. K. English. 2016b. "Classroom Experiments: Is More More?" *American Economic Review* 106 (5): 363–67. https://doi.org/10.1257/aer.p20161054.

Emerson, T., & B. Taylor. 2004. "Comparing Student Achievement across Experimental and Lecture-Oriented Sections of a Principles of Microeconomics Course." *Southern Economic Journal* 70 (3): 672–93. https://doi.org/10.2307/4135338.

Falk, A. & M. Kosfeld. 2006. "The hidden cost of control." *The American Economic Review* 96 (5): 1611–1630.

Filsecker, M., & D. T. Hickey. 2014. "A multilevel analysis of the effects of external rewards on elementary students' motivation, engagement and learning in an educational game." *Computers & Education* 75: 136–148.

Frank, B. 1997. "The Impact of Classroom Experiments on the Learning of Economics: An Empirical Investigation." *Economic Inquiry* 35 (4): 763–69. https://doi.org/10.1111/j.1465–7295.1997.tb01962.x

Freeman, S., S. L. Eddy, M. McDonough, M. K. Smith, N. Okoroafor, H. Jordt, & M. P. Wenderoth. 2014. "Active Learning Increases Student Performance in Science, Engineering, and Mathematics." *Proceedings of the National Academy of Sciences of the United States of America* 111 (23): 8410–15. https://doi.org/10.1073/pnas.1319030111

Giamattei, M., & J. G. Lambsdorff. 2015. "classEx: An online software for classroom experiments," *Passauer Diskussionspapiere*, Volkswirtschaftliche Reihe V-68–15, University of Passau, Faculty of Business and Economics.

Giamattei, M., & J. G. Lambsdorff. 2019. "ClassEx — an Online Tool for Lab-in-the-Field Experiments with Smartphones." *Journal of Behavioral and Experimental Finance* 22: 223–31. https://doi.org/10.1016/j.jbef.2019.04.008.

Giamattei, M., & H. Llavador. 2020. "Public goods game." Experiment 1 in The CORE Team, *Experiencing Economics*. Available at https://www.core-econ.org [Accessed on 14 May 2022].

Giamattei, M., & H. Llavador. 2022. "An Excise Tax in the Apple Market." Experiment 4 in The CORE Team, *Experiencing Economics*. Available at https://www.core-econ.org [Accessed on 14 May 2022].

Gneezy, U. 2005. "Deception: The Role of Consequences." *American Economic Review* 95 (1): 384–394. DOI: https://doi.org/10.1257/0002828053828662

Goeree, J., & Holt, C. 1999. "Employment and prices in a simple macroeconomy." *Southern Economic Journal* 65: 637–647. https://doi.org/10.2307/1060823

Gremmen, H. J. F. M., & G. van den Brekel. 2012. "Do Classroom Experiments Increase Student Motivation?" *SSRN Electronic Journal* 1997: 24–26. https://doi.org/10.2139/ssrn.1925777

Guest, J. 2015. "Reflections on ten years of using economics games and experiments in teaching." *Cogent Economics and Finance* 3 (1): 1–16.

Hansen, W. L., M. K. Salemi, & J. J. Siegfried. 2002. "Use It or Lose It: Teaching Literacy in the Economics Principles Course." *American Economic Review* 92 (2): 463–472. https://doi.org/10.1257/000282802320191813

Hauser, M., F. Cushman, L. Young, R. K.-X. Jin, & J. Mikhail. 2007. "A Dissociation between Moral Judgments and Justifications." *Mind and Language* 22 (1): 1–21. https://doi.org/10.1111/j.1468–0017.2006.00297.x.

Herrman, B., C. Thöni, & S. Gächter. 2008. "Antisocial Punishment Across Societies" Science Vol. 319 (5868): 1362–1367.

Holt, C. 1996. "Classroom games: Trading in a pit market." *Journal of Economic Perspectives* 10: 193–203. https://doi.org/10.1257/jep.10.1.193

Holt, C., & M. Capra. 2000. "Classroom games: A prisoner's dilemma." *The Journal of Economic Education* 31: 229– 236. http://dx.doi.org/10.1080/00220480009596781

Holt, C., & S. Laury. 1997. "Classroom games: Voluntary provision of a public good." *Journal of Economic Perspectives* 11: 209–215. http://dx.doi.org/10.1257/jep.11.4.209

Holt, C., & R. Sherman. 1999. "Classroom games: A market for lemons." *Journal of Economic Perspectives* 13: 205–214. https://doi.org/10.1257/jep.13.1.205

Jenkins, C. 2021. "Teaching with experiments online: reflections on how it went from a lecturer and student perspective." Center for Teaching and Learning Economics at University College of London. July 13. https://ctale.org/2021/07/13/teaching-with-experiments-online-reflections-on-how-it-went-from-a-lecturer-and-student-perspective-july-2021 [Accessed on 15 June 2022].

Kahneman, D. 2011. *Thinking, Fast and Slow*. Farrar, Straus and Giroux.

Kolb, D. A. 1984. *Experiential Learning: Experience as The Source of Learning and Development*. Prentice Hall, Inc. https://doi.org/10.1016/B978–0–7506–7223–8.50017–4.

Lambsdorff, J. G., & M. Giamattei. 2020. *International Monetary Economics. Lectures in Economics*. 1st English edition. E-book available at https://de.scribd.com/document/494261017/Macroeconomics-with-Games

Lantis, J. S., K. J. Kille, & M. Krain. 2010. "The State of the Active Teaching and Learning Literature." In *The International Studies Encyclopedia*, edited by R. A. Denemark and R. Marlin-Bennett. Oxford University Press.

Li, Z., P. H. Lin, S. Y. Kong, D. Wang, & J. Duffy. 2021. "Conducting Large, Repeated, Multi-Game Economic Experiments Using Mobile Platforms." *PLoS ONE*. https://doi.org/10.1371/journal.pone.0250668.

Madan, C. R. 2013. "Toward a common theory for learning from reward, affect, and motivation: the SIMON framework." *Frontiers in Systems Neuroscience* 7: 59.

Mehta, J., C., Starmer, & R. Sugden. 1994. "The Nature of Salience: An Experimental Investigation of Pure Coordination Games." *American Economic Review* 84: 658–73

Tila, D. 2021. "Economic Experiments in a Classroom Improve Learning and Attitudes toward Economics: A Case Study at a Community College of the City University of New York." *Journal of Education for Business* 96 (5): 308–16. https://doi.org/10.1080/08832323.2020.1812489.

10. Teaching economics online using cases

Cloda Jenkins

INTRODUCTION

Economics is about understanding how decisions are made and what impact they have. As researchers, we use theoretical models, empirical analysis, and what we observe in the real world to analyse decision-making. As educators, we want to pass on the ability to use integrated approaches to analyse questions to our students.

Economics provides a solid grounding for problem-solving in many different careers. Being able to bring what they have learnt in university and apply it to unseen problems is challenging for graduates. They need to identify which theory and empirical techniques to use when, understand how to apply the appropriate theoretical frameworks and critically adapt what is theoretical to what is feasible (Bhandari, 2020; Dalrymple et al., 2021).

In most work settings the problem-solving happens with others. The teamwork is often online, through cloud platforms for resource sharing and hybrid meetings. Graduates need to be able to work with others, be it online or in-person, or most likely, a mix of the two, to find rich and innovative solutions to problems (Jenkins, 2020; Jenkins and Lane, 2019; Tambe, 2023).

The skill of applying what you have learnt to problem-solving, with others, is not something that comes naturally to all students. They often need the opportunity to practice in a safe learning space. As emphasised by Hoyt (2017), the more relevant these opportunities are to the students' interests and lives the more likely they are to engage. Providing students with real world cases relevant to the content they are learning, and team-based discussion of them, is a direct way of enabling them to develop their knowledge and skills (Mahdi et al., 2020; Puri, 2022). It is a mini experiential-learning opportunity that gives them a taste of the problem-solving they can use their economics for and helps them to do well in their courses (Bonney, 2015; Nohria, 2019). The experience can be provided on campus or online, with scope for both live and asynchronous activities linked to case analysis (McLellan, 2004).

In this chapter we explore a broad definition of what we mean by 'teaching cases' and explain how they can be used for teaching in different ways in an online context. The examples discussed have been used across different courses, of different cohort size, primarily in micro-based policy courses but also in introductory overview economics courses for non-specialists.

WHAT DOES 'TEACHING WITH CASES' MEAN IN ECONOMICS?

When you mention that you teach with cases many assume that you give students a pre-written case study, produced by an external body such as the Harvard Business Review, ahead of a live class, ask them to read it and then have an active discussion about the case in class. Such case studies are very relevant, and excellent teaching resources, in many disciplines (see for examples The Case Centre [2023] and Columbia Case Consortium Resources [2023]). Finding pre-written formal case studies that connect well to economics topics, particularly current events, can be difficult. They may also be costly to acquire if your institution does not have a subscription.

The good news is you don't need a formal pre-written case to do case-teaching if we take a broader definition more aligned with problem-based learning and application to the real world (Servant-Miklos, 2019). Relevance is what matters most (Wooten et al., 2021). You can provide students with a reputable source of information about a situation in the economy that relates to the theories and empirical frameworks they are studying (ABL Connect Harvard, 2023; Volpe, 2002). It is the student's job to examine the source, extract key information and summarise it. They are expected to critically evaluate what they have reviewed through an economist lens. Reviewing the case can help them identify what the theory means, and even to come up with theories inductively through their own reasoning and discussions (Hult News, 2014). In a world of generative Artificial Intelligence (AI), using a mix of sources for non-standard cases also means that students can use AI tools to help with their research but are less likely to get a 'ready-made answer', assuming the lecturer varies their example situation or scenario.

When considered in this broad way, teaching with cases may seem like a standard approach to teaching economics. Open any textbook, or attend any economics class, and you will find examples discussed alongside the theory, perhaps linked to the lecturer's own research. Learning through cases is different. It is not about 'hearing' what others have done or reading someone else's summary of a situation. It is about examining the situation yourself and having to decide how best to connect what you are learning to the situation. The methodology used is very similar to that associated with teaching with media. Each type of 'case' – fiction and non-fiction – provides a useful base for developing application skills (Safapour et al., 2019).

Teaching with cases can stimulate the higher-order learning associated with Bloom's categories of analysis, synthesis, and evaluation (Persaud, 2023). These levels can be difficult for students as they are often faced with a lot of information that is not produced in a way that is directly related to the course material. They need to step back from what they have been taught, and what they think they already know, and consider how to use their knowledge to evaluate a situation.

Given how difficult the task is, there is significant value in working with others. Diversity of skills, ideas and lived experiences will enrich the solution and the process of getting to it (Swanson et al., 2019). The task is big and time consuming, and dividing it between a team can reduce the workload for an individual. Being able to talk through a situation with peers also allows students to see that nobody knows the answer at the outset, reducing potential stress.

Team-Based Learning and case teaching go hand in hand. The value of working in groups depends on having an appropriate question to engage with (Gibbs, 2009; Van Rheede and Oudtshoorn, 2004). The value of working with cases is that student-led perspectives within the group guide the analysis (Hult News, 2014). Teaching with cases delivers the benefits of both team-working and problem-based learning.

HOW CAN YOU TEACH ECONOMICS WITH CASES?

With this broad definition of 'teaching with cases' in mind, there are several different approaches to get students actively working in teams on concrete situations that link to core course materials. Those we have used in economics teaching are shown in Figure 10.1. Details of what each type of case teaching involves are provided in the Boxes 10.1–10.4.

The approaches vary in terms of how formal the 'case learning' is, whether the case learning happens in a live class or asynchronously and how much independent work students are required to do. What is common throughout is that students are actively thinking about and talking about a case, making the connections between the case and the economics theory and empirical methods they are learning. These approaches work well in a campus-based or online setting. We discuss in the next section particular things to consider when undertaking this form of teaching online. Here we focus on the methods in general (see Boxes 10.1–10.4).

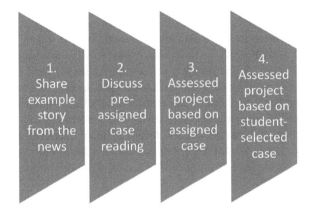

Figure 10.1   Types of case teaching in economics

BOX 10.1   SHARE AN EXAMPLE STORY FROM THE NEWS

Activity
Ask students every week to identify one recent news story that they see connects to the topic studied that week. They must explain the connection. The sharing can happen in a live class or on a discussion forum. The lecturer provides feedback live or on the forum, summarising the ideas using language and concepts from the course material. At the end of the course the students have a library of current real-world examples to connect to.

Nature of Team-Based Learning
The pre-work for this activity is informal and completed by students individually, although there is nothing to stop them discussing news stories with peers. Students get ideas from what is shared, in a live class or discussion forum.

Most relevant learning outcomes
- Explain connections between cases and models.
- Identify good quality sources of information.
- Compare and contrast experiences in different parts of the world, sectors, points in history.
- Communicate ideas with others.

Examples of use by author

Final-year undergraduate, Economics of Money and Banking module (100 students): At the start of all live classes, students were asked to give an example of something in the news that related to what we had worked on the previous week. After class, the lecturer shared links to some of the most relevant stories introduced by students in an open access document.

Final-year undergraduate, Economics of Regulation module (80 students): Students, studying remotely during the pandemic across the globe, were asked in an online discussion forum to share examples of a recent news story relating to one regulated sector from the country where they were born. Throughout the module the lecturer cross-referred to the examples provided in the forum.

BOX 10.2   DISCUSS PRE-ASSIGNED CASE READING

Activity

Give students a short case to read (e.g., an *Economist* or reputable newspaper article) and tell them in advance the questions that they will be discussing in live class or on a discussion forum. The assigned questions require them to use the economics concepts and models from the course to critically examine the case and to identify where they think theory is not sufficient for analysing the situation.

Nature of Team-Based Learning

The pre-work for this activity is completed by students individually, although there is nothing to stop them discussing the article with peers. Students can share their responses to the questions in class through plenary discussion (vocalised or in the chat), small group discussion (in breakout rooms online), or by commenting on the ideas of others on a discussion forum.

Most relevant learning outcomes
* Same as for 'Share an Example from the News'.
* Connect case and theory.
* Critically analyse the value and limits of economic theory.

Examples of use by author

Final-year undergraduate, Economics of Competition Policy (anti-trust) module (80 students): Students read a short *Economist* article on Uber before live class and were told they would be discussing whether Uber was good for competition in the taxi market or not. They first voted in a poll and then were asked to share ideas from the article, and their knowledge of the course material, on what the main factors to consider were. Ideas were shared verbally or in the chat. The lecturer wrote up the market features that came up in discussion on a shared document, summarising the connections to model assumptions.

MSc Economics, Economics of Public Policy (30 students): Students were asked to read two short blog-style commentaries on a recent tax policy announcement ahead of a live class. They were told that in class we would discuss which commentary was most convincing and why. Students shared their ideas in the class discussion, first in breakout rooms and then sharing those discussions with the whole cohort. The lecturer kept track of the points raised in a shared document which students could access afterwards for a summary of what they had read and what they thought made a policy review convincing, or not.

BOX 10.3   ASSESSED PROJECT ON AN ASSIGNED CASE

Activity
Give students a policy or commercial decision to analyse and ask them to produce an output on that case. The output can be a written report, a blog, a wiki, a live presentation, or a video presentation. The output requires a synopsis of the case. Students are also asked to compare what evaluation others have done on the case to what their knowledge of economics suggests could be done, considering why there might be a difference. Students should consider the context of the case and the availability of data and wider evidence.

Nature of Team-Based Learning
This is an assessed project that students work on in teams away from live sessions. They are provided with a starting link for their assigned case, for example a government report or an annual corporate report. Each team needs to work out for themselves how they want to work together, both in terms of the research required and the production of the final output. Office hour support is available and there are a small number of live classes where teams work on specific angles of the project with the lecturer available to answer any questions.

Most relevant learning outcomes

- Same as for 'Discuss pre-assigned case reading'.
- Learn how to extract most relevant material from lengthy documents and summarise for audience.
- Compare how markets are analysed in the real world with what economic models suggest.
- Critically appraise the approach taken by 'experts'.
- Appreciate the practical limitations of analysis undertaken in short time-frames and with imperfect data.
- Work in a team to collect and analyse information about the case.

Examples of use by author

Final-year undergraduate, Economics of Regulation module (80 students): Students are allocated to teams and each team is assigned a regulated sector (e.g., Northern Ireland gas transmission). They are provided with a link to a published regulatory decision for that sector. Each team produces a 10-minute video summarising the reasons why the sector is regulated and how it is regulated. They explain their points using economics concepts from the course. They also write a 3,000-word report analysing how the approach to regulation in the sector compares to the textbook models discussed in the course. This project has been completed by students on campus and fully online.

MSc Economics and Strategy for Business, Economics of Public Policy module (180 students): Students are allocated to teams and each team is asked to choose one policy to work on from a list of five provided. The policies relate to course material and span different policy areas and different countries. Each team writes a report (60% of mark) explaining what the policy is and why it was introduced, using their knowledge of the economics of market failures. Then each student writes a short individual review (40% of mark) on the extent to which economics informed the design and implementation of the policy. This project has been completed with students learning in hybrid format and fully on campus. In both scenarios they had the freedom to decide whether to meet online or in person as a team.

BOX 10.4 ASSESSED PROJECT ON A STUDENT-SELECTED CASE

Activity

Students are asked to identify a case themselves, with criteria provided to ensure their choice is relevant to the course. They produce an output linked to that case. This can be a written report, a blog, a wiki, a live presentation, or a video presentation. The output requires both a synopsis of the case and an evaluation of how economics can be used to analyse the case. Students apply the economics they are learning to the case.

Nature of Team-Based Learning
The team element of this activity is largely the same as for the activity where the case is assigned. The extra dimension is working together to identify a case they can all agree on. This step requires negotiation, persuasion, prioritisation, and compromise skills to be developed from the outset. Students value advice from the lecturer on how best to choose cases to help shape these discussions. The most important thing is finding a case that is doable.

Most relevant learning outcomes
- Same as for 'Assessed project on an assigned case'.
- Identify suitable cases that interest the team and are doable.
- Critically analyse commentaries from economists, incorporating their work with the ideas of the team.
- Negotiate professionally with teammates on choice of case and how to prioritise work.

Examples of use by author
Executive MBA, Economics for Business module (30 students): Students are allocated to a team and asked to analyse the relationship between real wages and labour productivity in a country they choose. They are expected to choose the country, find the data, and research literature. The output is a 2,000-word written report. Students work away from live classes and decide for themselves how to meet. As this is a blended degree, they are generally working in different parts of the world when doing the project.

Third-year undergraduate students taking a year in Business as part of their science or engineering degree, Management Economics Online module (220 students): This online module is taken by students from different degrees, with varied backgrounds, motivations, and timetables. Students are allocated to a team and asked to choose a market and analyse the factors that affect competition in that market. They are required to identify and explain relevant economic theory and empirical evidence. The output is a 1,500-word written report. Students decide for themselves how to meet and co-produce the output together.

First-year undergraduate, Economics capstone assessment (500+ students): Whilst working remotely, in late Spring 2020 when the Covid-19 pandemic first disrupted universities, the assessment for first-year students was changed from a set of coursework and exams to a single capstone piece of work. Students were asked to identify a research question linked to a theme such as inequality, climate change, or macroeconomic crisis. They had to explain how what they had learnt in their first-year compulsory modules (maths, statistics, economics and applied economics) could be used to help them answer the question. The output was a 1,500-word report. Students were given detailed written guidelines, including a template to use for their answers, and bespoke online office hours were held for students to check their understanding of what was required. Students worked on their own.

These four types of activities could of course be extended and adapted in many ways. They can be used in a wide range of economics courses, given the broad nature of what a 'case' can mean and the fact that across economics topics there is always an appropriate application. Whatever the course, the questions a lecturer needs to consider when deciding on what case to use and how to incorporate it into their teaching include:

- How deep do you want the case discussion and analysis to be?
- How much time do you expect students to spend on this activity, commensurate with the learning expected on the whole module?
- Is it best for students to work on the case on their own or in teams?
- Is there value in asking students to find their own case rather than assigning one?
- Is it best for the case work to be assessed or not?
- What type of materials are available for this type of activity in the field and how suitable are they for the way the module is taught and the level of the learner?

The answers to those questions will guide the lecturer to a design for their case teaching which allows for the details to be determined within a clear framework. These different types of case activities are not mutually exclusive. Indeed, there can be value in having more than one approach in a module or at least across modules to give students more practice at this method of learning.

As this chapter is about case teaching rather than teamwork, we have not spent time discussing the opportunities and challenges of getting students to work together, in classroom discussion and assessed assignments. For insights on Team-Based Learning, read Chapter 11 of this book. Students often find working in this way to be outside their comfort zone and need reassurance to be willing to put in the effort required. They need to understand why they are working in teams rather than on their own, and why that helps with case analysis. It is also important to consider the diversity of students when designing the activity, allowing for flexibility where possible and more support where not. Familiarising yourself with tips on how to design teamwork, and how to support students with teamwork, will make the activity more effective for learning (Gratton and Erickson, 2007; Mellor, 2015). Thinking about how best to design the teamwork element of the activity can take the focus off 'teamwork concerns' and back to the case analysis itself, for the lecturer and the students.

How to Make Case Teaching Effective Online

The different approaches to teaching cases can all be used when teaching on campus or online. The content of the case and the learning activity is largely the same. What varies is the specification of what students need to do and where. Here we consider specific aspects of design to enhance learning when teaching online, making a distinction between live interactions, when the lecturer and students are present simultaneously, and asynchronous interactions, where the students and the lecturer engage with activity in their own time, not in an allotted time slot.

Whether on campus or online it is important to consider the phases of the case activity, as illustrated in Figure 10.2.

Figure 10.2   Phases of case activity

For the case activity planning, a key decision to make as a lecturer is how to arrange the timing of the case and the timing of learning of theory. One option is to go with the case activity first, allowing students to discover ideas relevant to the theory. The alternative is to teach the theory first, asking students to connect specific theories they have learnt to the case. There is value in introducing the economics first if it will enhance the discussion on the case; and value in waiting if it makes the discussion narrow, overly focused on pre-learnt theory. If there are asynchronous activities – reading or watching videos – it is possible to break the learning up around an application case. For example, a high-level introduction of relevant theory can be provided before a case, followed by the case activity, and bringing in deeper analytical materials after.

For the case activity pre-work, it is most important that students are given clear instructions about what to do and by when. When online, student learning is enhanced if they fully understand what is expected of them given the more limited opportunity to ask questions. It is also harder for a lecturer to see if students are confused and make amendments to the instructions given to manage this. Lecturers should ensure they provide simple instructions and consider the value of how these are delivered – for example through video or written or both – and whether it is best to provide all information upfront or break into chunks (Savery, 2005).

The team interaction phase is the central point of learning for larger case projects. There are two elements of interaction to consider, interaction between peers in the team and interaction between the team and the rest of the class including the lecturer. When online, particularly if the team members do not know each other outside of the course, there is merit in providing a structure for them to meet and having a live event for the lecturer to check that teams have made contact. This could be as simple as establishing a platform 'norm' (e.g., MS Teams) for them to use, whilst allowing them to move to another platform if that is their preference. The live session – a class or a synchronous discussion forum – can be designed to require teams to work together on a specific case-related question, perhaps breaking down a large case and asking the team to connect it to a specific aspect of the course material. For maximum interaction it is important that the questions are posed in a way that facilitates different answers. Students can share what they have learnt in polls, online shared documents, comments on a forum or vocally in a live session. This method works best when there is a fixed window over which comments are posted to ensure genuine in-the-moment interaction. Providing lecturer-led support, such as online office hours, can help clarify uncertainties.

Case activities require participation by the lecturer and the students. The role of the lecturer is most clear in a live online class, resembling most closely what happens in a campus case activity. When activities are asynchronous or live in a discussion forum the lecturer needs to ensure that they are present and that their presence is valued by the students (Savery, 2005). As would happen in a campus classroom, the lecturer should moderate and guide discussion, helping the students connect ideas and helping them to align the case and theory by making links to what has been taught before and what is to come. Lecturer-led engagement can encourage student participation but additional incentives may be needed. Participation marking is one option. This requires a transparent and well-understood way of marking both the quantity and quality of engagement. An alternative related approach would be to have a linked activity, like a quiz or a short individual reflection on the case, that students can only get high marks in if they have engaged with the case. These activities help with the case-related activity and can enhance learning more generally (Argyriou et al., 2022).

The post-interaction phase is where students take their learning from the case activity and feed it forward to other learning. This could be in the module itself, in other modules or in wider areas of their professional life. Having a summary of what was discussed – e.g., the output of a forum, a shared document, or answers to a poll question – can provide a useful recap. Providing students with example exam questions or other questions that require them to use what they learnt from the case activity can help prompt their reflection. The lecturer reminding the students of what came out of their interactions on the case activity and connecting it to other topics in a course is also a useful mechanism for embedding the learning.

Table 10.1 provides an illustration of how these phases of case design could be organised for each of the four types of case activity when delivered online. There are of course variations on what could be done, depending on the objectives of the lecturer, the background and size of the cohort, and the role of the case activity in learning on the module.

Table 10.1   *Ideas on how to organise different types of case activities*

	Share news example	Discuss pre-assigned case	Assessed case project, with assigned case	Assessed case project, with student-chosen case
Preparation	Weekly reminder (email or forum) to post example online	Asynchronous video at start of term explaining role of case activity in course. For each case, email or forum post providing link to case online and document explaining questions to consider.	Instructions on case project in writing and asynchronous video. Guidance on working in teams online. Example output from previous year's students.	As for assessed project with assigned case. Additional guidance on selecting case with opportunity for feedback on ideas in office hours.
Pre-work	Students find an example in own time each week and share on online platform.	Students read case and prepare ideas on questions in own time.	n.a.	Potentially task to submit chosen case for approval

	Share news example	Discuss pre-assigned case	Assessed case project, with assigned case	Assessed case project, with student-chosen case
Interaction	Asynchronous: lecturer adds comments to shared examples, and peers encouraged to comment. Live class: lecturer summarises examples shared online and asks for volunteers to explain choice. Live discussion forum: lecturer and students pose comments and reply to them in interactive online forum.	Asynchronous discussion forum: thread for each case question. Students post their responses and comment on each other's. Lecturer contributes comments as well. Live class: breakout rooms for small groups to share ideas on case. Nominated spokesperson feeds back. Ideas from each room shared through plenary discussion, meeting chat and/or contribution to shared document. Live discussion forum: as for online class, but discussion happens in forum at whole class level, not in teams. Potential for team discussion if separate forums for different groups but can become complex.	Students meet away from lecturer-led time. Provide meeting platform default, for example, MS Teams, and deadline to meet for first time. Allow students to find their own approach to meeting after first meeting on suggested platform or elsewhere. Discussion forum and online office hours for support. Opportunities to ask questions and discuss linked material in any live sessions.	As for assessed project with assigned case

	Share news example	Discuss pre-assigned case	Assessed case project, with assigned case	Assessed case project, with student-chosen case
Participation	Incentive to find and share examples comes from requirement to have examples in coursework. This activity provides a way of crowd-sourcing relevant examples. Student engagement is observable by lecturer who can approach those who don't engage to check that all is okay.	Incentive to share comes from discussing with peers and close link to course material. Participation marks for contributing helpful idea in live discussion and/or on discussion forum can help with engagement.	Working on project is the main form of participation. Scope to have peer feedback on individual engagement with team effort, with adjusted mark for outstanding or poor peer feedback. Part of output could be presentation that allows for observing individual effort.	As for assessed project with assigned case. Marking criteria could include recognition for interesting and/or creative choice of case.
Post-interaction	Students have access to shared examples, with lecturer annotations/additions to put student suggestion into context of course. Assessment marking criteria include credit for use of relevant examples.	Students have access to shared answers on the case questions, with context and broader perspective added by the lecturer. This could be the discussion forum, pdf of poll answers, or shared document.	Consider sharing project outputs within class to allow everyone to learn from each other's. Having the whole class attend presentations or watch videos can help.	As for assessed project with assigned case.

As with all active learning and assessment strategies there is a lot of upfront work on the part of the lecturer to ensure that the use of cases delivers on the desirable learning outcomes and works effectively in the time available for the course. The returns, in terms of student engagement, student learning and lecturer learning from students, will generally outweigh the upfront cost over time. Being patient with yourself and students, as you all grapple with finding the best way to learn with cases online, is key to success.

REFLECTION ON WHY TO TEACH WITH CASES ONLINE

Teaching with cases brings benefits for both students and teachers in an economics course, with lecturer-student and student-student co-learning. There are set-up and running costs, both for the case activities and the design of wider materials. Once set up, based on this author's experience, the benefits of teaching with cases are significant and outweigh the upfront costs.

Students develop a deeper understanding of economics. This comes from being asked to identify connections to real world situations, to explain and critically analyse the connections and to explicitly use the theory in the context of the cases. As one student noted in feedback, 'The case study groups and methods are particularly effective in making the material more interesting and in encouraging you to think in different ways...makes it easier to learn and remember material'. The deeper understanding can lead to a greater interest in the subject.

Alumni also emphasise that the experience of using economics in the context of the case was very valuable practice for what they do at work. One graduate wrote to say, 'I've been referring to my notes from the ... module ... It's been very cool to translate the lectures into real-life work'. Similarly, students often recognise that interview questions are similar in style to cases, where they are asked to think on their feet and discuss an unfamiliar situation. This connection can make them more confident in these discussions.

As a lecturer, the main value of teaching with cases is that you learn a lot from student insights. The discussion of an open-ended case tends to be rich and diverse. Students are more engaged with what can often be seen as the drier material, for example derivations of model results, when they have an appreciation of the model usefulness.

These benefits are maximised when the lecturer invests the time to prepare for teaching with cases. The priority is designing clear instructions for students, and regularly reminding them of what is expected and why. Students need to know that the case learning, even if it appears informal, is an integrated part of their learning. For the cases that are discussed in class, or that provide the basis for assessment, the lecturer also needs to find recent cases and ensure they relate to the course content. Regular updating of cases is needed to keep the activity relevant.

It is also crucial to have the instructions for any assessed projects, including the marking criteria, ready at the start of term so that students and the lecturer have a shared understanding of what is required and can discuss any queries through the term. There is also a task of providing feedback on student input on the cases. For ideas that are contributed to forums, polls or in live discussions the lecturer needs to provide timely responses to shared thoughts and connect comments into an overarching class perspective on the case or cases. Supplementing asynchronous activities with opportunities to discuss live is an important way of providing feedback on student ideas, and ensuring students hear each other's and lecturer's ideas together. That live session can be online in a meeting, online synchronously in a discussion forum or in a lecture room on campus.

Online delivery has not curtailed any of the approaches that this author used mainly in person before the pandemic. A lot of the work was done outside the classroom and online tools like polls, discussion forums and shared documents enhanced and expanded the ways to share ideas. Many of these tools continue to be used in campus-based courses. Teaching with cases online works well, with all the value of experiential learning using cases and all the flexibility that allows students to adapt their learning to their context by being online.

REFERENCES

ABL Connect Harvard (2023). Make real world connections to course material. https:// ablconnect .harvard .edu/ make -real -world -connections -course -material #: ~: text = By %20providing %20real %2Dworld %20applications ,professionals %20in %20the %20field%20encounter.

Argyriou P, Benamar K, and Nikolajeva, M (2022). What to Blend? Exploring the Relationship Between Student Engagement and Academic Achievement via a Blended Learning Approach. Psychology Learning & Teaching, 21(2), 126–137. https://doi.org/10.1177/14757257221091512

Bhandari P (2020). Skills that employers who hire UCL SHS students are looking for, CTaLE Working Paper. https:// ctaleatucl.files.wordpress.com/ 2020/ 09/ skills -that -employers-who-hire-shs-graduates-are-looking-for_final-report.pdf

Bonney KM (2015). Case Study Teaching Method Improves Student Performance and Perceptions of Learning Gains. Journal of Microbiology & Biology Education, May, 21–28. http://dx.doi.org/10.1128/jmbe.v16i1.846

Case Centre (2023). Online case teaching. https://www.thecasecentre.org/caseTeaching/ guidance/onlineCaseTeaching

Columbia Center for Teaching and Learning (2023). Case Method Teaching and Learning. https:// ctl .columbia .edu/ resources -and -technology/ resources/ case -method/

Dalrymple R, Macrae A, Maïa Pal M, Shipman S (2021). Employability: a review of the literature 2016–2021. Advance HE Report. https://www.advance-he.ac.uk/knowledge-hub/employability-review-literature-2016–2021

Gibbs G (2009). The assessment of group work: lessons from the literature. Assessment Standards Knowledge Exchange. https://citeseerx.ist.psu.edu/document?repid=rep1&type=pdf&doi=008f41f48e442993736bafb12b66f67c732f2816

Gratton L and Erickson TJ (2007). Eight ways to build collaborative teams. Harvard Business Review. https://hbr.org/2007/11/eight-ways-to-build-collaborative-teams

Hoyt GM (2017). Great ideas for making economic principles relevant and engaging: A three-paper symposium from D Cutler, D Karlan, and C Rouse. The Journal of Economic Education, 48(3), 216–217. DOI: 10.1080/00220485.2017.1320615

Hult News (2014). The case study method or why 'Experience is the best teacher'. Hult Blog. https://www.hult.edu/blog/experience-is-the-best-teacher/#:~:text=If%20used%20correctly%2C%20it%20can,strategy%2C%20Hult%20International%20Business%20School

Jenkins C (2020). Desirable employability skills: a literature review of what the skills mean. CTaLE Working Paper. https://ctaleatucl.files.wordpress.com/2020/09/ctale-working-paper_literature-review-on-employability-skills.pdf

Jenkins C and Lane S (2019). Employability Skills in UK Economics Degrees. Economics Network Research Paper. https://economicsnetwork.ac.uk/research/employability/executivesummary

Mahdi OR, Nassar IA and Almuslamani HA (2020). The Role of Using Case Studies Method in Improving Students' Critical Thinking Skills in Higher Education. International Journal of Higher Education, 9(2), 297–308. https://doi.org/10.5430/ijhe.v9n2p297

McLellan, H (2004). The Case for Case-Based Teaching in Online Classes Educational Technology, 44(4), 14–18. http://www.jstor.org/stable/44428918

Mellor T (2015). Group work assessment: some key considerations in developing good practice. Planet, 25(1), 16–20. https://www.tandfonline.com/doi/full/10.11120/plan.2012.00250016

Nohria N (2019). What the case study method really teaches. Harvard Business Review. https://hbr.org/2021/12/what-the-case-study-method-really-teaches

Persaud C (2023). Bloom's Taxonomy: the ultimate guide. Top Hat Blog. https://tophat.com/blog/blooms-taxonomy/

Puri S (2022) Effective learning through the case method. Innovations in Education and Teaching International, 59(2), 161–171. https://www.tandfonline.com/doi/full/10.1080/14703297.2020.1811133

Safapour E, Kermanshachi S, Taneja P (2019). A Review of Nontraditional Teaching Methods: Flipped Classroom, Gamification, Case Study, Self-Learning, and Social Media. Education Sciences, 9, 273. https://doi.org/10.3390/educsci9040273

Savery JR (2005). BE VOCAL: Characteristics of Successful Online Instructors. Journal of Interactive Online Learning, 4(2), 141–152. https://www.ncolr.org/issues/jiol/v4/n2/be-vocal-characteristics-of-successful-online-instructors.html

Servant-Miklos VFC (2019). The Harvard Connection: How the Case Method Spawned Problem-Based Learning at McMaster University. Health Professionals Education, 5(3), 163–171 https://doi.org/10.1016/j.hpe.2018.07.004

Swanson E, McCulley LV, Osman, DJ, Scammacca Lewis N, and Solis M (2019). The effect of team-based learning on content knowledge: A meta-analysis. Active Learning in Higher Education, 20(1), 39–50. https://doi.org/10.1177/1469787417731201

Tambe N (2023). Top 20 Skills that Employers look for in candidates. Forbes Advisor. https://www.forbes.com/advisor/in/business/top-skills-to-get-a-job/

Van Rheede GP and Oudtshoorn V (2004). Group work in higher education: a mismanaged evil or a potential good?: perspectives on higher education. South African Journal of Higher Education, 18(2), 131–1489. https://journals.co.za/doi/epdf/10.10520/EJC37075

Volpe G (2002). Teaching with case studies. Economics Network Handbook. https://www.economicsnetwork.ac.uk/handbook/casestudies/

Wooten J, Al-Bahrani A, Holder K and Patel D (2021). The role of relevance in economics education: a survey. Journal for Economic Educators, 21(1), 11–31. https://libjournals.mtsu.edu/index.php/jfee/article/view/2025/1231

11. Teaching online with Team-Based Learning

Phil Ruder

INTRODUCTION

In order to engage students and promote learning in any course, instructors must adopt a structure that guides students to interact productively with the material, with each other, and with the instructor. An effective course structure is particularly important in an online environment where students can feel isolated and distractions beckon. Including frequent interactive learning exercises in a course can boost student engagement, though instructors must take care to ensure that the exercises focus student and instructor efforts in a manner that maximizes learning (Oliveira, Tinoca and Pereira 2011). Team-Based Learning (TBL) pedagogy offers an online course structure that leads to high student engagement and learning by offering students a high incentive to prepare independently for each course learning activity, regular opportunities to engage with course content in a small-group setting, frequent class-wide interactions, and prompt feedback from instructor and peers on their efforts in the course.

Garrison, Anderson and Archer (1999) identify the three elements of a Community of Inquiry that are necessary for an online educational experience of high quality. Participants must have a high level of *cognitive* and *social presence* and the instructor must have an effective *teaching presence*. Cognitive presence refers to the sustained effort by students to construct meaning from course materials and from their communication with peers and instructor. Social presence arises from frequent student opportunities to express their own knowledge, experiences and personalities to peers and to an instructor who are listening, providing feedback, and sharing of themselves. Teaching presence refers to both the instructor's design of the educational experience and her ongoing facilitation of learning activities to promote student cognitive and social presence.

TBL offers a structure that elicits sustained student cognitive and social presence in an online course by building a high level of individual accountability for both learning course material and interacting productively in group activities (Restall and Clark 2021). Instructor-created teams undertake activities designed carefully both to develop student mastery of the material under study and to foster team work skills. Regular timely feedback on student efforts both to learn course concepts and to engage with their group supports students' skill development. Freeman et al. (2014) document learning gains in STEM classes that feature frequent social learning activities. Haidet, Kubitz and McCormack (2014) report that TBL classes lead to student learning gains. The empirical literature on the effect of active learning pedagogy in general and TBL in particular in online courses remains in its infancy.

After student orientation, each of the six or seven modules of a TBL course follows the same learning sequence. Modules begin with a Readiness Assurance Process (RAP) in which students first work independently to learn basic concepts and applications, next take low-stakes individual and team quizzes with immediate feedback, and then receive direct instruction on the relatively difficult foundational concepts in the unit. The next phases of the learning sequence involve multiple "4S" application exercises (AEs) that each require students to apply concepts in the unit to a *significant* real-world example. All teams work on the *same* problem, which requires that teams make a *specific choice*; team choices are revealed *simultaneously* before a class-wide discussion among team reporters. The instructor facilitates the class discussion carefully to focus attention on key learning objectives and then closes each exercise by highlighting the lessons learned.

The emphasis in TBL classes on the application of course concepts to the concrete examples in the application exercises makes the pedagogy particularly useful in economics classes, where the struggle to help students master the technical aspects of the models under study often takes precedence over development of student intuition about "real-world" events. The regular in-team and class-wide discussions of economic concepts in a TBL class complement the direct instruction and individual effort on problem sets and exams that emphasize important computational skills.

Each module of a TBL course concludes with formative peer evaluations in which teammates assess each other's efforts in the group by assigning numerical scores on several aspects of performance and provide comments on teammate strengths and areas in which improvement could occur. Each student receives average scores and qualitative feedback.[1]

Implementing TBL in a fully synchronous online class poses similar challenges as those encountered in the traditional face-to-face mode. Michaelsen, Knight and Fink (2004), Sibley et al. (2014) and Sibley (2018) provide helpful general introductions to TBL. Ruder, Maier and Simkins (2021) offer guidance for implementing TBL in economics classes.

The asynchronous and hybrid online TBL course modes present unique logistical challenges. Given the need to expand the time allowed for the distinct steps in the TBL sequence in an asynchronous mode, completing a module in two weeks' time is difficult because all students and teams must complete each step before the next step can take place. This chapter suggests ways to achieve the learning gains available from adopting the highly structured TBL pedagogy in asynchronous and hybrid online courses while preserving some of the scheduling flexibility that students value. The next section discusses the first moments of a TBL course. Subsequent sections focus in turn on how to conduct the RAP online, the logistics of managing AEs online, an AE example, and the online peer feedback process.

ORIENTING STUDENTS AND MAKING TEAMS

Instructors must explain and demonstrate the TBL approach carefully to students as the course begins. Clark et al. (2021) recommend dedicating the first module of an asynchronous online TBL course to student and team orientation in order to provide students with information about the TBL structure itself as well as how content will be learned. During the first moments of the course, instructors will also form the teams and give them their first opportunities to work together. As in any course, student and instructor introductions will take place during orientation.

Costa and Pacansky-Brock (2020) offer excellent advice for communicating with students by means of short videos posted to the course Learning Management System (LMS). Darby and Lang (2019) and Boettcher and Conrad (2021) provide useful general guidance for teaching online and emphasize the importance of student first impressions in an online course. Given the importance of scheduled due dates for individual and team work in an online TBL course, instructors must be sure to communicate the required timing of course work throughout the semester with checklists and video reminders at the course LMS.

Team formation poses an orientation challenge specific to teaching strategies like TBL that rely on fixed, instructor-created teams. Forming the teams that will work together all semester must be accomplished in a transparent process that distributes diverse student resources across all teams. I have developed a process for making teams in an online course that mimics the first meetings of my face-to-face classes. I follow the recommendation by Clark et al. (2021) to send students an email before the course begins for the purpose of introducing myself and the course. In that letter, I direct students to the welcome activity at the LMS where I have students make and post video introductions. I also ask students to complete a very short survey in which I ask them the name by which they prefer to be addressed, their pronouns, and their intended major (I ask undecided first-year students to make their best guess). Then, to make teams, either in the first synchronous section or in a screencast, I project a spreadsheet with student first names and intended majors and, as students watch, I sort the list first by academic major and then by first name. I then add a column of repeating team numbers one through the number of teams.[2] I conclude the exercises by sorting the list by team number to get the team rosters for the entire semester that I then post on the LMS.[3]

When I conduct a synchronous orientation session, I launch breakout rooms immediately after forming teams for teammate introductions and several activities. The first activity asks students to evaluate past experiences working with groups and then develop ground rules for their work together in the course. The second activity has teams consider which learning activities should be prioritized during synchronous sessions and which should be accomplished by students working independently (Balan, Clark and Restall 2015).

In asynchronous classes, the teammate introductions can occur by means of an LMS discussion forum that is private to the team. I suggest giving teams the option of conducting this and other team activities throughout the course by means of synchronous videoconferencing sessions that they schedule themselves. Some instructors require teams to turn in recordings of such sessions. I generally specify the required output of the team work together and allow the teams to keep their synchronous sessions private. The orientation activities also take place by means of discussion forums or private team meetings.

THE READINESS ASSURANCE PROCESS (RAP)

The readiness assurance process (RAP) ensures that students ready themselves for the subsequent learning activities of the module. While individual preparation often consists of textbook readings, Dorius et al. (2021) suggest that in an asynchronous class it is important for instructors to shift some student preparation away from readings and toward preparation activities such as videos, podcasts, recorded lectures, simulations and games that take advantage of the expanded possibilities of the online mode. Preparation assignments that include engaging examples are particularly important in economics, where textbook readings tend to be highly abstract. Dorius et al. (2021) point out that a tool like the one offered by Thinkspace (thinkspace.org) can organize, scaffold, and build expert feedback into preparatory tasks for students. Danielson et al. (2006) found evidence that requiring students to complete regular summary tasks as they prepare leads to increased learning. Instructors can elevate the social and teaching presence embodied in reading assignments by using software tools like Perusall (perusall.com) or Hypothes.is (web.hypothes.is) to enable students to annotate texts, place their questions in the context of specific passages, and discuss key points in the reading with peers and instructor in the document under study. Miller et al. (2018) describe how social annotation platforms can enhance student pre-class reading assignments.

Instructors administer individual quizzes on basic student knowledge and comprehension online quite easily within the LMS or other tools. Dorius et al. (2021) suggest that individual RAP quizzes can be open-book and that imposing tight time limits for the quiz can maintain the student incentive to prepare carefully before taking the quiz. When the team RAP quiz is different from the individual quiz, student quiz scores and the correct answers can be revealed just before the team quiz. In my classes, I use the LMS to give each student a somewhat different quiz to limit the usefulness of shared screenshots.

The RAP in Asynchronous Courses

The team RAP quiz presents a scheduling challenge in an asynchronous class. The team quiz that happens in 20 action-packed minutes in a synchronous class must be stretched out in the asynchronous mode. Table 11.1 presents a possible timeline for a two-week module that could be expanded for longer modules. Instructors can implement the sequence using the course LMS alone, perhaps supplemented with additional tools as described below, or by means of a TBL support program such as those offered by InteDashboard (intedashboard.com) and FeedbackFruits (feedbackfruits.com/team-based-learning).

Palsolé and Awalt (2008) developed the 48-hour duration of the team RAP quiz that Table 11.1 depicts. At the beginning of the team quiz period – at the beginning of day 3 in Table 11.1 – the instructor posts the quiz. Because of the difficulty of conducting the discussion of RAP team quiz questions by means of LMS group discussion forums, I recommend a team quiz with just three or four questions.[4] The short team quiz should consist entirely of low- and medium-level application questions that will pose teams a greater challenge than students will have faced on the individual quiz. LMS quizzes can be set up to give students immediate feedback on whether their answer is correct and allow additional attempts on missed questions. Teams receive reduced credit when they need additional attempts to get the questions right.

Palsolé and Awalt (2008) recommend designating a team leader for the RAP team quiz on a rotating basis. The team leader submits the team's quiz answers at the LMS. Palsolé and Awalt (2008) require the team leader to document the team discussion of each RAP quiz question and post a synopsis of the team's reasoning for each choice. Prompt instructor feedback on the team leader's post that is directed specifically to the team conveys to students the instructor's attentiveness to their efforts.

Table 11.1   Sequence of events in a two-week asynchronous online TBL class

Days	1–2	3–4	5–7	8–9	10	11	12–13	14
Event	Individual prep and RAP quiz	Team RAP quiz	RAP challenges and individual prep work for 2–3 AEs	Team makes specific choices, produces any required exhibit and drafts rationales	Individual responses to other team choices	Team response to other team choices	Threaded class discussion of choices and responses	Peer evaluation

At the conclusion of the RAP quiz – the end of day 4 in Table 11.1 – the instructor posts explanatory videos on the most challenging concepts in the module and to respond to individual RAP quiz questions that were frequently missed, team quiz questions that required multiple attempts, and issues arising in the team leader explanations.

In TBL courses, students are allowed to consult course resources and other materials to make written challenges of individual or team quiz questions that they perceive to have more than one correct answer, have no correct answer, or require knowledge that is not reasonable to expect students to have. Any challenges that teams decide to make can be drafted and submitted before day seven in the suggested timeline in Table 11.1. Students can communicate about the challenge at the same discussion forum as they did for the team RAP quiz (or in a synchronous video conference). The team RAP quiz leader takes responsibility for writing and submitting the challenge.

The RAP in Hybrid Courses

I define a hybrid online course as one where the class meeting time has been reduced (relative to that of a synchronous online course) by shifting some learning activities to an asynchronous mode. One approach to teaching a hybrid online TBL class is to reduce synchronous class time by half or more, meeting weekly to conduct the learning activities that either must happen at the same time or involve whole-class communication. Table 11.2 depicts a recommended sequence of events in such a weekly hybrid class model. Students prepare textbook readings, videos, podcasts, etc., individually before taking an online individual quiz just before the first synchronous meeting of each module. In that first meeting, teams take the RAP team quiz and participate in an interactive lecture on key concepts. Teams compose any challenges asynchronously within a week of the first class.

The integrated online Team-Based Learning (IO TBL) offers an alternative hybrid approach in which a single synchronous class session occurs at the beginning of each course module, approximately every two or three weeks (Parrish, Williams and Estis 2021). The one synchronous session in an IO TBL course is identical to the first of the two meetings presented in Table 11.2 for a hybrid course that meets weekly. Students take the team quiz and receive instructor explanations in a synchronous session. The instructor conducts the AEs in an IO TBL course as they would in an asynchronous course. The IO TBL approach retains more of the flexible timing of an asynchronous course, but loses the student interaction offered by a synchronous whole-class discussion of the application exercises.

Table 11.2   Sequence of events in a two-week hybrid online TBL module with weekly synchronous meetings

Days	1–2	3	4	5–8	9–11	12	13–14
In-class	-	Class 1: Team quiz and instructor explanations	-	-	-	Class 2: Reports, debriefs and close	-
Out-of-class	Individual prep and individual quiz	-	Instructor sets up 2 AEs	Individual prep for AEs	Team decisions on 2 AEs	-	Peer evaluation

APPLICATION EXERCISES (AES)

After the RAP, individuals and teams in a TBL class prepare individually and work together on a series of applications that require teams to use the concepts under study to make increasingly challenging decisions. The quality of the application exercises (AEs) will determine the level of student engagement and learning achieved. TBL AEs require team decisions that satisfy the "4S" criteria: the economic application must be *significant* to students, all teams work on the *same* problem, teams make a *specific choice* among several defensible options, and team decisions are revealed *simultaneously*.

The "4S" criteria were designed to engage students in both the in-group conversation and the class-wide discussion that follows (Michaelsen, Knight and Fink 2004). Inherently interesting problems engage students better than do contrived examples that simply illustrate the computational mechanics. Having all teams working on the same problem creates the conditions necessary for a vigorous class-wide discussion among team reporters that follows students' work in their separate teams. When every team has worked on the same problem, all the students in the class – not just the team reporters – likely care about the discussion of the logic and evidence behind different team decisions.

For economists used to traditional practice problems that are highly computational and have a single correct answer, offering multiple defensible choices in a problem represents a departure from the norm. Yet the goal of TBL AEs is to require within-team and class-wide discussions in which students use the concepts under study to make an argument with logic and evidence to support the team's choice as the best one possible. In other words, the AEs strive to get students to "think like economists" through frequent practice articulating their understanding of economic concepts and receiving immediate feedback from peers and instructor. While the number of possible specific choices in an AE is limited to four or five, the central task of supporting the team choice with logic and evidence comprises an open-ended challenge. Computational problems that have a single correct answer do not motivate the conceptual thinking that AEs target. Moreover, such problems engage the one or two students in the group with high technical skills but largely exclude other students in the group.

Revealing team choices at the same moment commits each team reporter to explain and defend their team's choice rather than simply agreeing with the choice made by early reporters in a sequential process. Roberson and Franchini (2014) provide useful general guidelines for creating TBL AEs that boost student engagement and learning. Simkins, Maier, and Ruder (2019) describe AEs for TBL classes in economics and offer instructors over 200 AE examples, mostly for Principles classes.

AEs in an Asynchronous Course

At the conclusion of the team RAP quiz – the beginning of day 5 in Table 11.1 – the instructor posts materials that set up the two AEs in the module: the individual preparatory assignment, screencasts to provide any necessary context for the AEs, and the text of the AEs themselves.[5] In a face-to-face TBL course, there might be six to ten AEs in a module, including early ones that bolster foundational skills; however, given the need to expand the time allotted to each AE to allow student communication, fewer AEs are possible in the asynchronous mode. Clark et al. (2018) and Dorneich et al. (2021) offer suggestions for the design and timing of AEs in asynchronous TBL classes.

Robust individual student preparation before the application both develops foundational skills and provides team members with important information that the team will make sense of as they make the decision required by the AE. Working on their own, students will prepare for the AEs by reading related news articles, watching a news story or a clip from a documentary, or listening to podcasts that the instructor assigns. Individual preparation should also involve any computational work – graphing or calculation – necessary for the exercise. When teams are tasked with doing computational work, the conversation among students becomes dominated by the one or two students with the best quantitative skills. The individual pre-work might also include creating inputs that the team can consider as they make the decision required by the AE; for example, time series plots or other data analysis prepared by students beforehand can comprise important evidence to guide teams in their deliberation. Instructors should guide students in their preparations by posting clear assignment descriptions and instructions at the LMS and integrating the AE preparation with individual work on problem sets. Here, too, instructors might consider using a tool like Thinkspace (thinkspace.org) to support student AE preparation in an asynchronous course. We ask students to do a lot in this step and the full three days indicated in Table 11.1 for students to prepare for the team work on the AEs seems necessary.

Once the individual work to prepare for the AE has been completed, the team communicates via a group discussion forum at the LMS (or by synchronous videoconference) to make the decision required by the AE. A social annotation tool can be used instead of a discussion forum as the location for the team conversation about the AE. An online shared whiteboard offers another convenient tool for team collaborations. Shared whiteboards are also very useful when an AE report involves a "gallery walk" – graphs, maps, or other artifacts that are created and shared with the class during the reporting phase. Just as the instructor does for the RAP, I recommend assigning a team leader for each AE. The AE team leader has the responsibility of submitting the team's decision, the rationale and any gallery walk exhibit to the instructor before the deadline – the end of day nine in the suggested timeline of Table 11.1.

At the end of day 9, the instructor simultaneously reveals the choices, rationales and any "gallery walk" exhibits (Rodenbaugh 2015) of all teams for the AEs.[6] At this time the instructor also posts review guidelines or other materials (along with explanatory screencasts, if necessary) to specify the process for the required individual and team responses to the decisions and supporting materials of other teams. In the suggested timeline of Table 11.1, individuals post responses and gallery walk votes, if required, at a team discussion forum on day 10; the team then discusses the responses from the whole team that the team leader of each AE submits to the instructor by the end of day 11. The instructor reveals team responses at that time to the class and then facilitates a class-wide discussion of each AE during days 12 and 13 of the module. LMS tools enable the instructor to require each student to respond to instructor prompts before other comments in each forum are visible, thus ensuring a minimum level of participation by all individuals in these discussions.

During the class-wide conversation about the AEs at the end of the module, the instructor can identify areas of agreement and disagreement in the team choices and rationales as they emerge and provoke further discussion with questions about the different assumptions, interpretations of evidence, or team value judgments that led to the different decisions. During the discussion, the instructor can post as necessary to keep students on track but must take care to avoid squelching student discussion, as will happen once the instructor voices her own answers to the questions.

At the conclusion of the class-wide discussion – the end of day 13 in the suggested timeline – the instructor closes the work on the AEs by posting short videos that highlight the most important conceptual issues that emerged in the work on the AE and provide the instructor's expert view on the applications.

Students might be uncomfortable at first as they grapple with problems that lack a single correct answer. They will want to know how the understanding they develop through the AEs will appear on an exam. My own exams consist of a mix of computational problems that students will have worked on in individual problem sets and essay questions based on one or several AEs that they have worked on. I have found it helpful to relieve student anxiety and guide their study efforts by providing study guides in advance of exams that present one or two possible essay questions related to each AE.[7]

AEs in Hybrid Online Classes

In an IO TBL class, the AE sequence occurs asynchronously and, because the team RAP and instructor explanations occur in the synchronous class session, the individual preparation for the AEs can begin on day four in the asynchronous sequence in Table 11.1, allowing more time for one of the subsequent steps or for a rest on day 14.

In a weekly hybrid TBL class, following the first meeting of the module, the instructor posts individual preparatory assignments, videos that should be viewed before team work on each AE, and the AEs themselves. Just as in an asynchronous online course, individual students prepare readings and complete assignments before working with the team on the AEs. I usually load each AE into each team's shared whiteboard, where the team documents their reasoning and posts any supporting exhibits necessary to support the team decision in the AE.

The second class meeting in a two-week module of a hybrid course consists of team reports, facilitated discussion among team reporters, and instructor closing remarks for each of the two AEs in the module. When students return to the whole class session, the instructor selects a reporter through a random and transparent process such as the SpinnerWheel (spinnerwheel.com). Team credit is not awarded or deducted on the basis of right or wrong answers on the AE (often all choices are defensible); rather, points might be deducted from the whole team if the reporter cannot explain the reasoning behind the team's choice. I establish this incentive in the syllabus, explain it on the first day of class, and issue "warning citations" early in the semester. Later, I never actually have to deduct team points because the teams learn to orient their discussions toward making sure all members understand the reasoning rather than stopping once the decision has been made.

For the simultaneous revelation of the team's choice among a specific set of options, conduct a "ready-set-go" process (Bruff 2020) in which each team reporter types the letter corresponding to their team's choice in the chat and waits for the instructor's "go" before hitting return. Ideally, student responses are spread among numerous possible responses, which creates the conditions for a vigorous class-wide discussion about team choices.[8] Even when all teams select the same option, the instructor can give several team reporters the chance to explain their reasoning and the instructor can play "devil's advocate" to elicit student arguments against the options not selected. When responses are distributed across several possibilities, the instructor-facilitated debrief of the AE begins with team reporters explaining the reasoning behind each different choice. The instructor then uses facilitation questions that they have prepared in advance to guide a discussion of the economic concepts that they wish to emphasize.

When teams have been required to carefully assemble visual evidence to support AE choices in their shared whiteboards, the instructor has the option to have teams inspect each other's work in a "gallery walk" where a few minutes of the class period are set aside for teams in breakout rooms to view the exhibits prepared by other teams and vote on which team other than their own assembled the most compelling argument in favor of their answer (Rodenbaugh 2015). Team reporters are then tasked both to explain their own team's exhibit and their team's vote in the gallery walk.

The instructor closes each AE by summarizing the key points that emerged in the discussion. Students want an expert's take on the question and at this point their work on the AE has prepared them to gain a nuanced understanding of the concepts under study. To close an AE, instructors summarize the key takeaways that have emerged in the discussion. The instructor might also present additional information about the topic under study to the class; for example, a review of empirical findings related to the AE, a description of the empirical questions that remain unresolved, or a synopsis of the conversation among professional economists about the issue.

APPLICATION EXERCISE EXAMPLE

Table 11.3 presents an example of an AE that could be part of a Principles of Microeconomics unit on imperfect competition. Students will have studied textbook or other material related to the topic as part of the RAP. The instructor will have provided instruction on the topic in short videos following the team RAP quiz and in other text or video LMS postings in response to student questions on problem sets and exam study guides. As part of the individual preparation for the AE, students watch a short video about Amazon's purchase of MGM Studios and read a blog post that surveys the streamed video on demand (SVOD) market. The blog post provides some data on subscriber numbers and subscription fees that will inform team choices. Short essay questions that are part of individual student preparation ask students to think about why Amazon might value the assets in the deal more highly than MGM Studios did, adapt the central analytical framework of the unit to fit the specific case, and make a conjecture about households' willingness to pay for streaming services. Importantly, students will likely have substantial experience as customers in the SVOD market.

During individual and team work, the instructor will likely receive questions about the exercise. It is important that students post questions to a question-and-answer forum at the LMS so that the question and response are visible to all. Instructors must take care not to influence student responses to the exercise. The ideal response gives students enough information to enable them to make progress if they are stuck; however, an important part of the team work is to figure out a strategy to approach the problem and giving too much guidance limits the learning.

Table 11.3   *Example Team-Based Learning application exercise*

Exercise	Instruction/s
Learning objective	Upon completion of the activity, students will be able to explain the role of economies of scale and consumer demand in determining the level of competition likely to exist in an industry.
Individual student preparation	Watch news video on Amazon acquisition of MGM (ABC News 2022). Read blog post on streaming industry (Maglio 2022). Write two short essays in response to instructor prompts. Construct a graph of Amazon streaming service average costs and demand before and after acquiring MGM Studios.
Individual essay questions	We can infer from this news that Amazon's willingness to pay for MGM Studios' assets was greater than MGM's willingness to receive. Why do you think this was the case? (Answer in one paragraph typed in the text box for the assignment at the LMS.) Consider the budget of a typical household in the United States. What do you estimate the typical willingness to pay each month for all of the streaming service subscriptions? Which services could that budget support? (*Hint:* You might need to do some Internet research on subscription terms of various firms in the market.) Does your answer lead you to expect the number of firms in the SVOD market to change in the future? How?
Individual analysis	Use the general firm costs-firm demand framework to graph Amazon's average costs and demand before and after the deal for MGM Studios. Assume marginal costs are zero. Don't worry about actual numbers but do think carefully about the units on the *x*- and *y-axes* and, as always, label very carefully. (Attach your graph as a PDF to the assignment at the LMS. Drawing graphs neatly by hand or by means of a drawing program are both acceptable.)
The team AE	Your group is a team of consultants to the CEO of Vudu, a small player in the video streaming industry (10% of HHs subscribed in December 2020) and have been approached by the CEO of Hulu to discuss a possible buyout. The CEO asks you to predict will happen in the market for video streaming services during the next five years? How do you answer? Be ready to share your reasoning. A. Firms will continue to enter the market because consumers have a nearly insatiable appetite for video content and there are profits to be made. B. Some of the smaller firms in the industry will exit or be absorbed by larger firms because the economies of scale in the industry will allow only a few large firms to survive. C. The firms in the industry now will continue to exist but there will be considerably less entry in the future relative to recent years. Required exhibit: Team consensus graph of firm average costs and market demand.

Exercise	Instruction/s
Review criteria	Does the team base its answer on a technically correct analysis of the SVOD market using the appropriate framework studied in the unit? Does the team make a convincing argument to explain its prediction for the SVOD market? If your team made a different prediction, how did your analysis of the market differ from that of the team being reviewed?
Discussion questions	Did your examination of other teams' work cause you to change your prediction for the SVOD market or did other teams' work make you more confident in your own team's prediction? Explain. Do you think small firms will continue to exist in the SVOD market? Why or why not? Which of the streaming services in the market today seems *most likely* to flourish in the future? Explain. Which of the streaming services in the market today seems *least likely* to flourish in the future? Explain.
Close	Instructor should review basic concepts. Scale economies, minimum efficient scale, the importance of both firm costs and the nature of demand in determining market structure. Instructor might examine with the class measures of market concentration of the SVOD and other markets with which students are familiar. Instructor might examine some recent antitrust rulings, along with measures of concentration of the industries involved. Emphasize that the SVOD industry is very young and we will all observe it develop during the coming years.

The AE description should provide the specifications for the material to be submitted with the team's choice. Review questions should ask individuals and teams to evaluate how well the material submitted with the report meets the specifications. The goal of the threaded class-wide discussion that follows is to have students reflect on the economic concepts at the center of the exercise and to prod them to think about several finer points. Table 11.3 includes suggested prompts for the threaded class-wide discussion that are intended to improve student intuition about firm entry and exit when products are differentiated and the minimum efficient scale is large.

The instructor's closing remarks summarize the important economic concepts revealed in the AE, provide students a sense of empirical work that might shed light on some of the unresolved questions that emerged in the work on the AE, and perhaps point out to students how professional economists debate the issue in the professional literature on the topic.

PEER EVALUATION

Each module ends with peer evaluations that consist of a mix of quantitative and qualitative assessments. Michaelsen, Knight and Fink (2004) and Levine

(2008) provide several possible models for the peer feedback instrument. Students assign numerical ratings for teammates based on the perceived quality of individual preparation, engagement, and comportment during the team work on the module. Students also comment on areas in which each teammate excels and in which improvement is needed. Average teammate ratings and comments are provided to each student shortly after the conclusion of the module.[9]

Typically, the peer feedback serves a strictly formative purpose during the semester. The peer evaluation administered with the final exam does usually influence the student grade. In my classes, I adjust the team quiz and AE points based on the final summative teammate ratings, though I limit the magnitude of the adjustment to a maximum 5% inflation or deflation of those points, which amounts to about one percent of the course grade. If, however, a student receives aggregate teammate ratings of less than 60% of the maximum possible, that student fails the course. Students are notoriously easy graders and such a low rating is quite extraordinary. Even though that threshold is never breached, its existence conveys to students the importance of putting effort into the team's work and of treating teammates well.

The frequent peer feedback offers students the incentive to sustain a high level of engagement throughout the course. The feedback also helps students develop the team work skills necessary to work productively with others. This skill features prominently in the student learning outcomes of every course I teach and improving in this dimension is likely more important for student success in their careers and personal lives than mastering any content in economics or any discipline.

While some student teams work well together from the very beginning of the semester, most need four to six weeks to figure out how to work well together. Early AEs focused on developing team work skills and frequent peer evaluation helps students improve their contribution to their teams rapidly over the course of the semester.

CONCLUSION

Team-Based Learning offers a course structure capable of boosting student engagement and learning in online courses. By holding students accountable for regular individual work throughout the course, TBL motivates the sustained cognitive presence necessary for learning. Frequent, purposeful interactions with peers results in a vibrant social presence in the course while giving students frequent practice constructing meaning from course materials and learning activities. The TBL strategy gives students immediate feedback on their efforts from peers and instructor along with frequent opportunities to revise their understanding based on that feedback. In TBL courses, students develop team work skills that will help them succeed in future courses and their careers.

TBL's emphasis on applying course concepts to the concrete examples in application exercises works well in economics. Because of the mathematical rigor of many of the models, students and instructors in economics courses naturally emphasize the development of technical skills. The application of course concepts to real-world examples in so much of the work of a TBL course ensures that students develop sound economic intuition along with solid computational skills.

Implementing TBL does require a high level of instructor skill and effort, especially in the transition from lecture-oriented pedagogy with only infrequent episodes of social learning. Some scheduling flexibility is lost in online courses taught with TBL pedagogy. However, the gains in student engagement and learning justify the instructor effort. Further, making it harder for students to cram great effort into relatively few short bursts in online courses promises to generate desirable learning gains.

NOTES

1. In a face-to-face course, formative peer evaluation can occur just two or three times during the semester; however, in an online class, where students can disengage more easily and the reliance on text-based communication can lead to more frequent teammate misunderstandings, peer evaluation at the end of each module is necessary (Clark, Estis, and Farland 2020).
2. The number of teams is the class size divided by four, rounding down, so teams will generally have four members and some will have five. Team sizes online are smaller than the five-to-seven students recommended by Michaelsen, Knight and Fink (2004) and others, per the recommendation of Clark, Estis and Farland (2020).
3. Many instructors issue a more detailed survey at the beginning of class and carefully construct teams in order to maximize diversity by gender, academic strengths, etc. In my experience, the more transparent approach results in equally balanced teams. The benefit of the more transparent process results when teams have personality problems to work out. Students are far less likely to blame the instructor for putting the team together and far more likely to take responsibility for working through conflict themselves, sometimes with help from the instructor.
4. Even though teams can choose to schedule a private videoconference session to accomplish the team quiz, the course structure must allow the fully asynchronous work supported by a discussion forum.
5. A three-week module would allow for more than two AEs.
6. InteDashboard and FeedbackFruits offer a convenient infrastructure for the simultaneous reveal. The instructor can also post the team AE materials to the class using LMS tools, a shared whiteboard, or Google Docs.

7.   I find two-stage exams (McKee 2018) to be very helpful in TBL classes.
8.   If teams are unanimous in choosing one option, either the AE needs revision so that it creates better in-team and class discussions of the topics under study or the set-up process narrowed student choices. Either issue can be corrected in future iterations.
9.   The TEAMMATES website (https://teammatesv4.appspot.com/web/front/home) facilitates the peer feedback process free of charge. InteDashboard (https://www.intedashboard.com/) manages the peer feedback process as part of its TBL support package.

REFERENCES

ABC News. (2022, March 18). Video Amazon buys MGM Studios for $8.5M. *ABC News*. Retrieved November 17, 2023, from https://abcnews.go.com/GMA/Culture/video/amazon-buys-mgm-studios-85m-83524357

All in on Two Stage Exams - Teach Better. (2018, April 3). *Teachbetter.co*. Retrieved November 18, 2023, from https://teachbetter.co/blog/2018/04/03/all-in-on-two-stage-exams/

Balan, P., Clark, M., & Restall, G. (2015). Preparing students for Flipped or Team-Based Learning methods. *Education + Training, 57*(6), 639–657. https://doi.org/10.1108/et-07-2014–0088

Boettcher, J. V., & Conrad, R.-M. (2021). *The Online Teaching Survival Guide*. Jossey-Bass.

Brown, T., Rongerude, J., Leonard, B., & Merrick, L. C. (2021). Best practices for online team-based learning: Strengthening teams through formative peer evaluation. *New Directions for Teaching and Learning, 2021*(165), 53–64. https://doi.org/10.1002/tl.20436

Bruff, D. (2020). *Teaching in a Hybrid Classroom – What's Working, What's Not – Agile Learning*. Retrieved November 17, 2023, from https://derekbruff.org/?p=3676

Clark, M. C., Estis, J. M., & Farland, M. Z. (2020). *Experiences in moving TBL online*. Webinar, May 19, 2020. Team-Based Learning Collaborative. www.teambasedlearning.org

Clark, M., Merrick, L., Styron, J., Bender, H., Johnson, J., Chapman, J., Gillette, M., Dorneich, M., O'dwyer, B., Grogan, J., Brown, T., Leonard, B., Rongerude, J., & Winter, L. (2018). Off to On: Best Practices for Online Team-Based LearningTM. *Center for Excellence in Learning and Teaching*. https://www.teambasedlearning.org/wp-content/uploads/2018/08/Off-to-On_OnlineTBL_WhitePaper_ClarkEtal2018_V3.pdf

Clark, M. C., Merrick, L. C., Styron, J. L., & Dolowitz, A. R. (2021). Orientation principles for online team-based learning courses. *New Directions for Teaching and Learning, 2021*(165), 11–23. https://doi.org/10.1002/tl.20433

Costa, K., & Pacansky-Brock, M. (2020). *99 Tips For Creating Simple And Sustainable Educational Videos: A Guide For Online Teachers And Flipped Classes*. Stylus Publishing.

Danielson, J. A., Mills, E. M., Vermeer, P. J., Preast, V. A., Young, K. M., Christopher, M. M., George, J. W., Darren Wood, R., & Bender, H. S. (2006). Characteristics of a cognitive tool that helps students learn diagnostic problem solving. *Educational*

Technology Research and Development, *55*(5), 499–520. https://doi.org/10.1007/s11423-006-9003-8

Darby, F., & Lang, J. M. (2019). *Small teaching online: Applying learning science in online classes*. Jossey-Bass.

Dorius, C., Madeka, K., Bender, H. S., Johnson, J., Gillette, M. T., & Chapman, J. (2021). The readiness assurance process in online team-based learning classrooms. *New Directions for Teaching and Learning*, *2021*(165), 25–39. https://doi.org/10.1002/tl.20434

Dorneich, M. C., O'Dwyer, B., Dolowitz, A. R., Styron, J. L., & Grogan, J. (2021). Application exercise design for team-based learning in online courses. *New Directions for Teaching and Learning*, *2021*(165), 41–52. https://doi.org/10.1002/tl.20435

Freeman, S., Eddy, S. L., McDonough, M., Smith, M. K., Okoroafor, N., Jordt, H., & Wenderoth, M. P. (2014). Active learning increases student performance in science, engineering, and mathematics. *Proceedings of the National Academy of Sciences*, *111*(23), 8410–8415. https://doi.org/10.1073/pnas.1319030111

Garrison, D. R., Anderson, T., & Archer, W. (1999). Critical Inquiry in a Text-Based Environment: Computer Conferencing in Higher Education. *The Internet and Higher Education*, *2*(2–3), 87–105. https://auspace.athabascau.ca/bitstream/handle/2149/739/?sequence=1

Haidet, P., Kubitz, K., & McCormack, W. T. (2014). Analysis of the Team-Based Learning literature: TBL comes of age. *Journal of Excellence in College Teaching* 25 (3–4), 303–33.

Levine, R. E. (2008). Peer evaluation in Team-Based Learning. In Michaelsen, L. K., Parmalee, D., McMahon, K. K., and Levine, R. E. (eds.), Team-Based Learning for the health professions, 103–15. Stylus Publishing.

Maglio, T. (2022, March 16). *Who Is Winning the Streaming Wars? Subscribers by the Numbers*. IndieWire. https://www.indiewire.com/2022/03/how-many-subscribers-netflix-disney-plus-peacock-amazon-prime-video-1234705515

McKee, D. (2018, April 3). All in on Two Stage Exams. *Teach Better*. https://teachbetter.co/blog/2018/04/03/all-in-on-two-stage-exams/

Michaelsen, L. K., Knight, A. B., & Fink, L. D. (2004). *Team-Based Learning: a transformative use of small groups in college teaching*. Stylus Pub.

Miller, K., Lukoff, B., King, G., & Mazur, E. (2018). Use of a Social Annotation Platform for Pre-Class Reading Assignments in a Flipped Introductory Physics Class. *Frontiers in Education*, *3*. https://doi.org/10.3389/feduc.2018.00008

Millis, B. J., & Cottell, P. G. (1998). *Cooperative learning for higher education faculty*. Oryx Press.

Oliveira, I., Tinoca, L., & Pereira, A. (2011). Online group work patterns: How to promote a successful collaboration. *Computers & Education*, *57*(1), 1348–1357. https://doi.org/10.1016/j.compedu.2011.01.017

Palsolé, S., & Awalt, C. (2008). Team-Based Learning in asynchronous online settings. *New Directions for Teaching and Learning*, *2008*(116), 87–95. https://doi.org/10.1002/tl.336

Parrish, C. W., Williams, D. S., & Estis, J. M. (2021). Integrated online team-based learning: Using synchronous engagement and asynchronous flexibility to implement TBL online. *New Directions for Teaching and Learning*, *2021*(165), 91–105. https://doi.org/10.1002/tl.20439

Restall, G. C., & Clark, M. C. (2021). Team-based learning and the community of inquiry model. *New Directions for Teaching and Learning, 2021*(165), 65–76. https://doi.org/10.1002/tl.20437

Roberson, B., & Franchini, B. (2014). Effective task design for the TBL classroom. *Journal on Excellence in College Teaching, 25*(3–4), 275–302.

Rodenbaugh, D. W. (2015). Maximize a Team-Based Learning gallery walk experience: herding cats is easier than you think. *Advances in Physiology Education, 39*(4), 411–413. https://doi.org/10.1152/advan.00012.2015

Ruder, P., Maier, M. H., & Simkins, S. P. (2021). Getting started with Team-Based Learning (TBL): An introduction. *The Journal of Economic Education, 52*(3), 220–230. https://doi.org/10.1080/00220485.2021.1925187

Sibley, J. (2016). *Getting started with Team-Based Learning.* Stylus Publishing.

Sibley, J. (2018). *Learn TBL | Jim Sibley helping you learn more about TBL.* Retrieved November 18, 2023, from https://learntbl.ca/

Sibley, J., Ostafichuk, P., Roberson, B., Franchini, B., & Kubitz, K. A. (2014). Introduction to Team-Based Learning. In J. Sibley, *Getting Started With Team-Based Learning* (pp. 3-15). Routledge.

Simkins, S., & Maier, M. (2004). Using Just-in-Time Teaching Techniques in the Principles of Economics Course. *Social Science Computer Review, 22*(4), 444–456. https://doi.org/10.1177/0894439304268643

Simkins, S., Maier M., & Ruder, P. (2019). Team-Based Learning. *Starting Point.* Retrieved October 1, 2023, from http:// serc .carleton .edu/ introgeo/ interactive/ examples/morrisonpuzzle.html

PART IV

EXTRA- AND CO-CURRICULAR LEARNING ONLINE

12. A blended format for student conferences: the Explore Econ case study

Ramin Nassehi

INTRODUCTION

The post-COVID-19 world of higher education has made us rethink many of our pedagogical principles and practices, including the way we teach, assess, build knowledge networks, develop employability skills, etc. Perhaps it is time to rethink the way we hold academic conferences as well and explore new models to maximise engagement and access. This chapter discusses a blended format[1] of holding student conferences. This format transforms student conferences from a half-day event that often takes place on campus to a series of asynchronous and synchronous events. In other words, it *stretches* the notion of conference by changing it from a one-day event to an ongoing learning and community-building *process* that happens throughout the academic year. As will be explained, this format opens new doors for (a) promoting research-based education, (b) building student-staff relations and (c) empowering students by giving them new modes of expression and presence.

Before explaining our blended format, it is helpful to describe the conventional format of student conferences (Etzion, Gehman, & Davis, 2022). Normally, student conferences are held as a full-day live event on campus, where students present their works to internal academic staff, fellow students, and external guests. The conference may have a website that is used for uploading the selected papers and posters and making announcements in the lead up to the on-campus event. This format puts the main emphasis on the presentation of student papers/posters on the conference day. The conference's website is of secondary importance. In this format, the conference *is* a half-day live event happening on campus. Digital technologies such as the conference's website are only publicity tools around that event. This format suffers from three shortcomings. Firstly, it puts excessive emphasis on live presentations by students at the expense of celebrating and showcasing what they have *already* accomplished in their learning journey. Pedagogically, it emphasises synchronous engagement of the audience and misses out on the new possible modes of virtual asynchronous engagement. Secondly, and relatedly, this format does not take full advantage of digital technologies as it views them as mere marketing tools for the main on-campus event rather than an integral part of conference itself. Accordingly, the conference website is usually used merely for making announcements or uploading the final papers and posters of students, while it could be used as a platform for providing support to students in their learning journey and giving them empowering presence. Finally, this format is very costly because its organisation requires a lot of administrative planning and support.

In contrast, our blended format breaks down the conference into two stages:

1. The asynchronous stage, where we showcase students' papers/posters in the conferences' website, together with a pre-recorded video presentation of their work. We use different tactics to actively promote engagement with this asynchronous material. For instance, we ask internal and external academics and students to vote for their favourite submissions.
2. The synchronous stage, which is a live event that involves (a) showcasing the asynchronous material to the audience in the room (b) students giving an "elevator-pitch" of their research and (c) award giving. This live event, which lasts around two hours maximum, can be held virtually or in-person.

Right from the outset, our conference format embodies a dynamic application of digital technology, using the conference's website as a pedagogical hub rather than a static information repository or a mere marketing tool. This blended conference leverages the website as a nurturing ground for students' learning journey, providing them with motivation and support. On this platform, they can explore various materials on conducting literature reviews, data analysis, academic writing, and recording and editing video presentations. In addition, we hold virtual Q&A sessions and workshops throughout the year to inspire and support students. Gradually, as students finish their preparations and submit their work, the conference's website morphs into a showcasing platform. In the subsequent live event, we link our in-person activities such as student presentations or award giving to the material already uploaded on the website. We highlight the differences between conference formats in Table 12.1.

Table 12.1   Comparison of conventional and blended conferences

Conventional conference (full-day on-campus event)	Blended conference (asynchronous presentations then a live event)
Emphasis on live presentations	Emphasis on what students have already achieved
Little emphasis on digital technology (website is used merely as a promotional tool)	Digital technology as an integral part (website is used as a motivational and pedagogical tool)
Main organisational cost: finding and arranging venues	Main organisational cost: maintenance of the website
Accessible mostly to internal staff and students	Accessible to internal and external audience
A one-off presentation by students in the event day	Live and pre-recorded presentation by students (a more lasting presence for students)

This format has several advantages. First, it elevates research-based education by providing continuous support and motivation to students in their research throughout the year. In doing so, this format showcases the entire research process, not just the final outputs, through regular updates on the website, virtual workshops, and Q&A sessions. Second, it improves student-staff relations by combining the two modes of asynchronous and synchronous engagement. Previously, the only way for staff to engage with the students' conference was to attend the half-day on-campus event. However, our format opens a new digital doorway: staff can begin engaging with students' research well in advance of the live events. This early engagement opportunity allows for a richer, more iterative feedback loop between staff and students. The website becomes a living, interactive prelude to the live events that paves the way for a continuous dialogue that enriches both the students' research experience and the staff's involvement and understanding of the students' work. Third, this format empowers students as it provides them with new modes of expression and presence. In a conventional conference, great emphasis is put on live presentations, but in a blended format, students get a chance to record (and edit) a video presentation in addition to their live performance. This not only diversifies the mode of expression for students but gives them a more lasting presence in the conference as their video presentation is posted on the website. As will be discussed further, the website can be used creatively as a platform for giving more voice and presence to students, hence promoting student ownership of the conference. Additionally, the experience of recording and editing video presentations equips students with essential digital and employability skills that are increasingly valuable in today's digital-centric world (Arsenis, Flores, & Petropoulou, 2022). Finally, the blended format is economically efficient as it compresses the live event and saves on various administrative costs, as confirmed by Basken (2021) & Skiles et al. (2022). Moreover, the digital aspect of this format significantly enhances the inclusivity of the conference by allowing a broader audience to participate, regardless of geographical or financial constraints, thus extending the reach and impact of the conference as noted by Sipley (2021).

This chapter proceeds as follows. Section 1 briefly discusses the literature to which this project relates. The subsequent sections focus on a case study of a blended student conference: Explore Econ. This is an undergraduate student research conference in University College London's (UCL) Department of Economics, organised by the Centre for Teaching and Learning Economics (CTaLE). Section 2 traces the history and institutional context of this conference. Section 3 discusses different stages of this blended conference and outlines their pedagogical and practical implications.

LITERATURE REVIEW

The idea of a blended student conference speaks to four bodies of literature. Firstly, it links with the paradigm of research-based education (Blessinger & Carfora, 2014; Brew, 2010; Fung, 2017). According to this paradigm, the best way for students to learn economics is "by doing economics" (Chaudhury, 2020). This entails students undertaking their own independent economic research and inquiry. Research-based education can be fostered through various means, one of which is to hold an annual student conference as a co-curricular activity (outside modules). The new conference format discussed here can contribute to research-based education in novel ways. First of all, it makes it easier for academics (and fellow students) to engage with students' research as it opens a new model of asynchronous engagement. Secondly, by making digital technology an integral part, this format is more able to provide motivation and support for students' research journey throughout the academic year. For example, the virtual format makes it easier for instructors to hold Q&A sessions and workshops on an ongoing basis. Also, on the students' side, a blended platform opens the possibility of new forms of presentation (pre-recorded video and live elevator-pitch), which are nowadays considered essential digital skills (Arsenis, Flores, & Petropoulou, 2022; Montes, 2021).

The topic of this chapter also relates to the literature on community building in higher education (Blakeley, 2020; Gibson, 2020). It is now more important than ever for campus-based universities to create vibrant, inclusive learning communities. Arguably, the main role of such universities in the post-COVID-19 world of higher education is to act as social hubs that bring students, academics, and experts from business and public sectors together

(KPMG, 2020). A blended conference can contribute to community building by introducing new modes of engagement between students and staff and among students themselves. Additionally, the conference's website can function as a "virtual umbrella" that brings together all extra or co-curricular activities that take place in the department, strengthening the sense of community. Most importantly, because of being more accessible to external audiences (Sarabipour, 2020; Sipley, 2021), virtual conferences can help universities build a more global and inclusive learning community (Wu et al., 2022). The online format also makes it easier to invite alumni as well as speakers from private businesses and the public sector.

This chapter touches on the discussions around student empowerment as well (Bovill, Cook-Sather, & Felten, 2011). A blended conference makes students' work more visible and reachable to a general audience. This is because papers and posters are showcased in the conference's website together with a pre-recorded presentation (asynchronous material). So, students can refer to their presentation afterwards, which is not possible in a conventional conference. This creates a lasting presence for students, strengthening their sense of ownership of the conference as a result.

Finally, this chapter contributes to the growing literature on holding virtual conferences (Basken, 2021; Grove, 2021; Popovic & Kustra, 2020). As shown in Table 12.2, virtual technology opens the possibility for new conference formats: (a) a live virtual conference (with no asynchronous material), where the only difference between this format and the conventional conference is that it is held virtually; (b) a blended conference (asynchronous stage followed by a live event on campus); and (c) a virtual two-stage conference (asynchronous stage followed by a virtual live event). The main upside of all these formats is that they reduce organisational costs for host institutions (Wu et al., 2022). The blended formats have an additional benefit: they compress the duration of the conference's live event and, as a result, attract more attendance by reducing the time commitment. A shorter live event makes it easier to integrate the conference with other live activities (virtual or on-campus), hence creating more synergy.

An overall assessment of the literature suggests that an online conference, blended or not, offers new formats with high pedagogical values. Of course, institutions can pick and choose among these formats based on their goals and constraints, and further innovate.

Table 12.2   Student conference formats

Different formats	Asynchronous (virtual)	Synchronous (on campus)	Synchronous (virtual)
Conventional Conference	-	Yes	-
Blended Conference	Yes	Yes	-
Virtual two-stage Conference	Yes	-	Yes
Live virtual conference	-	-	Yes

EXPLORE ECON: CONTEXT AND BACKGROUND

Explore Econ is the annual undergraduate student research conference, organised by the Centre for Teaching and Learning Economics (CTaLE) in UCL's Department of Economics. The main purpose of this conference, which has been running since 2015, is to showcase the best research conducted by undergraduate students both within and outside the curriculum. The conference also tries to strengthen the sense of community in the department by bringing academic staff and students closer together. Since 2021, this conference has taken an innovative turn towards a blended format. This section gives a brief background to this conference and then focuses on the transition to a blended format. The aim here is to use Explore Econ as a case study to discuss the pedagogical implications and practicalities of holding an online or blended format student conference.

The institutional home of Explore Econ is University College London (UCL). With more than 40,000 students, UCL is a major public research university in the UK with a campus at the heart of Bloomsbury London. The university is active in research and teaching in almost every field including medicine, natural sciences, engineering, law, social sciences, and history. The UCL Economics department is part of the Faculty of Social and Historical Sciences, which has about 6,000 students and 800 academic staff. The Economics department itself has about 1,400 students and 50 academic staff, offering various programs at BSc, MSc, and PhD levels. The department is extremely active in terms of research and policy advice. There is a group of academics within the department who focus on developing teaching innovations and conducting research on economics pedagogy (Centre for Teaching and Learning Economics). The Explore Econ conference was introduced by this group in 2015 for the undergraduate level.

The undergraduate programs, especially BSc Economics, constitute the bulk of the student body in UCL Economics (80% of students). Similar to many leading undergraduate economics programs in the UK, our program follows a three-year structure. The initial two years are dedicated primarily to core modules, which encompass principles of economics, mathematics for economics, statistical methods, microeconomics, macroeconomics, and econometrics. The final year focuses on offering optional modules that are specialised in an economics field such as labour economics, financial economics, development economics, economics of inequality and economics of education. Each academic year is comprised of three terms where the first two terms are devoted to teaching and the final summer term to assessment. In addition to modules, we offer a variety of workshops called the "Skills Labs" that focus on developing essential employability and graduate skills like conducting literature reviews, data analysis, writing and presentations.

The primary aim of the Explore Econ conference is to enhance research-based education at the undergraduate level. Between 2014 and 2020, this conference followed the conventional format: there was a half-day event on campus (around five hours) where students presented their papers and posters to fellow students and departmental staff. This event was normally held towards the end of term 2 (mid-March) to ensure high student and staff attendance. The conference covered around eight paper presentations (10 minutes each) and ten poster presentations. The posters were printed and exhibited in a conference room and the papers were presented in three theme-based sessions. The climax of the conference was the award-giving ceremony at the end when the winners of top papers and posters were announced.

Unsurprisingly, the 2020 pandemic made it impossible for us to hold the conference in its usual format, so we decided to take an innovative and slightly risky turn towards holding a blended conference.

TOWARDS A BLENDED CONFERENCE

Since 2021, we have been holding Explore Econ as a blended conference composed of two stages. This section goes through different steps of organising this conference and discusses the pedagogical and practical implications of each step. But before doing so, it outlines the structure and timeline of the conference.

Structure and Timeline of the Conference

Our blended conference has two sequential parts:

Asynchronous part: In this stage we shortlist the submissions and showcase the selected papers and posters, together with their recorded presentations, on the conference's website. This shortlisting is conducted by the conference's Scientific Committee, which comprises two internal students, two internal academics and four external members, details of which will be elaborated upon later. Around six papers and eight posters are usually showcased. The main challenge at this stage is to make sure students, academics and external guests engage with the uploaded material on the website. Then, there is another round of selection, where the Scientific Committee selects the top three papers and posters from the shortlist to give "elevator-pitch" presentations (3 minutes) at the subsequent live event.

Synchronous part (the live event): This stage involves three activities: (a) showcasing the material already uploaded on the website to the live audience (linking the asynchronous and synchronous elements together), (b) students giving "elevator-pitches" of their research to the audience and (c) award giving.

In terms of timeline, as shown in Table 12.3, the live event is held after the exams in term 3 (mid-June). Working our way backwards from this date, we start advertising the conference to students from the very beginning of term 1 (early October). The call for papers and posters is sent at the start of term 2 (mid-January). We hold various virtual Q&A sessions throughout the year to provide support to students in preparing their research ideas and to provide feedback on their progress. The submission deadline is set at the start of term 3 (late-April). This leaves students a whole month to prepare their final submissions; that is, from late-March (when term 2 finishes) to late-April (when term 3 starts).

We officially launch the conference around late-May by starting the asynchronous stage. At this point we post the shortlisted papers and posters on the website and devise various promotional strategies to encourage students and staff, both within and outside UCL, to engage with the uploaded material. This creates a momentum for the live event, which is held after the exams, around Mid-June.

Of course, such a timeline is very much shaped by the specific term and degree structure of UCL economics. But putting specificities aside, organisation of this conference requires these general steps: initial promotion, helping students prepare their submissions, peer review of submissions, showcasing the shortlisted submissions (first stage) and the live event (second stage). The remainder of this section goes through the pedagogical and practical implications of each stage.

Table 12.3   *Online conference timeline*

Date	Event
October	Academic year starts
November	Motivating students to participate + Q/A session
December	Motivating students to participate + Research workshops
Mid-January	Call for paper and poster submissions
February	Research workshops
Late April	Submission deadline
Late May	Asynchronous stage (Shortlisted papers and posters are uploaded)
Early June	Popular vote opens
Mid-June	Live event

Initial Promotion

The very first challenge of running the conference is to motivate students to take part in the conference. It is important to recognise that students may not fully appreciate the significance of an academic conference and how engaging in one can enhance their employability and research skills. Students may narrowly perceive a "student conference" as a purely academic event, suitable only for students who want to pursue a PhD and an academic career. Indeed, the very notion of an "academic conference" may sound intimidating for many students. So as a first step we must motivate, or break the fear of, students to take part in the conference. We do this in a live event held during induction week. As a first step, we introduce the students to the conference's website and encourage them to keep an eye on the updates throughout the academic year. We stress that the conference is not a one-off event, but an exciting learning *journey*, with the conference's website acting as a guide and a host. For the blended format to work well, students need to be engaged with the conference's website from early on and see it as a source of support, learning and inspiration, rather than a mere announcement forum.

The next step is to convince students to embark on this optional journey. We highlight that a conference participation "would look good" on their resume/ CV as it signals their research, writing, presentation, and teamwork skills – all considered as essential employability skills (Jenkins & Lane, 2019). It is important to highlight that a blended conference makes the student's work more visible and accessible to a general audience because the papers and posters are showcased in the conference's website together with a pre-recorded presentation (asynchronous stage). This format not only allows students to refer to their presentations afterwards, unlike in the conventional format, but also enables them to build a digital portfolio of their work. Such a portfolio can be a valuable asset in the job market, showcasing their research, writing, and presentation skills to prospective employers. In essence, the blended format cultivates a lasting mode of presence for students' performances, providing an additional incentive for participation in the conference. In addition, since we have been running this blended format for two years, we can repost the past year's papers/posters and pre-recorded presentation videos on the conference's website, giving the new student cohort an idea what a blended conference would "look like" and enhance its visibility and reach. We also post interviews with past participants, titled "Spotlight on Students," where we ask students to reflect on their learning journey during different stages of the conference. The idea is that by listening to these interviews, students would not only get motivated to take part in the conference but also get a sense of the preparation journey.

In addition to the above tactics, we seek help from our student society, the Economist's Society,[2] in promoting the conference as they have a better reach to the student body and are more effective in communications. Arguably, students can better explain the merits of participation in an academic conference to a fellow student than a lecturer can. Also, involving students in this stage gives them more ownership of the conference: for instance, posting a promotional opening video message by a student representative on the conference's webpage can be empowering for new cohorts.

Finally, we mention to students that they can get involved in the organisation of the conference by applying for relevant research assistant opportunities or student helper positions. We normally recruit two students in the Scientific Committee of the conference for the peer review process of submission and two students in the Executive Committee to advise and help with the organisation of the conference. So, we ask students to keep an eye on the conference's website for the advertisement of these positions and apply for them. This again creates engagement with the conference's website throughout the academic year and encourages students to perceive it as a dynamic platform.

Support for Students

Holding a student conference entails supplying ongoing support to students at every stage, from topic selection to their final submission and presentation. For this purpose, we hold various online Q&A sessions and workshops (Skills Labs) in term 1 and term 2. Again, the conference's website acts as a crucial pedagogical tool in this stage. We post a variety of useful "how-to guides" and resources on the website and then draw students' attention to those materials in the live Q&A sessions and workshops. This going "back and forth" between the live sessions and the posted material on the website is a constant feature of our support delivery for students. Crucially, the conference's website must be seen by students as a *dynamic* educational tool that is going to support them during their research journey.

The first Q&A session, which is held right after the call for papers in term 2, is devoted to answering general inquiries about what sort of work can be submitted and how the submissions would be evaluated. This session is held online, and its recording is posted on the website afterwards. The online format makes attendance easier for students and allows those who miss the session to catch up by watching the recording.

The other aim of this Q&A session is to explain to students what a paper or a poster is and why we ask them to submit their research in those formats. Here, we direct them to the past paper and poster examples posted on the website (or in case of no precedence, one can show examples from other student conferences). The word limit for papers is 1,500 words and each paper needs to be accompanied by a recorded video presentation, no more than 5 minutes. Students are welcome to edit their recorded video presentations. This gives them an essential digital skill (Arsenis, Flores, & Petropoulou, 2022). A paper needs to present a well-defined question, explain why that question is important and use analytical and statistical tools of economics to answer that question. We open the paper submissions only to second-year and final-year students. Posters must be submitted with a three-minute video presentation, in which students simply explain their poster. We post various "how to" guides for making posters on the conference's website. The purpose of a poster is to take a concept like green monetary policy or an empirical trend such as proliferation of regional trade agreements and provide relevant conceptual analysis and/or some descriptive data or simple multiple regressions. In other words, we use a poster to function as a visual literature review around a theoretical or empirical topic. We open the poster submission for all students.

In addition to Q&A sessions, we hold various workshops throughout the academic year to provide students with training on literature review, data analysis, writing, and presentation. All these workshops are held online, with a mixture of asynchronous and synchronous sessions.

Peer Review of Submissions

The peer review of papers and posters is conducted by the Scientific Committee, which is comprised of two internal academics, four external judges and two internal students. The external judges are usually academics and professional economists from the corporate sector or civil service including the *Economist*, HSBC, UK Treasury and Bank of England. Involvement of these judges further motivates students to take part in the conference. As a promotional tactic, we announce the name of the judges on the conference's website as soon as they confirm their role. This invites students' engagement with the website from the outset. We also announce the student members of the Scientific Committee on the website and highlight their participation in the peer review process. The Scientific Committee evaluates the submitted papers and posters in two rounds. In the first round, it shortlists around six papers and eight posters, to be showcased in the conference's website as examples of "good" submissions. Then in the second round, it selects the top three papers and posters for giving elevator-pitch presentations in the subsequent live event. The criteria for shortlisting include academic merit, innovativeness, and popular appeal, ensuring a balanced representation of high-quality, creative, and engaging works that would resonate well with a wider audience.

The Asynchronous Stage of the Conference

The conference is formally launched at this stage. This is when we upload the shortlisted papers and posters, together with their pre-recorded presentations, to the conference's website. At this moment, the role of the website changes from a support platform to a showcase platform. The main challenge at this stage is to create excitement and engagement with the posted material. Having a planned marketing and communication strategy is essential. A useful tactic is to post the material gradually on the website and publicise the announcement plan in advance to create excitement and momentum. We also usually post a short video on the website by the Head of the Department, the Faculty Dean or Vice-Provost of Education, in which they formally open the conference and invite academics and students to engage with the asynchronous material that is, or will be, posted on the website. We widely advertise every upload in our social media platforms to generate momentum.

Once all the shortlisted submissions are uploaded, we employ strategies unique to the blended format to foster engagement: We ask students to vote for their favourite paper and poster, an interactive feature enabled by the digital nature of the conference. This voting not only promotes engagement with the posted asynchronous material but also enhances student ownership of the conference, leveraging the online platform to create a more interactive and student-centred experience.

On the conference's website, we also showcase other co-curricular activities of our department, such as our economics photo competition (EconFrame) and the First-Year Challenge, a multimedia competition designed by Spielmann and Chaudhury (2016). In this way, the website functions as a virtual umbrella that brings all the department's co-curricular activities together and showcases them to students and academics both within and outside UCL.

The other challenge at this stage is to ensure a smooth transition to the next stage of the conference, which is the live event. The aim is to channel the momentum gathered during the asynchronous stage towards the live event, ensuring a seamless connection between the two stages of the conference. This necessitates careful scheduling to avoid a large gap between the initial launch of the asynchronous part and the subsequent live event. The optimal gap we have identified is around three weeks. If the gap extends beyond three weeks, there's a risk that the excitement generated could cool down, diminishing the impact and engagement levels for the live event. Conversely, if the gap is shorter than three weeks, there may not be enough momentum built up, which could potentially lead to lower engagement during the live event. The uploading of papers and posters should be planned meticulously to create a lead-up momentum to the subsequent live event, capitalising on the anticipation and engagement generated during the asynchronous stage.

The Synchronous Stage Of The Conference (The Live Event)

This stage can be held either online or in-person. Let us turn to the in-person format first. In this format, the live event will consist of (a) elevator-pitch presentations by students, (b) showcasing the conference's website (asynchronous part) to the audience in the room and (c) award giving. The duration of the in-person event is around two hours, followed by a reception. This format provides a great opportunity for socialisation between students and staff and also among students themselves, across different year groups, programs, and departments.

The blended format allows for the live event to become shorter and thus more engaging and economically efficient. So instead of holding a full-day live event of presentations, the blended format makes it possible to focus more on showcasing and celebrating what students have already achieved (the asynchronous material). Also, a two-hour live program makes the conference more engaging for the audience and ensures a higher number of participants and a longer stay among students and academic staff. Moreover, a two-hour live event can be easily integrated with other events across the university such as career talks, workshops, festivals etc. For instance, one year we combined the Explore Econ's live session with a workshop on crypto currency and a career event, generating a synergy across these activities. And of course, holding a two-hour live event is more economically efficient than a conventional half-day conference on campus as it requires less administrative support.

Now, let us turn to the format where the subsequent live event is held online. I label this as a two-stage virtual conference (as opposed to a blended conference). Due to the COVID-19 pandemic, we chose this format for Explore Econ in 2021 and thus, held our live event on Zoom. But to avoid "Zoom fatigue", we kept the event to 90 minutes, containing it to showcasing the website, two elevator-pitches by students, and award giving. On the upside, thanks to holding the live event online we managed to attract a much higher number of attendees (90 people) than our previous face-to-face conferences. The virtual format also allowed us to reach new audiences, such as UCL students who have already received admissions offers and external students and academics from UK and overseas universities. This helped us in building a larger and more inclusive learning community for our students and academics. We should bear in mind that this virtual format also widens the possibility of inviting guest speakers or attendees from the corporate sector and public institutions.

Collecting feedback and self-reflection is the essential final step of our conference. This process not only helps us improve the quality of the conference but enables us to demonstrate its pedagogical impact. Thus, we collect various forms of feedback and self-reflections:

- Asking the live event audience to fill out a survey
- Monitoring the engagement with the conference's website (counting the number of visits)
- Holding a focus group with student representatives
- Conducting a video podcast with the conference's participants (Spotlight on Students), asking them to reflect on their learning journey
- Asking students who were involved in the peer review evaluation of submissions to reflect on the research skills they have learned in this process by writing a blog post
- Asking students who were involved in the organisation of the conference to write a blog post about the interpersonal and teamwork skills they have gained in this task

These pieces of evaluation and feedback can be helpful for subsequent promotion of the event to the next cohort of the students as well as demonstrating the pedagogical value of this project.

CONCLUSION

What should be the main role of campus-based universities in the post-COVID-19 era of higher education? It appears more crucial now for these universities to function as a social hub for bringing academics and students together to create vibrant learning communities. This means that it is essential for universities to take co-curricular activities such as holding conferences, competitions, or field trips seriously and try bold innovations by employing new digital technologies. This chapter focused on one such innovation: holding a blended student conference. This format tries to harness the best features of the asynchronous and synchronous modes of learning and engagement.

This format has two essential parts: a website that takes the students through an academic journey by giving them motivation and support and a subsequent live event (online or in person) that brings staff and students together to showcase and celebrate the students' journey. For this format to work properly students need to engage with the conference's website early on and, more importantly, perceive the website as a support hub and a place where they can find useful material for developing their research, writing and presentation skills. In other words, the website must be seen by students as a *dynamic* educational resource that would lead them in their learning journey throughout the academic year, rather than a mere platform for showcasing the final research outputs.

The other necessary element is that there needs to be a two-way connection (going back and forth) between the website and all live activities that take place throughout the academic year, such as Q&A sessions and workshops. Next, there needs to be a smooth and close transition between the asynchronous stage and the subsequent live event. Finally, activities in the live event need to be connected to the material already posted on the website, resulting in a synergy between the two stages of the conference.

This new format has several advantages. First, it enhances research-based education by providing continuous support and motivation to students in their research journey throughout the year by constantly posting material on the website as well as holding live virtual workshops and Q&A sessions. Second, it improves student-staff relations by combining the two modes of asynchronous and synchronous engagement. Previously, the only way for staff to engage with a student conference or other co-curricular activities was to attend a half-day event on campus. In the blended format, the website opens the door for another mode of engagement: the staff can start engaging with students' research well before attending the live event. In addition, the conference website can function as an umbrella that brings all co-curricular activities of the department together, further fostering community building and student-staff engagement. Third, this new format empowers students as it provides them with new modes of presence and expression. In a conventional conference, a lot of emphasis is put on live presentations, but in a blended format, students get a chance to pre-record a video presentation in addition to their live performance. This not only diversifies the mode of expression for students but gives them a more lasting presence in the conference as their video presentation is posted on the website. The blended format also allows the live event to focus more on celebrating and showcasing what students have already achieved in terms of research and other co-curricular activities throughout the academic year, in addition to the traditional emphasis on live presentations of papers and posters. Finally, the blended format is economically efficient as it compresses the live event and thus, saves on various administrative costs.

The blended conference format, however, introduces several challenges. First, it requires a solid technical setup, and participants need to be comfortable with the digital tools used. Second, maintaining engagement, especially during the online portion, could be difficult due to the lack of personal interaction embedded in traditional conferences. Third, transitioning smoothly from the online stage to the live event requires thoughtful planning and administrative support to keep the momentum going. Finally, preparing students for unique presentation formats like the elevator-pitch presentations requires some additional training and support.

All in all, the blended conference offers a novel format that can harness the best of the asynchronous and synchronous modes of engagement and learning.

NOTES

1. Blended learning, also known as hybrid learning, is an educational approach that purposefully combines in-class activities with online resources and interactions (Institute for Teaching and Learning Innovation, 2023).
2. The Economist's Society is the official student society for the UCL Economics Department, tasked with organising a range of social and academic events while representing the student body.

REFERENCES

Arsenis, P., Flores, M., & Petropoulou, D. (2022). Enhancing graduate employability skills and student engagement through group video assessment. *Assessment & Evaluation in Higher Education, 47*(2), 245–258. doi:10.1080/02602938.2021.18 97086

Basken, P. (2021, December 10). Online academic conferences showing wide benefit. *Times Higher Education.* https:// www . timeshighe reducation .com/ news/ online -academic-conferences-showing-wide-benefit

Blakeley, G. (2020, November 17). Developing students' confidence and sense of belonging online. *Times Higher Education.* https://www.timeshighereducation.com/ campus/developing-students-confidence-and-sense-belonging-online

Blessinger, P., & Carfora, J. M. (2014). *Inquiry-based learning for faculty and institutional development: A conceptual and practical resource for educators.* Emerald Group Publishing.

Bovill, C., Cook-Sather, A., & Felten, P. (2011). Students as co-creators of teaching approaches, course design, and curricula: implications for academic developers. *International Journal for Academic Development, 16*(2), 133–145. doi:10.1080/136 0144X.2011.568690

Brew, A. (2010). Imperatives and challenges in integrating teaching and research. *Higher Education Research & Development, 29*(2), 139–150. doi:10.1080/07294360903552451

Chaudhury, P. (2020). Best practice and innovations in economics education. In S. Marshall (Ed.), *A Handbook for Teaching and Learning in Higher Education: Enhancing Academic Practice* (5th ed.). Routledge.

Etzion, D., Gehman, J., & Davis, G. F. (2022). Reimagining academic conferences: Toward a federated model of conferencing. *Management Learning, 53*(2), 350–362. doi:10.1177/13505076211019529

Fung, D. (2017). *A connected curriculum for higher education / Dilly Fung*. UCL Press.

Gibson, M. (2020, November 4). Creating a welcoming and inclusive online learning community. *THE Campus*. https://www.timeshighereducation.com/campus/creating -welcoming-and-inclusive-online-learning-community

Grove, J. (2021, March 16). Research intelligence: the best and worst of a year of virtual conferences. *Times Higher Education*. doi:https://www.timeshighereducation.com/ career/research-intelligence-best-and-worst-year-virtual-conferences

Institute for Teaching and Learning Innovation. (2023). Blended teaching. The University of Queensland. Retrieved November 1, 2023, from https://itali.uq.edu.au/ teaching-guidance/learning-spaces-and-modes/blended-teaching)

Jenkins, C., & Lane, S. (2019). *Employability skills in UK economics degrees: Report for the Economics Network*. Retrieved from https://www.economicsnetwork.ac.uk/ sites/default/files/Ashley/Report%20for%20website%20-%20Final_0.pdf

KPMG. (2020). *Four building blocks for transforming and optimising universities*. Retrieved from https://assets.kpmg.com/content/dam/kpmg/xx/pdf/2020/10/future -of-higher-education.pdf

Montes, E. (2021). What is Digital Literacy: A Complete Guide. *D2L*.

Popovic, C., & Kustra, E. (2020, April 7). Tips on how to plan a virtual academic conference. *Times Higher Education*. Retrieved from https://www.timeshighereducation .com/blog/tips-how-plan-virtual-academic-conference

Sarabipour, S. (2020). Research Culture: Virtual conferences raise standards for accessibility and interactions. *Elife, 9*, e62668.

Sipley, G. (2021). The post-COVID future of virtual conferences. Retrieved from https:// po stpandemic university .net/ 2021/ 02/ 05/ the -post -covid -future -of -virtual -conferences/

Skiles, M., Yang, E., Reshef, O., Muñoz, D. R., Cintron, D., Lind, M. L., ... Kumar, M. (2022). Conference demographics and footprint changed by virtual platforms. *Nature Sustainability, 5*(2), 149–156. doi:10.1038/s41893–021–00823–2

Spielmann, C., & Chaudhury, P. (2016). Let's Make a Movie-Introducing Economics with a Multimedia Research Project. *Journal of Economics Teaching, 1*(1).

Wu, J., Rajesh, A., Huang, Y.-N., Chhugani, K., Acharya, R., Peng, K., ... Mangul, S. (2022). Virtual meetings promise to eliminate geographical and administrative barriers and increase accessibility, diversity and inclusivity. *Nature Biotechnology, 40*(1), 133–137. doi:10.1038/s41587–021–01176-z

13. The Econ Games: building a virtual co-curricular conference to create community and connect students

Abdullah Al-Bahrani, Darshak Patel, Daria Sevastianova and Brandon J. Sheridan

INTRODUCTION

Online learning has expanded substantially since the 2000s, with a particularly sharp increase in 2020 (National Center for Education Statistics, 2023).[1] The proliferation of online courses has offered many opportunities such as increased accessibility for those who may not otherwise be able to afford an education (Goodman et al., 2019). However, there are challenges that come along with that growth, namely that online courses are often viewed by both faculty and students as lower quality due to the lack of engagement (Allen et al., 2016). An integral part of a successful online course is the interaction between instructors and students, as well as among students themselves (Dixson, 2010).

Learning is often a social endeavor, whereby students benefit greatly from receiving feedback from subject matter experts and peers. Consensus definitions of engagement are elusive but Lamborn et al. (1992) offer a good starting point: "the student's psychological investment in and effort directed toward learning, understanding, or mastering the knowledge, skills, or crafts that academic work is intended to promote" (p.12). Studies vary widely in how they measure engagement, but the general idea is that students are actively doing something in their course rather than passively listening to a lecturer. For online classes, this could be submitting an assignment, completing a reading, or posting to a discussion forum, among many other possible activities. The pandemic likely amplified any pre-existing lack of engagement in online courses (Walker and Koralesky, 2021), so it is important to be mindful of ways to enhance engagement when designing courses. A well-designed online class or program can keep students engaged as well as any in-person class (Borup et al., 2020). Some of the disconnection with online learning can be mitigated by adopting strategies that put students in a position to have an authentic learning experience (Pühringer and Bäuerle, 2019).

These so-called experiential learning activities make students active participants by providing opportunities to apply theories learned in the classroom to real-world scenarios (Becker and Watts, 2001). These approaches, sometimes referred to as learning-by-doing, have been shown to increase student motivation and academic achievement (Redmond et al., 2018; Ziegert and McGoldrick, 2008). Economics continues to lag behind other disciplines in adopting experiential learning activities (Ghosh, 2013; Hansen et al., 2002; Ahlstrom et al., 2023), even though students express a strong desire to have more of these experiences (Hawtrey, 2007).

The flexibility of online learning has provided an avenue for collaborations across institutions locally and internationally. There are several variations to these collaborations. One example of such a collaboration is the use of Collaborative Online International Learning (COIL). COIL is an innovative pedagogical approach that connects students and professors from different cultural backgrounds and institutions through virtual means to engage in collaborative learning experiences. COIL is primarily a partnership between two institutions, involving an instructor at each institution working together to enhance a common course such as Principles of Microeconomics. Such online collaborations foster intercultural competency, global awareness, and cross-cultural understanding among students while enriching their academic learning (Rubin and Guth, 2022). Online collaborations are a wonderful way for professors to design a series of synchronous and asynchronous activities that encourage students to work together in international teams, leveraging a variety of digital communication and collaboration tools.

At the core of all online collaboration across institutions lies a strong emphasis on experiential student activities. These activities serve as the driving force behind the learning experience, with a central focus on students working together on various projects. From the initial stages, students are encouraged to actively interact with their peers from diverse backgrounds, participate in meaningful discussions, and engage in challenges leading up to the main activity. Good activities are designed to foster teamwork, communication, and the application of theoretical concepts to real-world scenarios. Through the integration of experiential student activities, students are active participants within their economics major, empowering them to develop valuable skills, embrace diverse perspectives, and succeed in an interconnected world.

In this chapter, we describe the 2021 Econ Games Online Edition (EGOE) as one such valuable activity that emphasizes online collaboration across institutions. The EGOE serves as a subsidiary of the in-person Econ Game event (Patel et al., 2024). The EGOE is a co-curricular experiential learning program that connects students across institutions around the world, provides workforce development skills, and increases student engagement across their various courses. The program partners with government and industry to provide real-world data for participants, which students then analyze and create a data story in a short period of time. With this program, students were challenged to apply classroom knowledge and economic theories to real-world problems. A similar program has been hosted in person. Even the in-person event involved a substantial online portion in the months prior to the competition, making it more of a blended format. In-person experiences are valuable, but the online education space continues to expand so it is important to also provide students with opportunities that are designed for an online format. Leveraging online communities allows students and faculty members to expand their network of connections and increase access for people who otherwise may not be able to join the experience.

The goal of the EGOE is to connect students with instructors, peers, and industry partners. While we do not yet have data available to indicate the efficacy of the program, the popularity of the program since its inception and the positive feedback from participants suggests that it is a valued opportunity. There are many ways one could gauge the efficacy of such a program and we encourage instructors to measure the things that matter most in their context, be it gains in economic knowledge, refining presentation and/or communication skills, development of data analysis skills, network-building, or student engagement, among many other possibilities. This chapter describes the program in detail.

THE ECON GAMES

The Econ Games is an annual event that provides undergraduate students the opportunity to participate in a data analytics and research event designed to challenge them to solve a data problem posed by participating business or government partners (Patel et al., 2024). The Econ Games are similar to a case competition and were developed in response to several important observations. First, students often struggle to clearly identify the connection between core economic theory and real-world applications, especially as it pertains to potential careers (Bayer et al., 2020). Second, students usually have limited experiential learning opportunities, especially within the context of a single course. Third, students and employers alike are often unaware of the types of jobs students with an economics major are qualified to do, stemming from the lack of connection between theory and practice in the classroom. Fourth, economics has struggled to increase diverse representation and efforts to do so have been focused at the postgraduate level (Al-Bahrani, 2022). The Econ Games provides an inclusive space for undergraduate students from all majors to participate, with hopes of attracting students to the field. Therefore, The

Econ Games serves as a window between students and employers: students can see the various types of jobs they are able to do and companies can see the rich skill set developed by economics majors. Finally, it allows students to network with each other, employers, and community stakeholders. Ultimately, the program aims to help students develop their skills beyond the classroom, including the technical and soft skills needed for careers in economic analysis.

A vital component of the event is that data is provided by a community partner/business, which is important for many reasons. First, a partner can provide an authentic dataset and research question. In doing so, the partner can help students and faculty deeply understand the challenges and/or problems faced by the business (or whomever the partner is). This is useful because students begin to see the connections between classroom theory and real-world challenges. Second, by creating and presenting a solution *to the partner/business* rather than to a professor, the students have an authentic audience and receive real, critical feedback. Finally, the partnership creates a talent pipeline for potential internships and job interviews.

THE ECON GAMES: ONLINE EDITION

The Econ Games have been organized in both in-person and online formats. The in-person event takes place annually in March, while the online edition offers flexibility, being open for hosting throughout the year, except for certain challenges mentioned later in the chapter. Despite the differences in the timing of the events, the planning process for both the online and in-person versions follows a similar approach. During the preceding summer, the organizers begin by selecting a data partner, which could be either from the private sector or government, responsible for providing a data problem for the students to solve during the event. In the fall semester, a call for participation is sent out to universities and colleges, aiming to attract students and form within-institution teams to participate in The Econ Games. All students from member schools are granted access to an online learning management platform to facilitate communication and increase engagement among peers.

In 2021, the Federal Reserve Bank of Cleveland (Cleveland Fed) collaborated as the data partner for the EGOE and also contributed judges for the competition. This event was meticulously planned and organized through joint efforts between faculty members and data partners. The primary component of the competition spanned a week, but The Econ Games offered activities over several months to incentivize comprehensive participation and engagement. The online nature of the event helped increase reach to create a bigger community of participants than in previous years. A total of 18 schools and 266 students participated: sixteen institutions from the US, one from Canada and one from England. The EGOE was held over several months and culminated with a virtual competition that lasted one week in early March. In the initial phase of the program, students received short challenges that helped develop their technical skills, build the team environment, and connect the overall community. In addition to challenges, the participants attended a speaker series that helped connect students to economists at higher education institutions, government, and industry.

All collaborations for the EGOE were facilitated through the free version of the Learning Management System (LMS) Canvas (https://www.instructure .com/). Organizers contacted faculty partners from participating institutions and included them on the Canvas platform. There were several methods for adding students to the event's Canvas website: 1) Faculty could provide the organizers with a list of student names and emails, and the organizers would manually add each student one by one. 2) Alternatively, each faculty instructor could be added to the event page as a Teaching Assistant (TA) or instructor, enabling them to add their respective students, and 3) An option was also available to share the Canvas event page sign-up link directly with the students. By using an online LMS, the organizers streamlined communication and coordination with faculty and students, ensuring a seamless and efficient experience for all participants.

The dataset is always a surprise to both students and faculty until the first day of the competition. Information about the dataset and the partner is released slowly as the competition approaches. This helps build anticipation and increase engagement among students, as they refine their preparation tactics. As the hype for the news on the data partner grows, students are asked to complete several challenges that will help them prepare for the main event. All challenges and communications are managed on the LMS. The first challenge is for students to introduce themselves via a video discussion board and engage with each other by connecting on the professional social media network LinkedIn. The introductions range from students sharing their passion for economics, their personal background such as where they are from, and their excitement on why they agreed to participate in The Econ Games. After students post their introductions, they are encouraged to respond to a few posts and deepen their connections on LinkedIn. This easy challenge has several benefits but the curiosity to know one another and connect with each other through LinkedIn is a high priority. Our other challenges focus on team building through solving several unique data challenges. Students must download publicly available data, with guidance, and then perform basic data cleaning, simple regressions, and some data visualization. Students are encouraged to create a narrative around their completed challenge and share their creation on LinkedIn. This reinforces the efforts to create community.

The release of the dataset, also known as the "data drop", is filled with anticipation and excitement. Students receive access to the dataset after a welcome event that includes a live virtual presentation from the sponsor. The EGOE welcome remarks covered several items, in this case: What does the Federal Reserve do? What are some of the projects the current Cleveland Fed research associates are working on? What are some of the career opportunities for current students and recent graduates? Finally, the Cleveland Fed shared the much awaited data, a large dataset on the US economy. Given the timing (early 2021) they tasked students with developing COVID-19 recovery policy recommendations. Students had to use data analysis and visualization skills, and produce an eight-minute video with their recommendations. Students had an entire weekend to work with their groups to solve the policy problem and communicate their solutions and recommendations via a recorded video. The Cleveland Fed also provided four Research Assistants (RA) who hosted virtual office hours as a resource for students to contact with any questions concerning the data.

Some schools fielded multiple teams but only one submission per school was allowed. This enhanced participation, but also meant that some schools had to choose the best video internally prior to submitting their video to the EGOE. This approach allowed schools to engage their alumni, board members, and stakeholders by including them in the judging process. After receiving the online submissions, The Econ Games executive team then submitted each school's entry to the Cleveland Fed. Judges from the Cleveland Fed reviewed the submissions over the next 48 hours, chose the top three submissions, and provided those teams with feedback and questions. The top three teams were then given the next two days to prepare amended presentations that took place live on the final day of the competition. The final presentations were twelve minutes each, followed by Q&A with the judges. The institutions that did not make the top three were not informed about their placement to motivate their students to be present in attendance for the final presentations, which were followed by a prize ceremony.

EXPERIENCE OF PARTICIPATING INSTITUTIONS

The format of the EGOE was a necessity given COVID-19 public health guidelines, but it also provided participating students and faculty advisors with flexibility in program promotion, preparation, and time management. Students were free to participate on their own terms and engage as much as they deemed appropriate in practice challenges, while mostly concentrating their effort in the final stage of the challenge, the week of the competition.

Most of the institutions used the EGOE as a co-curricular opportunity rather than incorporating it as part of a class – though the latter is certainly a possibility. Promotion is important when asking students to voluntarily participate in a learning activity outside of a typical course. The Econ Games organizers assisted institutions, if needed, with creating promotional materials, including flyers and posts for social media. In addition to using social media, some instructors also created a short video to share with interested students near the beginning of the semester. The event was advertised as a mini-internship where business majors would have the opportunity to apply their skills and knowledge to solving a real-world problem. The combination of the video/ personal message from the instructor/faculty advisor and the social media push generated significant interest. An added advantage was the flexibility of virtual training along the way, with the bulk of the workload concentrated during the weekend before the final challenge. Of course, another feature that attracts participants is the data partner. Students love the idea of having an authentic experience, particularly if it is with a business or government agency such as the Cleveland Fed. Students are able to clearly see the bridge between being a college student and joining the workforce. The networking opportunities of such a competition are invaluable.

Faculty advisors also had the freedom to set the frequency and agenda for virtual meetings with their own student teams. In this way, the experience was customizable based on the previous preparation of the students and the time that faculty had available. Many institutions were able to form multiple teams, representing various business majors. While having economics majors on board was valuable, the diverse representation of majors is a strength of participating in The Econ Games. Consideration was also given to students' compatibility, based on their prior interactions in business courses. In addition to Canvas, regular training sessions were held over Zoom to keep students' morale and momentum going. When multiple teams were formed, there was an internal contest to select one team to represent an institution in the final round of the challenge. This allowed participating institutions to recruit judges from Deans and Provosts across campus, to economics faculty, as well as alumni. The judges were given a rubric according to which a finalist was selected to advance to the final challenge. The internal competition allowed for further advertising the event, which in turn was important for continuity in future years. It also allowed students to enhance their resumes. Additionally, fielding multiple internal teams allowed for students to be recognized within their institution via the institution's website and posts on social media.

Benefits

Students
The Econ Games is often described as "interning for a day/weekend." This data analytics and research experience allows students to explore careers in economics while solving real-world problems. According to the National Association of Colleges and Employers, desired soft skills include critical

thinking, problem-solving, oral and written communication, collaboration, and digital technology. The Econ Games provides an opportunity for students to strengthen these skills as they work with big data, team members, and technology, all under time constraints. With hands-on experience, students practice data cleaning, coding, and importantly, they learn to tell an effective story using economics, data analysis, and data visualization. Successful students possess technical data analysis skills and know how to use them effectively for diverse, non-expert audiences. The experience condenses valuable learning into a few days, equivalent to what some gain from a three-month internship.

By the end of the program, students feel comfortable working with data, creating data visualizations, and solving real-world problems. As a result, they gain a strong foundation for advanced learning in the workplace and develop skills to advance their majors and careers. Multiple students have received job offers because of The Econ Games experience. The Econ Games also helps answer students' questions about what economists do, while simultaneously building their skill sets and portfolios.

Economics discipline

The EGOE has opened doors for a wide and diverse range of students, removing many barriers for participation. Regardless of academic abilities, gender, major, class year, or academic performance, all students have the chance to take part in this event. Because promotional videos recorded by faculty advisors can be circulated to a wider audience, recruitment took place amongst all business majors, and even other social science majors. Participating students represented different years of study, different majors and minors, international and domestic students. Their practice time with their faculty advisor helped create long-lasting connections with faculty and fellow participants alike. Much positive feedback was received on the power of the EGOE to create engagement at a time when students felt disconnected from campus life, faculty and one another due to implemented safety measures. In the 2021 edition, an impressive 44% of the participants were female, far surpassing the average representation of females in economics, which typically hovers around 30%. This inclusivity and representation underscore the program's commitment to fostering a diverse and equitable environment for all participants.

Institutions and community

At the institutional level, the EGOE demonstrated a strong commitment to inclusivity and community engagement through various initiatives. Faculty members actively participated in the program, engaging with a diverse set of students, and fostering a supportive environment that encouraged collaboration and learning across different academic backgrounds. One of the notable aspects of community involvement was the inclusion of more faculty and external community members as judges for the event. This not only added a valuable perspective to the competition but also allowed students to receive feedback and mentorship from seasoned professionals, enriching their learning experience and expanding their network of contacts.

In addition to faculty and external judges, some institutions took it a step further by involving local businesses from the community. These businesses were invited to be present during the internal presentations, providing students with a real-world audience and an opportunity to showcase their problem-solving skills and economic insights directly to potential employers. This interaction not only gave students a taste of the professional world but also facilitated potential job offers and internships, fostering a strong bridge between academia and the business community. Furthermore, the importance of telling the student story at the university level cannot be overstated. The Econ Games provided a platform for students to shine, demonstrating their talents, expertise, and creativity to a broader audience, including representatives from the business community. As the students' stories resonated with these professionals, it opened doors for potential career opportunities and partnerships.

WHAT FACULTY NEED TO KNOW

The Econ Games is a wonderful opportunity for faculty to engage their students in an extracurricular, experiential learning activity with a relatively low time investment for the participating faculty member. Demands on faculty time are always high so The Econ Games is designed, and continually refined, with the busy faculty member in mind. A faculty advisor can put as much or as little time into the experience as they have available. The Econ Games incorporates synchronous and asynchronous online activities via an LMS available to all member schools. This allows students to participate in data exercises, speaker events, and network with exercises in-person on their respective campuses as a way to practice and build camaraderie. Faculty advisors can help in these stages by offering feedback along the way or assessing the final product. Faculty could also host viewing parties for the speaker events and encourage/ incentivize students to ask questions.

ASSESSING THE ECON GAMES

There are several ways to measure the efficacy of online experiential programs such as The Econ Games:

1. Survey students: After the event, the organizers survey the participating students to get feedback on their experience. They ask about the useful-

ness of the skills they learned, whether they felt more prepared for their future careers, and whether they would recommend the program to others. The organizers also collect information on the diversity of student participation: race, gender, discipline, etc.

2. Employer feedback: Organizers can gather feedback from the participating business partners to see if they were impressed with the quality of work produced by the students, quality of the program, and if they would be interested in hiring them in the future.

3. Faculty feedback: Organizers can gather feedback from the participating faculty to see if they were impressed with the quality of work produced by the students, quality of the program, and if they would be interested in participating in the future.

4. Student success: The organizers can track the success of the participating students after they graduate, such as the percentage that are hired by the partner companies, or the percentage that pursues further education in economics or a related field.

5. Competitiveness: The organizers can track the competitiveness of the program, such as the number of participating schools, the level of engagement from students, and the number of business partners interested in participating.

6. Long-term impact: Finally, the organizers can evaluate the long-term impact of the program, such as whether it helps to address the pain points mentioned earlier, such as connecting economic theory to careers in the real world, providing experiential learning opportunities, and increasing awareness of the types of jobs economics majors can pursue.

Assessment is important to ensure continuing success of such events and these are all elements that we monitor, some formally and some informally. However, different institutions likely have different goals so it is important for participating institutions to consider these goals prior to competing in the EGOE or another such experience.

Challenges

Whether you are contemplating participating in the EGOE or starting a new venture on your own, there are several challenges we encountered that future organizers should consider. The time investment for participating faculty can vary based on their level of involvement in preparing for the main event. However, it's worth noting that faculty organizers of the EGOE, who take the lead in coordinating the event, face a substantial time commitment. As a result, replicating the success of the 2021 EGOE has proven challenging, with only a small online event held in May 2022. The primary reason for this limitation is the significant time investment required from the organizing group. To address this issue and potentially reduce the burden on the organizing group, collaborative efforts from participating institutions' faculty members could be explored. By sharing responsibilities and working together, the workload could be distributed more evenly, leading to a more feasible and sustainable organization of future EGOE events.

Additionally, it is crucial to consider differences in academic calendars and time zones across international and local institutions when determining the final count of participating schools. For instance, schools in the UK often have a break in the month of April, while schools in the US have varying weeks for spring break in March/April. These variations must be taken into account to accommodate as many institutions as possible. The success of the 2022 EGOE was evident, but the number of participating schools was limited to seven, mainly because the event took place in May. During this time, many schools in the US were on an academic break for the summer, resulting in only one participating school from the US. To ensure broader participation in the future, it might be necessary to schedule the event during a time when academic breaks are less common across different regions. Lastly, the timing of the official welcome and presentation days must be thoughtfully planned to consider the time differences among all participating institutions. This ensures that all schools can actively engage in these critical events without significant disruptions due to time zone variations. Proper coordination in this aspect enhances the inclusivity and overall success of The Econ Games for all participants.

CONCLUSION

This chapter presents The Econ Games as a valuable and innovative experiential learning program for online collaborations across institutions in the field of economics. We highlight the increasing importance of online learning and the challenges associated with engagement in virtual environments. Experiential learning activities, such as The Econ Games, play a crucial role in enhancing student engagement, motivation, and academic achievement. These activities allow students to actively apply economic theories to real-world scenarios, fostering teamwork, communication, and the development of essential skills.

The 2021 EGOE demonstrated the potential and flexibility of hosting experiential learning events virtually. With the shift to an online format due to the COVID-19 pandemic, the program expanded its reach to a more diverse set of students and institutions, fostering a larger and more inclusive community of participants. The event provided students with an opportunity to engage in a real-world data analytics and research challenge, solving problems posed by collaborating business partners. This experience not only strengthened their technical and soft skills but also exposed them to potential career paths and internship opportunities.

Looking forward, this chapter serves as a guide and inspiration for future EGOE organizers. It emphasizes the importance of creating a well-designed online program that connects students with instructors, peers, and industry partners. Faculty members can play a vital role in facilitating and guiding students through the competition, ensuring their engagement and success. To further enhance the program's reach and sustainability, collaborative efforts among participating institution faculty members could be explored, distributing the workload and promoting broader participation. With careful consideration of academic calendars, time zones, and inclusive event planning, future iterations of The Econ Games have the potential to continue empowering students, bridging the gap between theoretical concepts and practical applications, and creating a supportive community for aspiring economists in an interconnected world.

NOTE

1.   Data from the National Center for Education Statistics show the number of students taking any distance education course increased from 15.6% in 2003–04 to 37% by Fall 2019. This percentage doubled to 74% in Fall 2020.

REFERENCES

Ahlstrom, L. J., Harter, C., & Asarta, C. J. (2023). Teaching Methods and Materials in Undergraduate Economics Courses: School, Instructor, and Department Effects. *International Review of Economics Education*, 100270.

Al-Bahrani, A. (2022). Classroom management and student interaction interventions: Fostering diversity, inclusion, and belonging in the undergraduate economics classroom. *The Journal of Economic Education*, *53*(3), 259–272.

Allen, I. E., Seaman, J., Poulin, R. & Straut, T. T. (2016). *Online Report Card: Tracking Online Education in the United States*. Babson Survey Research Group and Quahog Research Group, LLC, p. 47.

Bayer, A., Bhanot, S. P., Bronchetti, E. T., & O'Connell, S. A. (2020, May). Diagnosing the learning environment for diverse students in introductory economics: An analysis of relevance, belonging, and growth mindsets. In *AEA Papers and Proceedings* (Vol. 110, pp. 294–298). American Economic Association.

Becker, W. E., & Watts, M. (2001). Teaching methods in US undergraduate economics courses. *The Journal of Economic Education*, *32*(3), 269–279.

Borup, J., Graham, C. R., West, R. E., Archambault, L., & Spring, K. J. (2020). Academic communities of engagement: An expansive lens for examining support structures in blended and online learning. *Educational Technology Research and Development*, *68*, 807–832.

Dixson, M. D. (2010). Creating effective student engagement in online courses: What do students find engaging? *Journal of the Scholarship of Teaching and Learning*, 1–13.

Ghosh, R. (2013). Mentors providing challenge and support: Integrating concepts from teacher mentoring in education and organizational mentoring in business. *Human Resource Development Review, 12*(2), 144–176.

Goodman, J., Melkers, J., & Pallais, A. (2019). Can online delivery increase access to education? *Journal of Labor Economics, 37*(1), 1–34.

Hansen, W. L., Salemi, M. K., & Siegfried, J. J. (2002). Use it or lose it: Teaching literacy in the economics principles course. *American Economic Review, 92*(2), 463–472.

Hawtrey, K. (2007). Using experiential learning techniques. *The Journal of Economic Education, 38*(2), 143–152.

Lamborn, S., Newmann, F., & Wehlage, G. (1992). The significance and sources of student engagement. *Student engagement and achievement in American secondary schools*, 11–39.

National Center for Education Statistics. (2023). Postbaccalaureate Enrollment. Condition of Education. U.S. Department of Education, Institute of Education Sciences. Retrieved March 4, 2023, from https:// nces .ed .gov/ programs/ digest/ current_tables.asp

Patel, D., Al-Bahrani, A., & Hoyt, G. (2024). Facilitating Authentic Practice and Content Acquisition through Competition: The Econ Games. *American Economist*. Forthcoming.

Pühringer, S., & Bäuerle, L. (2019). What economics education is missing: the real world. *International Journal of Social Economics, 46*(8), 977–991.

Redmond, P., Abawi, L., Brown, A., Henderson, R., & Heffernan, A. (2018). An online engagement framework for higher education. *Online Learning Journal, 22*(1), 183–204.

Rubin, J., & Guth, S. (Eds.). (2022). *The Guide to COIL Virtual Exchange: Implementing, Growing, and Sustaining Collaborative Online International Learning* (1st ed.). Routledge. https://doi.org/10.4324/9781003447832

Walker, K. A., & Koralesky, K. E. (2021). Student and instructor perceptions of engagement after the rapid online transition of teaching due to COVID-19. *Natural Sciences Education, 50*(1), e20038.

Ziegert, A. L., & McGoldrick, K. (2008). When service is good for economics: Linking the classroom and community through service-learning. *International Review of Economics Education, 7*(2), 39–56.

14. Teaching economics to professional learners online

Parama Chaudhury and Cloda Jenkins[1]

INTRODUCTION

In the ever-evolving landscape of post-compulsory education, Continuing Professional Development (CPD) courses have emerged as transformative avenues for lifelong learning. They are increasingly important in a world where professionals need to upskill in a fast-changing world. University academics have a potential comparative advantage to deliver such courses, bringing expertise in both their subject and in teaching adults. This advantage is a great starting point, but only goes so far. University teachers need to adapt what they do to the specific characteristics of professional learners. This is even more relevant when moving between traditional campus-based teaching and online CPD.

This chapter delves into the intricacies of designing and delivering effective online and blended CPD courses, exploring their unique attributes and the two-way synergies with traditional university course and programme design. Lessons from literature and the authors' experiences delivering CPD economics courses inform the discussion.

CPD courses typically cater to a more diverse group of learners compared to traditional university degree programmes. These can include new entrants to the job market looking to complement the skills acquired at university as well as seasoned professionals from various fields looking to enhance their knowledge for personal or professional reasons. Each of these groups has a different set of goals, motivations, and preferences. This key feature of CPD participants makes a tailored and intentional course design even more important but also less straightforward than the design of a university course. Despite this, there are striking similarities with the motivations, learning objectives and challenges of university students. Understanding these commonalities is essential for creating an engaging, learner-centric educational experience for professional learners.

In this chapter, we use our experience of designing and delivering successful online CPD courses for public sector organisations to develop principles of good practice for education provision for nontraditional learners. We also rethink related lessons for the typical university course. This experience includes a blended course for more than 1000 civil servants spread across the world, which spanned a traditional university undergraduate course in terms of the content covered, as well as a more targeted online course for public sector workers in the UK in economics-adjacent roles. These courses ran the gamut from mostly online and asynchronous to online preparation with live and in-person classes.

Delivering CPD courses provides an opportunity for academics to extend their impact to professional learners and to try out new approaches before implementing in a potentially more constrained institutional environment in university. It is also an opportunity for universities to expand their revenue sources and their engagement with professional organisations, locally and globally. They can also develop expertise in flexible learning options for the modal student of the future. Given the shifting paradigm of funding and provision in higher education, particularly in the UK and the US, CPD and executive education programs can act to better prepare universities for the future. As more and more universities move to deliver short online courses for professional learners, knowing how to be excellent in online CPD design and delivery is important.

UNDERSTANDING PROFESSIONAL LEARNERS

Adults engage, post formal school education, with learning in different ways and for a variety of reasons. The spectrum of lifelong learning opportunities ranges from signing-up for a short course linked to a hobby (e.g., golf lessons), attending regular classes to develop a new interest (e.g., conversational Italian) and engaging with courses to enhance work-related skills (e.g., a Python course). Professional learners are those that are looking for a course to enhance their career, within an organisation or in the wider labour market. These learners may find an online open access course that links to a self-identified knowledge gap, attend a course organised by their employer or seek out a specialist professional course independently. University teachers have a comparative advantage in delivering expert courses across all these routes. However, these courses will only be successful if the specific needs of the professional learners are recognised in the design.

Professional learners in a short online economics course have different objectives and motivation to those who engage with economics as part of a structured degree programme (Williams et al., 2018; Cercone, 2008). The learners are filling a knowledge gap in economics specifically rather than expecting to enhance their wider learning or seeing the course as a way to meet people and enhance their life experience. They identify a stand-alone course that contains material they need to do their jobs better – either working this out for themselves or being told this by an employer as a requirement. Taking the course may help them move up the ladder in an organisation and/or move across to a new role within or outside their organisation. Christensen et al. (2013) found that in Massive Open Online Courses (MOOCs), particularly for social sciences and business, more than 50% of participants said they took the course to "gain skills to do my job better." The proportion is likely even higher where an employer requires or highly recommends the training. This work-related focused approach makes the professional learners highly motivated to learn economics. They are looking for something time-limited, low cost and practical that helps them connect their work with their learning, that is tailored to their specific objectives.

Unlike university students, who enrol in a programme of study with required entry standards and structured community, professional learners are not necessarily part of an identifiable cohort. If the economics course is provided as part of an organisational training scheme they will be learning with a group of colleagues with similar interests to them, although with a variety in their background in economics. When the learner is joining a course by themselves, say a MOOC, they will not know who else is taking the course with them. There will be little tying the learners together other than a common interest in studying some economics. They are even more likely to have different backgrounds in economics, with most professional courses having no or very limited entry requirements and learners self-selecting into the level that they think is appropriate for them. It is possible that some learners will sign up for a course that is at too low, or too high, a level for them and that learners are working at a very different pace from each other on the same course.

Whether part of an organisational CPD opportunity, or an independent sign-up to a course, the professional learner will be working, often full time, alongside taking the course. Learners also have non-work life commitments that reduce their available time (Williams et al., 2018; Christensen et al., 2013; Cercone, 2008). They are looking for a way to learn that fits alongside their other commitments.

The design and delivery of online short courses is heavily influenced by these characteristics of the demand-side. The value of the CPD opportunities is also heavily dependent on the course being well-designed. We turn our attention next to the value of delivering CPD online and then look at what needs to be considered for effective design and delivery.

THE VALUE OF ONLINE LEARNING FOR CPD

Other chapters in this book have emphasised the value of being online for university learners. The benefits might be even greater for CPD. In many circumstances, the needs of professional learners can be best met through online, or blended, provision.

The obvious advantage of online education is that it allows for greater flexibility in terms of when and where individuals can access the content and engage in learning activities. According to a recent study (European Commission, 2021), online and blended learning can improve the accessibility of learning opportunities for a diverse range of learners, including those with disabilities or who live in remote locations. Additionally, learners can study at their own pace and schedule, which can be a particular advantage for working professionals who have busy schedules (Cercone, 2008). These benefits of flexibility, convenience, and accessibility make online and blended learning an excellent choice for CPD, where professionals need to balance their work and learning needs.

Organisations we have worked with to design and deliver economics training online for professional learners have emphasised the need for allowing professional learners to choose the level of study and the topics they focus on. Online education can facilitate the development of more personalised learning experiences. For example, online courses can use adaptive learning algorithms to adjust the content and pace of the course to the learner's abilities, or track learning analytics to identify areas where learners need additional support. This can be especially beneficial for CPD courses, as it allows professionals to focus on the areas of the course that are most relevant to their specific needs, rather than having to spend time on topics that they are already proficient in. It is also useful in a situation where learners may have very different backgrounds and motivations for engaging (Zamecnik et al., 2022).

Online education can also enable the development of more interactive learning experiences. For example, online courses can incorporate interactive elements such as quizzes, simulations, and discussions to engage learners and promote active learning (Hew, 2016). This can be especially beneficial for CPD courses, as it allows professionals to apply the concepts they are learning to real-world scenarios, which can help them to better retain the information and apply it in their professional practice. If cohort-based learning is possible within the context, these interactive learning experiences can be extended to peer groups focused on areas of work, geographic location or background experiences through discussion forums or live online sessions facilitated by course tutors. In our blended course for the British government, we included workshops led by a subject specialist. These built on the online part of the course with an interactive "deep dive" discussion session into a particular topic.

An obvious benefit of online education is the potential to democratise access to learning. By making educational content available online, a wider range of individuals can participate, regardless of their geographic location, socioeconomic status, or other factors. This can be especially beneficial for CPD courses, as it can enable professionals from underserved or remote communities to access educational opportunities that may not have been available to them before. If learners in the course are quite disparate in geography, background and other characteristics, the online course can also provide an opportunity for them to connect with content and people they would not have otherwise come across. This extends beyond simply content or curriculum, as online and blended learning can facilitate collaboration and communication among learners and between learners and instructors. Online discussion forums, chat rooms, and social media platforms allow learners to share their experiences and knowledge with one another (Liu et al., 2007). These skills are particularly important for professionals who need to work collaboratively and communicate effectively with their colleagues and clients in diverse organisations. Where the online course is tailored for a particular organisation, being online opens access to a wider group of employees, particularly in a world of hybrid working, and creates a space to discuss economics with colleagues. For example, providing economics courses for the UK diplomatic service online, for staff at all levels located around the world, ensured that they all had equal access to the same quality training, they had a common learning experience and they could share experiences from working in different contexts.

Finally, online and blended learning can be cost-effective compared to traditional university programs and compared to in-person professional training. For professional learners, such courses can be less expensive due to lower tuition fees and reduced travel costs. This cost-effectiveness can be particularly beneficial for professionals who need to invest in their CPD themselves but have limited financial resources. Organisations with reduced training budgets also find that they can provide support to a greater number of employees with online provision. A key reason for the lower cost of online CPD courses provided by universities is that they can adapt what they already do in traditional degree programmes relatively easily. They can expand their impact and establish a source of revenue.

It is important to note, however, that online CPD does have its limitations. One potential disadvantage is that it can be more difficult for individuals to build relationships with their peers and instructors, which can be an important aspect of learning, particularly where the CPD is not required by the employer and therefore needs to be self-motivated. The efficacy of online education may also depend on the type of learner with, for example, those who learn best with hands-on experiences or those who struggle with self-directed learning requir-ing more support. These issues can be at least somewhat alleviated through appropriate learning design, to which we turn our attention in the next section.

LEARNER-CENTRED DESIGN OF ONLINE CPD

The specific challenges of CPD, including time-constrained professional learners, different motivations, and the need for applicability of course content, mean that online design needs to be calibrated for those not learning within a traditional university degree setup. In short, an economics course that is taught to university students cannot be directly transferred to a new home for professional learners without thinking about the design and delivery.

Delivery Model

The biggest decision is about the best model of delivery to use. Broadly speak-ing there are three general models of online courses which vary in the range of their online vs in-person blend as well as the extent to which the courses are or can be tailored.

Traditional in-person courses with online materials are at one end of the spectrum with a blend of face-to-face interaction and online resources. These courses typically involve access to online resources such as videos, articles, and discussion forums which provide the background preparation for the in-person sessions with a teacher. This type of course may be best for learners who prefer a more structured learning environment and value face-to-face interaction with instructors and peers. Additionally, learners who may not have reliable internet access may find this type of course more accessible.

MOOCs (Massive Open Online Courses) are open to anyone who has inter-net access and can enrol for free or at a low cost. They are not connected to a particular cohort of professional learners from a particular organisation, and as such are not tailored to the needs of any one set of employees, or employers. These courses may be self-paced, potentially with a time limit schedule, and can cover a broad range of topics. This type of course can be most suitable for learners who prefer a self-directed learning approach and have the motivation to complete the course on their own (Turan et al., 2022). Additionally, learners who want to explore new topics or gain a broader perspective on their field may find this type of general course beneficial.

In between these two extremes are purely online or blended courses on bespoke portals which are designed and delivered by organisations for their employees or members. These courses may be delivered synchronously or asynchronously, and the content is tailored to the specific needs of the organ-isation. This type of course may be most suitable for organisations that need to develop specific skills or knowledge within their workforce. This more tailored course can be an excellent option for professionals who need to complete CPD as part of their job requirements and where it is important that groups of employees have received similar training.

Whatever format is selected, the online course needs to be flexible, allowing professional learners to engage when and for how long they want to through the course period. Being online on a reliable platform helps enormously, as does allowing enrolment for a long time window within which learners choose how to work through the material. This window allows learners to self-pace, but having an end date ensures they do not put off engaging forever; deadlines help (Miller and Schmidt, 2021). It is also important to have "teaching presence" online, which enhances the sense of community and learning outcomes (Shea et al., 2006). This can be done through welcome induction sessions, active discussion forums, responsiveness to online questions, regular communications from the teaching team and optional live workshops (Dyer et al., 2018; Liu et al., 2007; Moore, 2014).

Content and Activities

Whatever the delivery model, the professional learner will only engage if the content is relevant to them, and it is made clear how it can be applied in different contexts. Where a course is being tailored for a particular organisation, connecting the materials to the typical work of that organisation is relatively straightforward. For open courses, where learners join from a mix of organisations and sectors, it is important to provide opportunities for learners to connect what they are learning to their own job through the online teaching. This goal requires providing a mix of resources and content.

Materials need to be accessible, recognising that the learners are busy and want to get straight to the content. Making the design of the course and the content "simple to understand" and easy to access helps with engagement (Hew, 2016). Providing support on an ongoing basis also helps learners move their learning forward, particularly when working remotely without timed live sessions.

There also need to be different entry levels, which are clearly signposted, to meet the varied background of learners within and across organisations. Hill (2006) emphasises that flexibility allows an individual learner to engage with the content that is best for them. Cercone (2008) also notes that learners can do better when they are presented with different options in terms of goals and instructional opportunities. It is important that everyone feels they are working at their level from the outset. If they don't, they are likely to stop the course, either because it is too easy or too complex depending on the individual. Allowing for different pathways means that more learners can meet their individual objectives to progress.

The different characteristics and objectives of the professional learner means that what economics is taught, and how it is taught, in CPD courses will not map directly to what happens in a traditional degree programme. There are of course synergies to delivering a university economics course and delivering a short course for professionals, but the content will require adaptation to make it relevant to professional interests and applications. It needs to be focused on more practical, applied learning than traditional university economics courses, stepping back from technical tools and concepts to key principles and messaging.

Bringing the Design Principles Together

The choice of delivery mode, and the decisions about what to teach and how to embed activities in the course, are best taken during the planning process and in discussion with the key stakeholders. This is what we did, as the Centre for Teaching and Learning in Economics (CTaLE), when setting up a blended suite of CPD courses for the British government called Economics for Foreign Policy. Topics included the basics of understanding how the economy works, how to identify underlying instability in a country's economic structure and training on the use of data for programme evaluation. There were also courses focused on more targeted topics such as the economics of the environment, globalisation, and macroeconomic crises.

The key to developing an appropriate design was understanding the target learners and their employer's motivation in setting up such a course. In this case, the learners were civil servants of different levels of seniority and from different disciplinary backgrounds. What they all had in common was the need to work in proximity with trained economists and therefore to have a good understanding of the fundamentals of how a country's economy works and perhaps more importantly, how to interpret and query the work produced by economists within the government and elsewhere. We were not trying to turn the learners into professional economists, but rather equipping them with the tools to work with economists and economics.

Most learners in this course were employees or contractors of the Foreign, Commonwealth and Development Office, meaning that many of them were working in posts around the world. This meant that the blended course with the majority of the content materials online, either synchronously or asynchronously, was most appropriate. Each course was broken up into 2-hour long units, and each unit into 30 to 45-minute sections to ensure that learners could do a "chunked-up" bit of learning at the end of a day of work without losing continuity. Each course had between 4 to 6 units, which meant that a course would take between 8 to 12 hours of learning to complete.

The learning material included relevant academic materials alongside policy and media reports, and podcasts and videos where applicable. At the end of each section, there was a mini quiz to help consolidate the material in the section before moving on to the next section. At the end of the unit and the course, learners were asked to complete a short, written assignment to apply their learning to a current work project.

Once the learner had completed the online course, they were able to sign up for online or in-person workshops with a subject area specialist to deepen their understanding of the online content and to expand their application of the material to current issues. This structure was developed in consultation with the client with constant feedback and revision to ensure that we were aligned in our understanding of the learning design and its desired outcomes (Dyer et al., 2018).

The initial setup of the course gave each learner 12 months on the bespoke platform to complete a minimum number of courses. They were also able to take more courses if they chose. While this flexibility was a key benefit of the online modality, we soon found that many learners ended up not completing the course after a few initial weeks of activity. In response to this, we carried out surveys and focus groups to identify the barriers learners were facing, and consulted with the client to better understand what changes might improve engagement. Paradoxically, it appeared that a shorter period to complete the course would provide learners with the focus and commitment device they needed to engage fully with the course (Miller and Schmidt, 2021). Given this, we altered the timeline of the course. Learners could sign up for 6, 8 or 12 weeks, during which they would need to complete 2 courses but could do more if they had time. We also refreshed the content to focus it on questions most relevant to the organisation's work and reshaped the sections to signpost fundamental learning material as opposed to optional "if you have time" elements. Finally, we introduced a live induction session at the start of each cohort, and automated reminders at key points during the course to nudge learners along. This process of reviewing the experience and adapting to the needs of the professional learners was key to the longer-term success of the blended course.

At the end of the nearly 5-year contract, nearly 1100 learners had enrolled in the course, and the completion rate had increased from approximately 15% to 60%. The redesign of the course helped significantly with this, but we also needed to provide more explicit incentives and support to our professional learners.

Incentivising Professional Learners

As we found, a blended online course provides a high amount of valued flexibility to professional learners but left to their own devices there is a tendency to start late and/or engage for a short period and drop out. Adapting the course design to take account of the characteristics of the professional learners helps with enthusiasm and engagement but more incentives may be needed to get them over the finishing line.

Completion rates for online courses, for example MOOCs, are significantly lower than for traditional in-person teaching. Reich and Ruipérez-Valiente (2023) find, based on data for MITX and HarvardX MOOCs, that completion rates of around 5% are typical, although this includes a high proportion of people who sign up for a course and then never actually engage with it. Of those that "participate" more actively, completion rates were closer to 15%. Even where learners are professionals and have a career-related reason for engaging with an online economics course, there is a high risk of them not completing their learning. They have many demands on their time and the course, which is not part of a potentially expensive qualification, can be the activity that gets pushed down their to-do list. This is more likely when the learner is taking the course independently – that is, it is not part of their organisation's required training – and when the course is online with a relatively long window for completion.

Professional learners need incentives to complete and these need to be designed taking account of their specific circumstances. The lack of external accountability puts more of an onus on the learner to direct themselves to completion. Building in some motivation in the form of an incentive can help redirect them when they are on the balance of a decision to stay or go. Reeves et al. (2017) found that intrinsic incentives, such as providing a free certificate for completion of a MOOC or connecting completion to access to another learning experience, can have significant positive effects on completion.

When we first designed our blended course for the British government, we expected learners to be engaged because they were professionals with an interest in economics for their jobs, and because the course was part of wider professional development expectations of their organisation. Initially, the asynchronous learning did not incorporate any specific incentive mechanisms to progress, although the expectation of completing by the time of the in-person workshop did provide some form of deadline. We found that those who enthusiastically signed up at the beginning did not always complete. This included low rates of registering on the platform on the first day of the course – procrastination – and evidence of learners starting and not completing. Of those that had signed up via their employer's formal training platform, 10–20% had not logged in at all or had logged in at the start date but did not engage afterwards. Amongst those that did engage, completion rates were also disappointing, with only 10–15% of the cohorts passing the course. Others that engaged along the way but did not pass tended to not complete assignments.

After the first three cohorts of learners had been through the course, we discussed how to improve completion rates with the organisation that we were delivering the course for. It was clear that learners needed more guidance through the process and needed to be motivated by more than the personal satisfaction of getting the course done. In more ways than originally envisaged, professionals were like university students learning asynchronously online. We were therefore able to adopt and adapt several tools that we used at university to incentivise engagement through the CPD course.

Engaging in the first two weeks of the course is key (Jordan, 2015) and learners need to be comfortable with the technology they are using (Onah and Sinclair, 2014). We therefore held a live induction session on the first day of the course, explaining to learners how to enrol on the platform and talking them through the structure of the course. This helped increase the rate of enrolment on day one and we found more learners engaging early in the course period.

Structuring the course in a way that learners could follow when going at their own pace was also important (Yukselturk and Yildrim, 2008). Alongside the induction we provided clearer information about the student learning journey, a roadmap of the materials and how they connected and advice on how to manage the timing of different chunks of learning. Allowing learners to see their progress clearly through the course, for example with a progress bar, helps students monitor if they are keeping up. The teaching team can also check the analytics on progress and send reminders as needed.

Supporting students is key to them progressing (Bingöl et al., 2020), as true for professionals as for university learners. We provided opportunities to engage with other learners and tutors through the Economics for Foreign Policy course, providing touch-point reminders to make progress. For example, we had live question-and-answer drop-in sessions with a tutor where learners could ask questions and hear those of others. There was also an online discussion forum to post questions, with replies provided by tutors within a short time.

We shortened the length of a course period, consistent with Jordan (2015), reducing the scope for delaying starting, and made the start and end dates more evident on the online platform and in all correspondence. Whilst we had thought there was most merit in flexibility over a long period, it transpired that leaving it too long increased the risk of procrastination.

The flexibility of the blended model was retained however, as most learners could not engage unless they had scope to complete the material in their own time. This was particularly relevant as they were working all around the world in a wide range of jobs and contexts. For example, one learner may have had a week dealing with an international crisis and another learner may have had a quiet period at work at the same time.

Conscious that a busy person is more likely to disengage if they find the material is not relevant to them immediately, we made small updates to the materials for each new cohort to ensure that applications for the organisation were up-to-date and of current interest. The connections to the organisation's goals and strategic areas of work were particularly emphasised. In parallel, we reduced the technical material recognising that our focus should be on what they needed to know rather than what we thought they should know about economics. Using a variety of interactive materials was also important for engagement (Zapalska and Brozik, 2006). This included videos, quizzes, case studies, and group discussions to change up the pace and modality of learning materials and activities.

Having regular opportunities to engage with activities is important for learner engagement and successfully passing a course (Soffer and Cohen, 2019). Learners, and tutors, were able to evaluate how their learning was progressing through the use of self-directed quizzes. This allowed for any particularly difficult parts of the course to be identified and for questions to be answered through a discussion forum. There was also a clear deadline for submission of a final assignment that needed to be discussed with a learner's line manager and overseen by the organisation that set-up the blended course. A requirement to explain progress with a manager provided a useful external incentive. Other incentives to complete included the ability to earn a certificate or online badge (e.g., to share on social media), a useful way to signpost an achievement (Rughiniş and Matei, 2013). Having a follow-on live workshop or seminar, where the online learning had to be complete to enrol, also incentivised those who were most interested in the topics.

After these incentive measures were introduced we found more engagement through the course period and higher completion rates. By the final cohort in our course, we had completion rates of nearly 60%, and active engagement for most of the course of around 80–85% in the last four cohorts. As teachers, we had also learnt a lot about incentivising learning that we could build into our university courses as well.

TAKING LESSONS FROM ONLINE CPD BACK TO ONLINE UNIVERSITY EDUCATION

When organisations and individuals are considering an economics course for CPD they often look to universities, and experienced academic economists, as the best source of such training. There are of course positive spillovers from expertise in university teaching to CPD, particularly when the need to tailor the course to the characteristics of professional learners is recognised.

The spillovers work in the other direction as well. The economies of scope are particularly evident when taking lessons from online CPD to online or blended university courses. Institutional constraints may make it difficult to trial teaching and learning techniques and technologies in a university setting. Being involved with CPD allows for potentially more freedom to try things out both in the design and delivery of online courses.

These lessons start from the technical aspects – familiarity with the functionalities of an online learning platform outside the restrictions of university priorities and subscriptions can help academics to understand the capabilities of a portal. This can inform discussions around what kinds of technological solutions might be useful to the university. Lecturers can provide feedback, based on experience, to current technology providers in their institution and feedback to those who purchase technologies on behalf of the university about what functionalities they should be looking for with new providers.

In addition, for individual academics, exposure to a portal different from the university's makes them more adaptable, a valuable skill when required to make changes to their teaching either in the same institution or when moving to a new institution. The tutors on our course for the British Government felt better prepared for the emergency shift to online teaching in 2020 than colleagues because of their experience with a blended CPD course.

Embedded in the use of new technologies is the potential gain from a deeper understanding of how to engage and motivate learners. To a certain extent, university rules on attendance might mean that students are a captive audience in a traditional setting. Since professional learners tend not to be in this position, instructors need to think more carefully about design to motivate and engage them. These techniques can be used to develop a more intrinsic kind of engagement for university students as well. This may include the use of quizzes and other assessments for learning (rather than just assessment of learning), and frequent feedback or dialogue channels to evaluate student progress and to tweak any problematic elements of the course. Student engagement in universities has become more "complex" (Hulene et al., 2023), increasing the need to design university courses that will motivate learners, rather than assuming this is the default. Experience with motivating busy and distracted learners in an online CPD course can inform what happens in university.

The second set of lessons which carry over into university economics education have to do with the content. Delivering an online or blended CPD course requires economics teachers to seek out different types of materials, including multimedia formats and sources that are written for a non-technical audience. These materials prove as useful for university students, particularly in online teaching where the same principles of engaging a self-directed learner apply. Building on this, the teacher may have created their own videos or podcast style recordings for their CPD course that can be reused for university teaching, particularly with the increase in blended delivery since the pandemic.

Feedback from and interaction with learners on a CPD course can help academics to bring experiences and perspectives from the world of work into their university classrooms. Teaching on a CPD course also forces the instructor to think about the main messages, and intuition, that they want learners to take away. Authentic real-world examples and a focus on key messaging are both important tools for effective teaching in university. Once using a mix of different formats for delivering content and thinking about the core messages that they want learners to take away, economics teachers are able to open up the possibility of delivering some of their content online, in asynchronous chunks for example, and other parts in live sessions. They can also think about whether they want live sessions to be more about big questions than technical analytical tools. Exposure to creating and curating online content for a CPD course can make it easier to adapt teaching in university courses as much of the set-up work and nervousness about trying something different have been dealt with.

LESSONS FOR ECONOMICS INSTRUCTORS AND UNIVERSITIES

The evolving landscape of the university sector, marked by shifting funding dynamics and changing demands, along with the pandemic experience starting in 2020, has provided an opportunity to rethink the traditional higher education model. As universities strive to foster deeper engagements with enterprise and professionals, the significance of bridging academia and real-world impact has gained prominence. While the impact of university research in economics is often measured by its adoption or use by policy makers or businesses, CPD courses provide a chance for connecting with and influencing this group through an alternative avenue. This particular benefit extends to the more standard in-person CPD provision as well but given that by definition such learners have full time jobs, the additional flexibility provided by the online modality is likely to increase engagement and therefore impact.

Universities can only succeed in this space if economics courses are adapted when moving between university students to professional learners, both in their design and their mode of delivery. This chapter has emphasised the need to understand your professional learners when designing an online CPD course, and to adapt as information is revealed about the nature of learning in different contexts. The online course needs to be reliable and user-friendly, with accessible and relevant materials that meet the learners' interest in learning economics to help them do their job better. When the course is run for a particular organisation, working closely with senior staff can help get insights on learners. Where learners are joining independently, having them fill out a pre-survey and navigating learning analytics early in the module can help. Incentives matter and are enhanced by a design that makes it straightforward to engage with the course in chunks in a time-limited period. Obtaining regular feedback from the professional learners, and responding to it, will enhance the value for all.

Success in delivery of online CPD courses can also lead to enhanced learning for students in the university as well. The interaction with professional learners provides teachers with authentic real-world examples on current topical issues for their university courses. Feedback from CPD courses can also benefit the pedagogical approach in the university setting, particularly for the growth of online components in otherwise traditional, in-person higher education programmes. For example, designing an online CPD course builds expertise in educational technology. Finally, in a time of financial uncertainty, CPD courses and online CPD can provide a potential revenue stream for public universities.

Involvement in the provision of online CPD courses can also benefit individual academics as it builds their own impact and expertise, but it is important to note that this comes at a cost. Adapting existing materials to develop an effective course for professional learners is time consuming and needs to be done on top of the usual university research and education workload. The design needs to involve both subject expertise and expertise in the design of online courses. Universities interested in reaping the benefits of CPD courses will need to think carefully about their investment in developing such courses, starting with the time required from academics, technical and professional support staff. New online portals, potentially a range of them for different purposes, may also be needed to ensure a smooth experience both for learners and for instructors. The investment should pay off in the sense that online CPD provision, which by its nature is scalable, will be most successful if it is carefully designed. The upfront cost needs to be balanced with the longer-term benefits in terms of potential income and improved teaching in the university.

NOTE

1.   The professional training project this chapter describes would not have been possible without the incredible effort of colleagues from various universities who led the development and delivery of the various courses, Madeleine Adamson and the UCL Consultants team who managed the project expertly, and the teams of economists in various UK government departments whose input and feedback were essential.

REFERENCES

Bingöl, I., E. Kursun and H. Kayaduman. (2020). Factors for Success and Course Completion in Massive Open Online Courses through the Lens of Participant Types. *Open Praxis, 12*(2), 223–239.

Cercone, K. (2008). Characteristics of Adult Learners With Implications for Online Learning Design. *AACE Review (formerly AACE Journal), 16*(2), 137–159.

Christensen, G., A. Steinmetz, B. Alcorn, A. Bennett, D. Woods and E. Emanuel. (2013). *The MOOC Phenomenon: Who Takes Massive Open Online Courses and Why?* Retrieved from https://ssrn.com/abstract=2350964

Dyer, T., J. Aroz and E. Larson. (2018). Proximity in the online classroom: engagement, relationships, and personalization. *Journal of Instructional Research, 7*, 108–118. Retrieved from https://files.eric.ed.gov/fulltext/EJ1188336.pdf

European Commission. (2021). *Blended learning: Building more resilient education and training systems*. Retrieved from https://education.ec.europa.eu/news/blended-learning-building-more-resilient-education-and-training-systems

Hew, K. (2016). Promoting engagement in online courses: What strategies can we learn from three highly rated MOOCS. *British Journal of Educational Technology, 47*(2), 320–341.

Hill, J. (2006). Flexible Learning Environments: Leveraging the Affordances of Flexible Delivery and Flexible Learning. *Innovative Higher Education, 31*, 187–197.

Hulene, G., S. Cronshaw, E. Davies, L. de Main, H. Holmes, A. Hope, C. Odindo, R. Page-Tickell, A. Rawal, S. Roberts, D. Talbot, S. Vieth and P. Wolstencroft. (2023). *Student Engagement Guidelines: Learning from innovative practices introduced in response to COVID-19*. Retrieved from QAA: https://www.qaa.ac.uk/docs/qaa/members/qaa-report-on-student-engagement---gh-02–05–23.pdf?sfvrsn=639aa81_8

Jordan, K. (2015). Massive open online course completion rates revisited: Assessment, length and attrition. *International Review of Research in Open and Distributed Learning, 16*(3), 341–358.

Liu, X., R. Magjuka, C. Bonk, and S. Lee. (2007). Does sense of community matter? An examination of participants' perceptions of building learning communities in online courses. *Quarterly Review of Distance Education, 8*(1), 9–24, 87–88.

Miller, L. and J. Schmidt. (2021). The Effects of Online Assignments and Weekly Deadlines on Student Outcomes in a Macroeconomics Course. *The American Economist, 66*(1), 46–60.

Moore, R. (2014). Importance of Developing Community in Distance Education Courses. *Tech Trends, 58*, 20–24.

Onah, D. and J. Sinclair. (2014). Dropout rates of massive open online courses: behavioural patterns. *EDULEARN14 Proceedings* (pp. 5825–5834). Barcelona, Spain.

Reeves, T. A., Tawfik, F. Msilu and I. Şimşek. (2017). What's in It for Me? Incentives, Learning, and Completion in Massive Open Online Courses. *Journal of Research on Technology in Education, 49*(3–4), 245–259.

Reich, J. and J. Ruipérez-Valiente. (2023). The MOOC pivot. *Science, 363*, 130–131.

Rughiniş, R. and S. Matei. (2013). Digital Badges: Signposts and Claims of Achievement. *HCI International 2013 - Posters' Extended Abstracts. Communications in Computer and Information Science* (pp. 84–88). Springer.

Shea, P., C. Li and A. Pickett. (2006). A study of teaching presence and student sense of learning community in fully online and web-enhanced college courses. *The Internet and Higher Education, 9*(3), 175–190.

Soffer, T. and A. Cohen. (2019). Students' engagement characteristics predict success and completion of online courses. *Journal of Computer Assisted Learning, 35*, 378–389.

Turan, Z., S. Kucuk and S. Cilligol Karabey. (2022). The university students' self-regulated effort, flexibility and satisfaction in distance education. *International Journal of Education Technology in Higher Education, 19*, 35.

Williams, K., R. Stafford, S. Corliss and E. Reilly. (2018). Examining student characteristics, goals, and engagement in Massive Open Online Courses. *Computers & Education, 126*, 433–442.

Yukselturk, E. and Z. Yildirim. (2008). Investigation of Interaction, Online Support, Course Structure and Flexibility as the Contributing Factors to Students' Satisfaction in an Online Certificate Program. *Journal of Educational Technology & Society, 11*(4), 51–65.

Zamecnik, A., V. Kovanović, S. Joksimović and L. Lin. (2022). Exploring non-traditional learner motivations and characteristics in online learning: A learner profile study. *Computers and Education: Artificial Intelligence, 22*, XX.

Zapalska, A. and D. Brozik. (2006). Learning styles and online education. *Campus-Wide Information Systems, 23*(5), 325–335.

Index